Differences That Work

The Harvard Business Review Book Series

Designing and Managing Your Career, Edited by Harry Levinson

Ethics in Practice: Managing the Moral Corporation, Edited by Kenneth R. Andrews

Managing Projects and Programs, With a Preface by Norman R. Augustine

Manage People, Not Personnel: Motivation and Performance Appraisal, With a Preface by Victor H. Vroom

Revolution in Real Time: Managing Information Technology in the 1990s, With a Preface by William G. McGowan

Strategy: Seeking and Securing Competitive Advantage, Edited with an Introduction by Cynthia A. Montgomery and Michael E. Porter

Leaders on Leadership: Interviews with Top Executives, With a Preface by Warren Bennis

Seeking Customers, Edited with an Introduction by Benson P. Shapiro and John J. Sviokla

Keeping Customers, Edited with an Introduction by John J. Sviokla and Benson P. Shapiro

The Learning Imperative: Managing People for Continuous Innovation, Edited with an Introduction by Robert Howard

The Articulate Executive: Orchestrating Effective Communication, With a Preface by Fernando Bartolomé

Differences That Work: Organizational Excellence through Diversity, Edited with an Introduction by Mary C. Gentile

Reach for the Top: Women and the Changing Facts of Work Life, Edited with an Introduction by Nancy A. Nichols

Global Strategies: Insights from the World's Leading Thinkers, With a Preface by Percy Barnevik

Command Performance: The Art of Delivering Quality Service, With a Preface by John E. Martin

Manufacturing Renaissance, Edited with an Introduction by Gary P. Pisano and Robert H. Hayes

The Product Development Challenge: Competing through Speed, Quality, and Creativity, Edited with an Introduction by Kim B. Clark and Steven C. Wheelwright

The Evolving Global Economy: Making Sense of the New World Order, Edited with a Preface by Kenichi Ohmae

Managerial Excellence: McKinsey Award Winners from the *Harvard Business Review*, 1980–1994, Foreword by Rajat Gupta, Preface by Nan Stone

Fast Forward: The Best Ideas on Managing Business Change, Edited with an Introduction and Epilogue by James Champy and Nitin Nohria

First Person: Tales of Management Courage and Tenacity, Edited with an Introduction by Thomas Teal

Differences That Work

Organizational Excellence through Diversity

Edited with
an Introduction by
Mary C. Gentile

Foreword by
R. Roosevelt Thomas, Jr.

A Harvard Business Review Book

Published by the Harvard Business School Press in hardcover, 1993; in
paperback, 1996

The *Harvard Business Review* articles in this collection are available as
individual reprints. Discounts apply to quantity purchases. For information
and ordering contact Operations Department, Harvard Business School
Publishing Corporation, Boston, MA 02163. Telephone: (617) 495-6192, 9
a.m. to 5 p.m. Eastern Time, Monday through Friday. Fax: (617) 495-6985,
24 hours a day.

The paper used in this publication meets the requirements of the American
National Standard for Permanence of Paper for Printed Library Materials
Z39.48-1984

Library of Congress Cataloging-in-Publication Data

Differences that work : organizational excellence through diversity / edited,
with an introduction by Mary C. Gentile : foreword by R. Roosevelt
Thomas, Jr.
     p.   cm. — (A Harvard Business review book)
     Includes bibliographical references and index.
     ISBN 0-87584-499-5 (alk. paper) (hc)
     ISBN 0-87584-735-8 (pbk)
     1. Organizational effectiveness, 2. Multiculturalism.
     I. Gentile, Mary C.   II. Series: Harvard business review book series.
     HD58.9.D54 1994
     658.3—dc20   93-37088
                                                                         CIP

Contents

Foreword   **xi**
R. Roosevelt Thomas, Jr.

Introduction   **xiii**
Mary C. Gentile

Part I Differences at Work:
Where We've Been, Where We Are, Where We Go from
Here

**1 Global Work Force 2000: The New World Labor
Market**   **3**
William B. Johnston
International demographic trends will have a
profound impact on national strategies of employment
and competitiveness. A growing imbalance between
the world's labor supply and demand has resulted in
greater relocation of workers from developing
countries to more developed countries, creating a
more diverse work force. The author predicts changes
in immigration regulations, increased standardization
of labor-management relations, and a greater
government role in managing the new global work
force.

2 From Affirmative Action to Affirming Diversity   27
R. Roosevelt Thomas, Jr.

The author argues that our traditional image of assimilating differences—the melting pot—is no longer valid. Affirmative action policies have often proved insufficient for optimizing the skills, commitment, and competitiveness of a multicultural workplace. Thomas profiles several corporations wrestling with diversity and offers an alternative model for program development.

Part II   Racial Difference in the Workplace: How It Feels and What It Means

1 What It's Like to Be a Black Manager   49
Edward W. Jones, Jr.

The author's personal experience, moving from a management trainee position to area manager in a traditional corporate environment, highlights the inner conflicts faced by minority employees struggling to advance in a resistant atmosphere.

2 Black Managers: The Dream Deferred   65
Edward W. Jones, Jr.

Interviews with over 200 black professionals illustrate the widespread disappointment, frustration, and anger they feel despite the progress resulting from equal opportunity policies. Top leadership must not only be committed to promoting equal opportunity but also to creating a culture that allows employees to discuss openly their concerns about discrimination in the workplace.

3 Racial Remarks in the Workplace: Humor or Harassment?   85
Terry L. Leap and Larry R. Smeltzer

Increasingly, employees are bringing cases involving

teasing and joking at work before the Equal
Employment Opportunity Commission and the courts.
The authors provide useful observations for helping
employers recognize harassing behavior and set
appropriate corporate policies to prevent it.

Part III Women in the Workplace:
New Ways to Think About Work

1 Two Women, Three Men on a Raft   93
Robert Schrank
A rafting trip with Outward Bound gives a male
executive insight into the relationship between men
and women at work. Reflecting on his experiences,
the executive illustrates the many levels on which
men subvert the authority of women in their
organizations, while reinforcing attitudes of mutual
male support.

2 Coping With Comparable Worth   107
George P. Sape
Cases of inequity in compensation and employment
practices are increasingly being brought to the courts.
The author reviews the recent pattern of legislative
rulings and judicial decisions, offers a case study of
one firm's efforts to review its own practices, and
concludes with a set of general guidelines for other
firms to follow.

3 Women as a Business Imperative   123
Felice N. Schwartz
The author offers some tough talk about the
limitations of current corporate efforts to integrate
women effectively into the managerial ranks. In a
memo to a fictional CEO, she identifies the costs firms
pay for failing to develop women as an essential
resource.

Part IV   AIDS in the Workplace:
The Organizational and Individual Experiences

1 Uncommon Decency: Pacific Bell Responds to AIDS   **141**
David L. Kirp
AIDS confronts companies with new issues, including
employee benefits and fears, education and
prevention programs, and public image. The story of
Pacific Bell's examination and transformation of its
own culture and policies illustrates the kind of
leadership that business can take in dealing with this
disease.

2 Nothing Prepared Me to Manage AIDS   **163**
Gary E. Banas
Over a period of four years, the author had to deal
with two consecutive cases of AIDS in his
management team. The challenges of balancing
employee and company needs forced the author to
reevaluate his managerial assumptions.

Part V   Emerging Issues in Workplace Diversity

1 Dealing with the Aging Work Force   **179**
Jeffrey Sonnenfeld
In light of demographic trends, the author refutes
stereotypes about older workers and identifies key
challenges to organizations that wish to maximize the
productivity of employees as they age.

2 Business and the Facts of Family Life   **199**
Fran Sussner Rodgers and Charles Rodgers
With a focus on shifting demographics, evolving
employee attitudes and expectations, impacts on
productivity, and concerns about the future of the
nation's youth, the authors illustrate the need for new
attitudes and policies concerning working families,

positioning the issue of work and family interaction within the broader one of corporate responsibility and purpose.

3 How Technology Brings Blind People into the Workplace **215**
Julia Anderson
The author offers a provocative glimpse of the ways in which visually impaired individuals can make significant contributions to businesses as well as the reasons employers shy away from giving them the opportunity. At a broader level, this article illustrates a shared reticence to deal with people who are "different."

Part VI   Managers Wrestle with the Issues

1 The Case of the Unequal Opportunity **223**
Mary C. Gentile
A major producer of small appliances and yard equipment faces deeply engrained attitudes when a proposed international appointment for a high-performing product manager is resisted because of the candidate's race. Four experts comment on the case and suggest action plans for the characters.

2 A Case of AIDS **239**
Richard S. Tedlow and Michele S. Marram
In this three-part case, the authors follow the manager of a sales and customer service team as he makes a series of decisions about the promotion of a person with AIDS. Three experts offer guidance and personal experience regarding the concerns of employees and managers as they confront the wide range of issues presented by this situation.

3 Is This the Right Time to Come Out?   **253**
Alistair D. Williamson
How should a manager at a conservative business
respond when a gay employee requests permission to
bring his partner to a major company/client event? As
the manager tries to sort his own personal feelings
from his concerns about the firm's reaction, seven
commentators help place these issues in a wider legal,
social, and competitive context.

Suggested Further Reading   **267**

About the Contributors   **271**

Index   **275**

Foreword

R. Roosevelt Thomas, Jr.

When I started speaking about diversity ten years ago, some executives feared that my motive was to promote a narrow, politically charged agenda. They were unconvinced that my interests transcended traditional concepts of civil rights and affirmative action. Instead, they saw my efforts with the concept of managing diversity as a cover-up or disguise to make "black issues" in the workplace more palatable.

Over the past ten years, many of those same executives and their companies have had some profound realizations. They have discovered that managing diversity is much more than a concept, much more than a program, much more than an initiative. They have come to know it as a process that goes far beyond the interests of a particular individual or group of individuals. In the context of today's environment, they see managing diversity as providing a perspective that can enhance creativity and growth—not only with respect to the work force, but also synergistic progress in other arenas such as diverse functions, acquisitions, and multiple lines of business.

I have seen a significant evolution of thought regarding diversity. For example, I recently listened to managers discuss diversity issues with only a rare mention of race and gender. Rather, they focused on diversity as it relates to functions, acquisitions, and change in general. Similarly, executives at one corporation used diversity management as a vehicle to facilitate teaming, and delayed addressing race and gender as diversity dimensions. Their thinking was that this "teaming and diversity" program would later facilitate consideration of the more traditional subjects.

Differences That Work is a collection of articles which marked milestones in the evolving field of diversity. Individually and collectively, they establish a taxonomy that serves to expand our theoretical constructs while legitimizing inquiry around diversity and placing it on the managerial agenda. Most important, this anthology demonstrates the importance of discussing diversity issues, and contributes to the acceptance and understanding of differences. It recognizes differences as a reality in the business environment and sets the stage for further progress.

What can we expect in the future? Relatively little has been done to understand diversity and its dynamics independent of the work force. It is inevitable that as we expand our consciousness about diversity and managing diversity issues, we will give greater attention and effort to developing frameworks for understanding and addressing diversity outside of the work force. Once we understand diversity in a generic sense, I suspect that we will have a conceptual framework that will be useful in many areas, on a national as well as a global level.

Furthermore, we will begin to focus more on the collective mixture of differences and similarities, rather than on the differences themselves. The task of managing diversity is not only to address issues that have resulted in individuals being underutilized or excluded, but also to consider those who traditionally *have been* fully utilized and included. This will give us insight into how we can apply strategies of utilization to the entire work force.

We must increase our ability to operationalize the concept of work force diversity to include the white male. Managing diversity does not simply mean white males grappling with the opportunities and challenges of diversity. It also encompasses the incorporation of white male experiences along with those of minorities, women, immigrants, and a host of other visible and invisible contributors to the diversity "stew" into the mixture of similarities and differences that is known as today's work force.

In the context of this dynamic environment, *Differences That Work* reflects past accomplishments and the potential for exciting progress in the future. We will come to see diversity as relevant to any situation where there are differences and similarities—in the work place and beyond. However, while we celebrate this collection and its implications, we must keep in mind that much work remains to be done. Managing diversity is only the beginning of infinitely more to come.

Introduction

Mary C. Gentile

What is it that we hope to find when we pick up yet another book about managing diversity in the workplace? These texts abound now, many of them quite useful and a number of them written by authors represented in this collection. Nevertheless, it is probably safe to say that we come away from most of the books and articles on this topic yearning for something more. Why, and how can this volume help us move beyond dissatisfaction?

In many cases, our disappointment reflects not the inadequacy of the texts we are reading, but rather the breadth and bias of our questions. The questions triggered by diversity in the workplace exist at the intersection of our work lives and the rest of our lives, the intersection of the workplace and wider society, the intersection of our national identity and our global citizenship. They go to the heart of some of our most cherished assumptions about our organizations and perceptions about ourselves: meritocracy, equal opportunity, fair treatment, unbiased standards of performance, and so forth. And, painfully, they point out seeming contradictions and inconsistencies in these assumptions and perceptions.

When confronted with these difficult questions and contradictions, we have typically responded by focusing on the messenger, not the message. Diversity becomes a "problem" to be solved, rather than the herald of a new creative energy and the necessary announcement of heretofore unseen fault lines in the foundation of our workplaces. By defining diversity as a problem, we predetermine and constrain the structure our responses can take.

In *Differences That Work: Organizational Excellence through Diversity*, the

Harvard Business School Press has gathered together thirteen articles and three case studies, published in the *Harvard Business Review* over a 20-year period, on the subject of diversity. All the critical themes, the ongoing debates, and the familiar and the not-so-familiar intellectual and emotional responses are represented, making this collection important not only for its clear-eyed, practical approach to morally and managerially complex issues, but also for its historical documentation of business organizations' and managers' changing experience of difference.

Most significant, however, this book is an illustration of the whole being greater than the sum of its parts. By juxtaposing these responses to growing diversity in the workplace, this collection points the way to a new formulation or *framing* of diversity, not as a problem but as a resource and a process. It identifies a new *locus* for addressing the issue, not merely between individuals but within them. And it reveals a new *motivation* for responding to differences in the workplace, moving beyond moral and competitive drivers to the creative energy born of learning, personal and organizational growth, and innovation.

If we begin by taking an overview of the essays, we will quickly recognize an historical shift in the focus and approach they illustrate. The earliest pieces, whether written by individuals who identify as members of a majority or a minority, tend to be rooted in an analysis of individual and group culpability. Growing out of the civil rights and the women's movements, a heightened sensitivity to issues of fairness and morality engenders a focus upon the specific behavior and attitudes of individuals in the workplace. As time passes we see a petition to legal arguments in the essays, as their focus shifts from appeals to fairness and morality to an emphasis upon compliance.

And finally, as we come up to the present, the emphasis shifts again toward an outright appeal to self-interest, first from a defensive and reactive posture in response to demographic projections and competitive pressures, and second from a more proactive position as the authors begin to suggest initiatives born of diversity that can result in a more human and stimulating work environment for all. This developmental shift is not linear and unidimensional, but rather it is layered. It does not suggest that there is no place for appeals to morality or to the law in the discussion of diversity in the workplace, but rather that these are incomplete, and ultimately insufficient, approaches to such an historically, managerially, and psychologically complex issue. The juxtaposition of these articles reveals both the change and progression in our approach to workplace diversity as well as the consistencies. Just as we began in a place of moral imperative, we still find ourselves there in the most recent articles. The difference is that the benefits and the experience of obligation are more broadly defined in the more contemporary essays. The historical overview of the 20 years of thought represented in this anthology enables us to *reframe* the issue of diversity in the workplace, not as a moral or legal "problem" but rather as a resource and a process that can trigger innovation and new learning in business organizations.

Similarly, a review of these articles also broadens our definition of the site of inquiry for addressing the issues of workplace diversity. We begin to identify the different perspectives, priorities, anxieties, and commitments that exist not only *between* individuals or groups of individuals separated by gender or race or some other identification, but also those differences that exist *within* individuals and so-called homogeneous groups. For example, reading the compellingly candid accounts of Edward W. Jones, Jr., in "What It's Like to Be a Black Manager" and of Robert Schrank in "Two Women, Three Men on a Raft," we start to understand the conflicting impulses and identifications to which we all are subject.

Jones powerfully portrays the resistance and barriers with which he is confronted again and again in his career path. At the same time, he wonders to what degree his own personal style or his simple human frustration with repeated obstacles may have contributed to his challenges. For his part, Schrank participates in the gender stereotyping and exclusive male bonding he describes on the raft, even as he expresses doubt and discomfort with the needs and emotions which lead him to do so. It is this honesty and sophisticated self-insight that allow us to see the ways in which we are all called upon to resolve the conflicts triggered by diversity within our own identities on a regular basis.

In order to find and maintain a sense of personal coherence and integrity, we need to—and we do—find ways to balance the multiple identities we all experience inside ourselves: identities of race, gender, age, culture, religion, and sexual orientation as well as the more subtle and situational identities as members of a particular group or organization. This internalization of diversity allows us to begin to formulate a definitional model of "difference" that preserves the recognition of historical and personal and power distinctions even as it allows for acknowledgment of the continuities and commonalities of experience among us all.

Our definitional model of diversity or "difference" might begin with the following six observations. First, we can acknowledge that we all have multiple identities, one or another of which we may identify with more strongly at different moments in our lives and in different contexts. When I am with a group of women, I may be more cognizant of the commonalities of our experience based upon gender, whereas when I am with a mixed gender group of colleagues at work, I may identify more strongly as an individual with a particular educational and professional experience held in common with my peers in that context. Nevertheless, I negotiate, as we all do, a coherent, although complex, personality.[1]

Second, we often experience contradictory urges or needs for a sense of belonging or "fitting in" as well as a feeling of uniqueness or "specialness."[2] In some contexts, I may tend to emphasize my identity as an Italian-American, for example, in order to feel special or different. In other contexts—family gatherings for instance—I may emphasize the same ethnicity as a means to feel part of the group. These conflicting urges can trigger complicated reactions of loyalty, rejection, pride, oppositionality, and guilt within the same individual and between different individuals.

Third, we can acknowledge that some identities exact a higher and/or different price for the bearer in a particular societal, historical, or even situational context than others. In the United States, for example, the historical experience of African-Americans has had very real implications, generally speaking, for access to education, information, and financial resources. In a group of African-Americans, however, the lone white individual may experience a situational cost for being/feeling different that, if understood and explored, can serve as a foundation for empathy for all present.

Fourth, we can acknowledge that some individuals have a choice of becoming recognized as members of a particular identity group in a particular setting, and that choice brings certain costs and benefits.[3] Some identities, such as gender, race, and age, *tend* to be immediately evident. Other identities, such as religion or sexual orientation, *tend* to be less evident. For example, gays and lesbians often can choose whether or not they wish to reveal their sexual orientation. It is useful to understand the potential advantages and disadvantages of so-called invisible diversity. As a gay person, one can choose to "pass." This choice gives gay people greater control over the impression they make on others at the same time that it creates personal and political dilemmas. They may wonder if their discretion is actually a manifestation of internalized homophobia and a lack of self-confidence, or if it is a betrayal of gays and lesbians more generally because it allows others to assume they are not working and depending on homosexuals in their daily lives.

Fifth, we can recognize that our individual identities are always developing, that we are continually negotiating, defining, and redefining the internal coherence of our original values, our new experiences, and our multiple identities. If I can remain aware of the process of self-definition that requires a reconciliation of the aspects of my identity that present me with "privilege" in some circumstances and with "exclusion" in others, I can be more open to the same process in those with whom I work.

Sixth, we can acknowledge that identity differences do not preclude the development and pursuit of "shared goals" among and across identities. Managing diversity in the workplace is absolutely dependent upon the acceptance of some primary objectives to which all employees are willing to commit such as the survival of the firm.

These insights and acknowledgments, all of which are illustrated in this volume, can serve as the foundation and the impetus for both internal and external dialogue and inquiry about diversity. They give us a way to talk about diversity as a learning process in which we all are—or can be—engaged. Which brings us to perhaps the most significant contribution of this volume, a new *motivation* for responding to differences in the workplace.

Taken together, these essays demonstrate an energy and excitement about a new and untapped potential for growth, learning, and innovation—both individual and organizational. By opening ourselves and our organizations to the perspectives of individuals and groups who have had less managerial voice in the past, we can step outside the traditional frame of business decision making. We breathe a new life into our competitive brainstorming and our organizational definitions. We make the inside world of our corporations look more like the outside world of customers, competitors, and operating contexts. And we allow . . . no, *require* . . . ourselves to question the status quo.

This can be frightening, but ultimately it is perhaps the most compelling reason for proactive efforts to respond to diversity in the workplace. This is not to say that moral or legal reasons are not important, but rather that, when the rubber hits the road, real change comes from internal impetus. And the most powerful internal impetus is one that comes not from self-defense but from desire. I dare anyone to immerse themselves in the conversation created between the authors assembled in this text without becoming excited about the opportunities for communication and innovation they evoke.

Let's turn now to the individual articles and take a look at the themes that emerge within and between them. In Part I: Differences at Work: Where We've Been, Where We Are, Where We Go from Here, two opening essays offer a demographic and an ideological framework within which we can position the rest of the book. In "Global Work Force 2000: The New World Labor Market," William B. Johnston presses well beyond the by now familiar presentation of expected demographic changes in the U.S. workforce—more women and minorities, an aging labor pool—to present an integrated picture of the world's population growth patterns, education trends, and employment opportunity developments. His major contribution is to identify a fundamental "mismatch" between the site of new job development and that of the greatest population growth. He predicts greater relocation of workers from developing countries to more developed countries, causing pressures on unfavorable immigration regulations. He also predicts increased standardization of labor practices regarding employee rights and benefits, with governments playing a greater role. Johnston places his discussion of diversity in a context of demographic and competitive necessity.

R. Roosevelt Thomas, Jr.'s "From Affirmative Action to Affirming Diversity" builds on this foundation, reframing the issue of workplace diversity, placing it in an historical continuum, and sounding the first notes of a refrain which will be repeated in different keys throughout this text: our goal in managing diversity in the workplace is no longer to "assimilate" but rather to "optimize" differences. Thomas argues that affirmative action policies were a necessary but "transitional intervention" and that changing demographics and competitive realities have shifted the challenge from getting into the workplace to getting ahead. He explains that many corporations have hired a more diverse work force, but then neglected to attend to its orientation and development, and that of its supervisors. He illustrates this self-defeating cycle by offering a model of typical corporate diversity initiatives and how they founder, and then counters that reality with an alternative model of ten guidelines for corporate diversity efforts with a greater chance of success. Thomas also contributes five profiles of major corporations wrestling with the challenges of diversity: Avon, Corning, Digital, Procter & Gamble, and Xerox. Thus Part I has provided a multifaceted review of the historical and ideological context for discussions of diversity as well as the global and the corporate experience as background. In Part II: Racial Difference in the Workplace: How It Feels and What It Means, we turn to a more focused discussion of race in the workplace.

In "What It's Like to Be a Black Manager" and "Black Managers: The Dream Deferred," Edward W. Jones, Jr. offers two views, a dozen years apart, of the experience of black managers in corporate America. The consistencies are striking and disturbing. Jones' candor makes the earlier piece a valuable educational experience for anyone who wants to understand, from the inside out, the experience of being a visible minority in a traditional corporate environment. Jones allows us to see the subtle interplay of his own righteous anger with an answering self-doubt, the experience of being unjustly treated juxtaposed with a questioning of his own performance. His willingness to share this uncertainty offers a rare and generous insight into the insidious impact of discrimination on one's capacity for self-criticism and personal growth.

In "Black Managers," Jones broadens and deepens his analysis, presenting representative career histories from a larger sample of black managers and drawing conclusions which we will see echoed in subsequent essays. Perhaps most significant, he raises the fundamental problem of *undiscussability*: that is, that the penalties for naming concerns about discrimination (i.e., backlash, scapegoating) are perceived to far outweigh the rewards. If we are to unleash one of the greatest benefits of diversity in the workplace—its capacity to serve as a catalyst for individual and organizational learning and innovation—we must first make it safe and acceptable to talk about.

Part II concludes with a brief but useful piece by Terry L. Leap and Larry R. Smeltzer. In "Racial Remarks in the Workplace: Humor or Harassment?," they raise issues of compliance with the antiharassment laws and rulings of Title VII of the Civil Rights Act and the Equal Employment Opportunity Commission, and ask: "What constitutes harassment?" and "When is an employer responsible for the actions of its employees?" Their answer includes a lucid taxonomy of the types of racial remarks that surface in the workplace and a discussion of the legal requirements and precedents regarding each. This article provides some very usable distinctions and a kind of checklist for considering the climate in a particular organization, but perhaps more important, it opens the door for more subtle discussions in the wake of recent events such as the Clarence Thomas/Anita Hill congressional hearings. The observations here apply more broadly across discussions of harassment based upon gender, as well as race.

In Part III: Women in the Workplace: New Ways to Think About Work, the focus turns to gender and Robert Schrank opens the section with his personal account of an Outward Bound expedition in "Two

Women, Three Men on a Raft." Not only is this essay written from the perspective of a male, it implicitly assumes a male audience. Its reference point is male experience, and it becomes visible as such largely because of the juxtaposition with other essays written from the point of view of women or members of different minorities. This recognition is perhaps one of the most valuable lessons of the piece; we become aware of the way gender can be seamlessly knitted up in the presentation of experience, such that we do not always notice the degree to which it determines the "facts" of the situation. Schrank reveals the subtle, unspoken pressures to ally with one's own identity group (in this case, gender), even against another. Interestingly, this pressure to stand together with the other men seems derived both from the recognition of a power advantage (i.e., there were more men than women; the rafting "expert" was male), and from a tacit sense that the women were a potential threat if they stepped outside traditional gender roles. As Jones does in his piece, Schrank stresses the importance of being able to *name* and talk about these dynamics as the key to resolving them: "Things might have been different on Raft No. 4 had we been willing to confront each other." It is such self-inquiry that allowed Schrank to see and question his own behavior and that of his peers.

George P. Sape moves the focus from an analysis of interpersonal behavior to one of organizational experience in his discussion of the concept of comparable worth. He lays out the problem of pay disparity between men and women, citing Bureau of Labor Statistics figures for 1981, when women were making 62 cents against the dollar earned by men. (This article was published in 1985, but in 1992, women were making only 75.4 cents against that same dollar.) Sape presents the pattern of federal and state government rulings on this issue as well as the key court decisions, arguing that although government and court statements were evolving and somewhat sporadic, they pointed the way for a growing concern. In response, he offers a case study of one firm's efforts to review its own job classification and compensation systems for equity, and then concludes with a set of general guidelines for other firms to follow.

Although Sape's "Coping With Comparable Worth" limits its legal and regulatory analysis to the United States (as do most of the pieces here), it is useful to note that this issue is very much alive in the global business community. Although U.S. efforts to legislate comparable worth met with limited success throughout the 1980s, quite a number of states adopted measures to review their municipal payrolls, and a significant number of large firms took on similar projects. As Sape points out, with or without legislation and regulation, this is an issue that will not go away, particularly as the presence of women in the work force grows and as the United States interacts with international work forces.

In "Women as a Business Imperative," Felice N. Schwartz has written a capstone essay that integrates the interpersonal with the organizational perspectives presented by Schrank and Sape. She offers some tough talk about the limitations of current corporate efforts to integrate women effectively into the managerial ranks. Framed as a consultant's report to the CEO of the fictitious Topform Corporation, the article self-consciously and deliberately violates the taboo against naming the problem. Schwartz writes: "You don't voice your concerns for fear of litigation, and you are joined in this conspiracy of silence by women who don't want to be seen as different from men." She then enumerates a compelling list of the costs firms pay for failing to develop women, and the key actions firms can take to begin to capture these underutilized human resources. Here Schwartz has moved beyond the controversial arguments she presented in her 1989 essay, "Management Women and the New Facts of Life" (see HBR volume, *Reach for the Top*) now arguing for a flexibility in the workplace around parenting that can apply to and benefit all employees (men and women). Her 1992 arguments stem less from a focus on the ways women managers' experiences are different from men's, and more from an awareness of the way women's presence in the workplace was simply the herald, or the leading edge, of a new societal—and therefore a new workplace—reality. Changing labor pool demographics, changing attitudes about gender participation in parenting, changing possibilities for telecommuting, changing expectations about job mobility . . . all of these trends, and more, are facts of doing business today.

In Part IV: AIDS in the Workplace: The Organizational and Individual Experiences, we view firsthand the impact of a powerful and relatively new workplace reality. AIDS, or Acquired Immune Deficiency Syndrome, may not, at first glance, appear to be an aspect of workplace diversity, but upon closer look we see that it raises many very pertinent questions. Although quite particular in many aspects of its history and impact, in some ways AIDS can serve as a proxy for any health or ability-affecting condition to which employees are subject. It focuses attention on issues of reasonable accommodation, health and disability benefits, employee confidentiality, and the sometimes conflicting needs and wishes of individuals and work groups. On the other hand, the association of AIDS with homosexuality has added another prejudice to the experience of many persons with AIDS (PWAs), rendering earlier analyses of stereotyping and differences particularly relevant.

David L. Kirp's "Uncommon Decency: Pacific Bell Responds to AIDS" is a detailed and dramatic narrative of the transformative impact of diversity when an organization openly and honestly confronts and responds to it. AIDS was the catalyst and the occasion for genuine culture change at Pacific Bell, a culture change whose impact went far beyond AIDS and positioned the firm more effectively for dealing with its changing competitive context. Similarly, in "Nothing Prepared Me to Manage AIDS," Gary E. Banas presents a first-person account of dealing with two consecutive cases of AIDS in his management team. We see that the reality he faced refined and changed his managerial sensitivity and ability in ways that went well beyond dealing with AIDS. One of the more valuable contributions of this account, aside from its usefulness as a training vehicle for managers, is its demonstration of the fact that not all PWAs are the same. When we discuss a particular group of people along one similar dimension, we run the risk of assuming homogeneity along all dimensions . . . and that assumption just doesn't hold true.

In Part V: Emerging Issues in Workplace Diversity, the topics of an aging workforce, the impact of family on the workplace, and some exciting possibilities for enhancing the contributions of persons with disabilities are discussed. The three essays in this section only begin to suggest the rich possibilities for viewing the workplace in new ways. They reveal the ways that differences in the labor pool can be a catalyst for new perspectives on old problems, and the ways that apparent new problems can really be harbingers of new competitive enhancements.

In "Dealing with the Aging Work Force," Jeffrey Sonnenfeld presents research findings concerning the expectations, desires, and the capabilities of older workers, refuting stereotypes and identifying the key challenges to organizations that wish to maximize the productivity of employees as they age.[4] Perhaps most interesting, however, is that Sonnenfeld's description of employment trends, written in 1978, foreshadows changes firms are dealing with today regarding employees' needs to find greater balance between their work lives and the "rest of their lives" as well as changes in organizational structure from the traditional pyramid hierarchy to more matrixed, team-managed patterns. Once again, an attention to the differences in the workplace yielded useful signposts for the future.

We can draw the same conclusion from Fran Sussner Rodgers and

Charles Rodgers' "Business and the Facts of Family Life." Here the authors show how an attention to the needs of women employees reveals the leading edge of concerns that will be shared by larger numbers of employees as time passes. Flexible work schedules are no longer a concern only for working mothers, for example. Similarly, dependent care as a concept is expanding to include care for elders. Rodgers and Rodgers give a series of *"business* reasons" for corporate attention to the interrelation of work and family, including shifting demographics, shifting employee attitudes and expectations, impacts on productivity, and finally, but by no means least, concerns about the future of the nation's youth. They offer examples of corporate responses to dependent care assistance and working condition options, such as flextime, part-time work, and career path choices. Finally, they position the issue of work and family interaction within the broader one of corporate responsibility and purpose. Reflecting that in many other countries government regulates the provision of child care, Rodgers and Rodgers indicate that the United States' choices about business and government relationships imply certain self-imposed obligations regarding the well-being of its children, its future work force.

Finally, in "How Technology Brings Blind People into the Workplace," Julia Anderson offers a brief but provocative glimpse of both the ways in which visually impaired individuals can make significant contributions to businesses as well as the reasons that employers and managers sometimes shy away from giving them the opportunity. She uses anecdotes and field observations to identify and debunk unfounded stereotypes and to reveal the ways in which employers' reluctance to hire the visually impaired is often an attempt to protect themselves from their own discomfort. She illustrates the usefulness of presenting potential employers with a sense of what it will actually be like to work with the visually impaired: What kind of accommodations will be needed? How will their workstations fit into the existing space? What kind of interpersonal issues can be expected to come up? Honest questions and honest answers are key to moving beyond discomfort and prejudice. And as we have seen, we share a learned reticence about asking questions of those who are different from us. But this reticence can and must be "unlearned."

The concluding section, Part VI: Managers Wrestle with the Issues, demonstrates the wonderful discipline imposed upon our authors' analyses by the case study, with its implicit tests and challenges to each of the insights and approaches to diversity presented in preceding articles.

In my contribution, "The Case of the Unequal Opportunity," a group

marketing director for ARPCO, Inc.—a major producer of small appliances and yard equipment—must decide whether to recommend a
high-performing product manager for a choice international position.
The supervisor overseas resists the hire because of the candidate's race,
and the recommending manager fears that insisting on the promotion
will create a no-win situation for the candidate, for herself, and for
the firm. Yet, she believes he is the best candidate and should not be
denied the opportunity. The case illustrates how unfair and discriminatory practices are *expressed* (often through "coded" language), ra-
tionalized (often through an appeal to worst-case scenarios based
upon projection of one's own worst fears/biases or upon a failure to
imagine beyond the status quo), and *maintained* (often through organizational disincentives to action and the inability or unwillingness to
communicate about conflict). Four respondents, managers and academics, comment on the case and suggest action plans for the case
characters.[5]

In "A Case of AIDS," Richard S. Tedlow and Michele S. Marram
follow the manager of a sales and customer service team as he makes
a series of decisions about the hiring of a person with AIDS, the
management of confidentiality, work team dynamics, and, later,
whether to promote this employee to a more responsible position.
Three experts—Jonathan Mann, director of the International AIDS
Center of the Harvard AIDS Institute; James W. Nichols, an assistant
vice president of American Security Bank who has since died of AIDS;
and Lee Smith, president of Levi Strauss International—offer guidance
and personal experience regarding the concerns of employees and
managers as they confront such situations.

Finally, in "Is This the Right Time to Come Out?" Alistair D. Williamson portrays a manager struggling with the appropriate response
to a gay employee who intends to bring his partner to a major com-
pany/client social event. The manager tries to sort his own personal
feelings from his concerns about the firm's reaction, the response of
customers, and the impact of his actions on the commitment of a
promising and valued employee who just happens to be gay. Seven
commentators—academics in communications, anthropology, and
law, as well as human resource professionals and lawyers—put this
situation into a legal, social, and competitive context, offering both
advice and their opinions of likely outcomes for the case protagonist.

Stepping back from the insights and analyses presented in these
sixteen articles, we as readers can begin to take our collective pulse,
to get a sense of the overall impact of these assembled works on our
attitudes, our approach, and our commitment to the questions raised

by diversity in the workplace. There are a number of themes repeated, in different ways and from different points of view, throughout this text. We have seen the importance of *discussability*, of creating an environment and developing the personal characteristics necessary to enable managers and employees to name the issues surrounding race, gender, sexual orientation, and so on. We have seen the *inseparability* of our professional lives and our wider lives, the fact that family realities, health realities, and interpersonal realities affect the workplace even when we try to deny it. We have seen that diversity in the workplace, if attended to, can serve as a *bellwether* of and a *lever* toward inevitable change and potential opportunity. We have begun to develop a capacious and sophisticated *definition* of diversity, recognizing that it affects and includes us all, and that, as R. Roosevelt Thomas, Jr. suggests, to treat individuals equally does not necessarily mean treating them the same. Perhaps the most valuable thing we can take away from this collection is an *excitement and energy for new knowledge*. We learn that to really understand the differences among us means broadening our harvest of life's experience, and that "differences work" precisely when and because they are the channel to new learning, innovation, and individual and organizational growth.

Notes

1. C. D. Alderfer, "Intergroup Relations and Organizations," in J. R. Hackman, E. E. Lawler, and L. W. Porter (eds.), *Perspectives on Behavior in Organizations* (New York: McGraw-Hill, 1983), p. 410.
2. Mary C. Waters, *Ethnic Options: Choosing Identities in America* (Berkeley, CA: University of California Press, 1990), p. 147.
3. Ibid., pp. 155, 156.
4. In 1986, eight years after Sonnenfeld's article was first published, a mandatory retirement age was eliminated entirely in the United States.
5. As of November 21, 1991, the Civil Rights Act of 1991 extended protection from discrimination in employment to U.S. citizens working in foreign countries while employed by U.S. firms. This act extended coverage of Title VII of the Civil Rights Act of 1964 and of the Americans with Disabilities Act to such employees. Before this—during the period when this case study is set—the applicability of Title VII to U.S. employees on foreign soil had been a contested area of the law. Thus, the case raises the issue of making decisions in areas where the law offers no clear guidance.

Differences
That Work

PART

I

Differences at Work: Where We've Been, Where We Are, Where We Go from Here

1

Global Work Force 2000: The New World Labor Market

William B. Johnston

For more than a century, companies have moved manufacturing operations to take advantage of cheap labor. Now human capital, once considered to be the most stationary factor in production, increasingly flows across national borders as easily as cars, computer chips, and corporate bonds. Just as managers speak of world markets for products, technology, and capital, they must now think in terms of a world market for labor.

The movement of people from one country to another is, of course, not new. In previous centuries, Irish stonemasons helped build U.S. canals, and Chinese laborers constructed North America's transcontinental railroads. In the 1970s and 1980s, it was common to find Indian engineers writing software in Silicon Valley, Turks cleaning hotel rooms in Berlin, and Algerians assembling cars in France.

During the 1990s, the world's work force will become even more mobile, and employers will increasingly reach across borders to find the skills they need. These movements of workers will be driven by the growing gap between the world's supplies of labor and the demands for it. While much of the world's skilled and unskilled human resources are being produced in the developing world, most of the well-paid jobs are being generated in the cities of the industrialized world. This mismatch has several important implications for the 1990s:

It will trigger massive relocations of people, including immigrants, temporary workers, retirees, and visitors. The greatest relocations will involve young, well-educated workers flocking to the cities of the developed world.

It will lead some industrialized nations to reconsider their protectionist immigration policies, as they come to rely on and compete for foreign-born workers.

It may boost the fortunes of nations with "surplus" human capital. Specifically, it could help well-educated but economically underdeveloped countries such as the Philippines, Egypt, Cuba, Poland, and Hungary.

It will compel labor-short, immigrant-poor nations like Japan to improve labor productivity dramatically to avoid slower economic growth.

It will lead to a gradual standardization of labor practices among industrialized countries. By the end of the century, European standards of vacation time (five weeks) will be common in the United States. The 40-hour work week will have been accepted in Japan. And world standards governing workplace safety and employee rights will emerge.

Several factors will cause the flows of workers across international borders to accelerate in the coming decade. First, jet airplanes have yet to make their greatest impact. Between 1960 and 1988, the real cost of international travel dropped nearly 60%; during the same period, the number of foreigners entering the United States on business rose by 2,800%. Just as the automobile triggered suburbanization, which took decades to play out, so will jumbo jets shape the labor market over many years. Second, the barriers that governments place on immigration and emigration are breaking down. By the end of the 1980s, the nations of Eastern Europe had abandoned the restrictions on the rights of their citizens to leave. At the same time, most Western European nations were negotiating the abolition of *all* limits on people's movements within the boundaries of the European Community, and the United States, Canada, and even Japan began to liberalize their immigration policies. Third, these disappearing barriers come at a time when employers in the aging, slow-growing, industrialized nations are hungry for talent, while the developing world is educating more workers than it can productively employ.

These factors make it almost inevitable that more workers will cross national borders during the 1990s. Exactly where workers move to and from will greatly influence the fates of countries and companies. And even though those movements of people are not entirely predictable, the patterns already being established send strong signals about what is to come.

The Changing World Labor Force

The developments of the next decade are rooted in today's demographics, particularly those having to do with the size and character of various countries' work forces. In some areas of the world, for instance, women have not yet been absorbed in large numbers and represent a huge untapped resource; elsewhere the absorption process is nearly complete. Such national differences are a good starting point for understanding what the globalization of labor will look like and how it will affect individual nations and companies.

Although looming labor shortages have dominated discussion in many industrialized nations, the world work force is growing fast. From 1985 to 2000, the work force is expected to grow by some 600 million people, or 27% (that compares with 36% growth between 1970 and 1985). The growth will take place unevenly. The vast majority of the new workers—570 million of the 600 million workers—will join the work forces of the developing countries. In countries like Pakistan and Mexico, for example, the work force will grow at about 3% a year. In contrast, growth rates in the United States, Canada, and Spain will be closer to 1% a year, Japan's work force will grow just .5%, and Germany's work force (including the Eastern sector) will actually decline. (See Exhibit I.)

The much greater growth in the developing world stems primarily from historically higher birth rates. But in many nations, the effects of higher fertility are magnified by the entrance of women into the work force. Not only will more young people who were born in the 1970s enter the work force in the 1990s but also millions of women in industrializing nations are beginning to leave home for paid jobs. Moreover, the work force in the developing world is also better and better educated. The developing countries are producing a growing share of the world's high school and college graduates.

When these demographic differences are combined with different rates of economic growth, they are likely to lead to major redefinitions of labor markets. Nations that have slow-growing work forces but rapid growth in service sector jobs (namely Japan, Germany, and the United States) will become magnets for immigrants, even if their public policies seek to discourage them. Nations whose educational systems produce prospective workers faster than their economies can absorb them (Argentina, Poland, or the Philippines) will export people.

Beyond these differences in growth rates, the work forces of various

Exhibit I.

The World Work Force Is Growing Rapidly   (in millions)

Country or Region	Labor Force 1970	Labor Force 1985	Labor Force 2000	Labor Force Annual Growth Rate 1985-2000
World*	1,596.8	2,163.6	2,752.5	1.6%
OECD*	307.0	372.4	401.3	0.5%
United States	84.9	122.1	141.1	1.0
Japan	51.5	59.6	64.3	0.5
Germany	35.5	38.9	37.2	-0.3
United Kingdom	25.3	28.2	29.1	0.2
France	21.4	23.9	25.8	0.5
Italy	20.9	23.5	24.2	0.2
Spain	13.0	14.0	15.7	0.8
Canada	8.5	12.7	14.6	0.9
Australia	5.6	7.4	8.9	1.3
Sweden	3.9	4.4	4.6	0.3
Developing Regions*	1,119.9	1,595.8	2,137.7	2.1%
China	428.3	617.9	761.2	1.4
India	223.9	293.2	383.2	1.8
Indonesia	45.6	63.4	87.7	2.2
Brazil	31.5	49.6	67.8	2.1
Pakistan	19.3	29.8	45.2	2.8
Thailand	17.9	26.7	34.5	1.7
Mexico	14.5	26.1	40.6	3.0
Turkey	16.1	21.4	28.8	2.0
Philippines	13.7	19.9	28.6	2.4
South Korea	11.4	16.8	22.3	1.9
USSR	117.2	143.3	155.0	0.5%

*Totals include some countries not listed in table.
Sources: For OECD nations except Germany: OECD, Department of Economics and Statistics, *Labor Force Statistics, 1967-1987*; U.S. Bureau of Labor Statistics; The World Bank, *World Development Report, 1987*. For developing nations and Germany: International Labour Office, *Economically Active Population, 1950-2025*; The World Bank, *World Development Reports, 1987*.

nations differ enormously in makeup and capabilities. It is precisely differences like these in age, gender, and education that give us the best clues about what to expect in the 1990s.

Women will enter the work force in great numbers, especially in the developing countries, where relatively few women have been absorbed to date. The trend toward women leaving home-based employment and entering the paid work force is an often overlooked demographic reality of industrialization. As cooking and cleaning technologies ease the burden at home, agricultural jobs disappear, and other jobs (especially in services) proliferate, women tend to be employed in the economy.

Exhibit II.

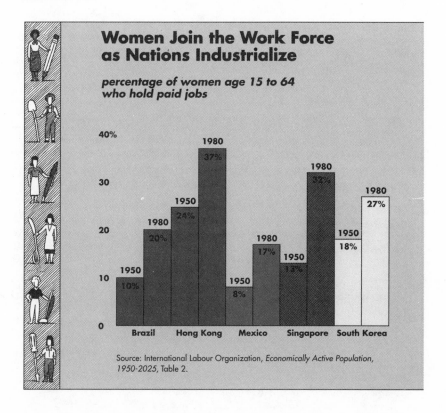

Women Join the Work Force as Nations Industrialize

percentage of women age 15 to 64 who hold paid jobs

Brazil: 1950 — 10%, 1980 — 20%
Hong Kong: 1950 — 24%, 1980 — 37%
Mexico: 1950 — 8%, 1980 — 17%
Singapore: 1950 — 13%, 1980 — 32%
South Korea: 1950 — 18%, 1980 — 27%

Source: International Labour Organization, *Economically Active Population, 1950-2025*, Table 2.

Their output is suddenly counted in government statistics, causing GNP to rise. (See Exhibit II.)

More than half of all women between the ages of 15 and 64 now work outside the home, and women comprise one-third of the world's work force. But the shift from home-based employment has occurred unevenly around the world. The developed nations have absorbed many more women into the labor force than the developing regions: 59% for the former, 49% for the latter. (See Exhibit III.)

More telling than the distinction between the developed and developing worlds, though, are the differences in female labor force participation by country. Largely because of religious customs and social expectations, some developed countries have relatively few women in the work force, and a small number of developing nations have high rates of female participation. The fact that women are entering the

Exhibit III.

Women Hold More Than One-Third of the World's Jobs

Country or Region	Working Women 1985 or 1987* (in millions)	Female Share of Work Force (percentage of total work force)	Female Labor Force Participation (percentage of all females age 15 to 64)
World†	790.1	36.5%	51.3%
Developed Regions‡	156.5	40.9%	58.6%
United States	53.9	44.1	66.0
Japan	24.3	39.9	57.8
Germany	11.1	39.3	51.3
United Kingdom	11.7	41.4	62.6
France	10.2	42.5	55.2
Italy	8.9	36.9	43.4
Spain	4.8	32.6	37.5
Canada	5.7	43.2	65.4
Australia	3.1	39.7	54.1
Sweden	2.1	48.0	79.4
Developing Regions‡	554.2	34.7%	48.6%
China	267.2	43.2	75.5
India	76.8	26.2	32.3
Indonesia	19.8	31.3	38.0
Brazil	13.5	27.2	32.2
Pakistan	3.4	11.4	12.1
Thailand	12.2	45.9	74.8
Mexico	7.1	27.0	31.1
Turkey	7.3	34.0	47.4
Philippines	6.4	32.1	39.2
South Korea	5.7	34.0	42.2
USSR (1985)	69.2	48.3%	72.6%

*For developed regions, 1987 figures were used; for developing regions, 1985 figures.
†Totals include some countries not listed in table.
‡Developed and developing regions as defined by the International Labour Office.
Source: International Labour Office, *Economically Active Population, 1950-2025*, Table 2.

work force is old news in Sweden, for instance, where four-fifths of working-age women hold jobs, or in the United States, where two-thirds are employed. Even in Japan, which is sometimes characterized as a nation in which most women stay home to help educate their children, about 58% of women hold paid jobs. Yet highly industrialized countries like Spain, Italy, and Germany have fairly low rates of female participation. And for ideological reasons, China, with one of the lowest GNPs per capita of any nation, has female participation rates that are among the world's highest.

The degree of female labor force participation has tremendous implications for the economy. Although a large expansion of the work force cannot guarantee economic growth (Ethiopia and Bangladesh both expanded their work forces rapidly in the 1970s and 1980s but barely increased their GNP per capita), in many cases, rapid work force growth stimulates and reinforces economic growth. If other conditions are favorable, countries with many women ready to join the work force can look forward to rapid economic expansion.

Among the developed nations, Spain, Italy, and Germany could show great gains. If their economies become constrained by scarce labor, economic pressures may well overpower social forces that have so far kept women from working. In developing countries where religious customs and social expectations are subject to change, there is the potential for rapid expansion of the work force with parallel surges in the economy.

Women are unlikely to have much effect in many other countries—Sweden, the United States, Canada, the United Kingdom, and Japan, all of which have few women left to add to their work forces. They may be able to redeploy women to more productive jobs, but the economic gains will likely be modest. Also, countries that maintain their current low utilization of women will have a hard time progressing rapidly. It is hard to imagine Pakistan, for example, a largely Moslem country where 11% of women work, joining the ranks of the industrialized nations without absorbing more of its women into the paid work force.

As more women enter the work force worldwide, their presence will change working conditions and industrial patterns in predictable ways. The demand for services like fast food, day care, home cleaners, and nursing homes will boom, following the now-familiar pattern in the United States and parts of Europe. Child rearing and care for the disabled will be increasingly institutionalized. And because women who work tend to have more demands on them at home than men do, they are likely to demand more time away from their jobs. It is plausible, for example, that some industrialized nations will adopt a work week of 35 hours or less by the end of the 1990s in response to these time pressures.

The average age of the world's work force will rise, especially in the developed countries. As a result of slower birth rates and longer life spans, the world population and labor force are aging. The average age of the world's workers will climb by more than a year, to about 35, during the 1990s.

But here again it is important to distinguish between the developed and the developing countries. The population of the industrialized nations is much older. Young people represent a small and shrinking fraction of the labor force, while the proportion of retirees over 65 is climbing. By 2000, fewer than 40% of workers in countries like the United States, Japan, Germany, and the United Kingdom will be under age 34, compared with 59% in Pakistan, 55% in Thailand, and 53% in China. (See Exhibit IV.)

The age distribution of a country's work force affects its mobility, flexibility, and energy. Older workers are less likely to relocate or to learn new skills than are younger people. Countries and companies that are staffed with older workers may have greater difficulty adapting to new technologies or changes in markets compared with those staffed with younger workers.

By 2000, workers in most developing nations will be young, relatively recently educated, and arguably more adaptable compared with those in the industrialized world. Very young nations that are rapidly industrializing, like Mexico and China, may find that the youth and flexibility of their work forces give them an advantage relative to their industrialized competitors with older work forces, particularly over those in heavy manufacturing industries, where shrinkage has left factories staffed mostly with workers who are in their forties and fifties.

Most industrialized nations will have 15% or more of their populations over age 65 by the year 2000, compared with less than 5% for most developing nations. The challenge that industrialized nations may face in preserving their competitive positions as their work forces age may be stiffened by the high costs of older workers and older societies. Older workers typically have higher wages because of seniority systems, and their pension and health care costs escalate sharply

Exhibit IV.

The World's Work Force and Population Are Aging

Country or Region	Share of Work Force Under Age 34		Share of Population Over Age 65		Labor Force Participation of Workers Over Age 65
	1985	2000	1985	2000	1985
World*	57.1%	51.7%	5.9%	6.8%	32.8%
Developed Regions†	46.9%	40.7%	11.2%	13.3%	9.0%
United States	50.4	39.5	12.3	12.9	10.3
Japan	33.8	33.9	11.1	15.8	26.0
Germany	45.7	37.4	14.2	16.0	3.2
United Kingdom	43.6	38.8	15.5	15.4	4.6
France	47.0	41.5	13.6	15.6	3.0
Italy	48.0	44.6	14.0	16.7	3.9
Spain	49.9	49.0	9.1	11.5	3.8
Canada	50.9	39.7	11.1	13.1	7.1
Australia	50.7	44.4	10.7	11.6	5.1
Sweden	38.7	36.3	16.9	17.2	5.4
Developing Regions†	60.7%	54.9%	4.2%	5.1%	26.3%
China	63.7	53.3	5.5	7.3	16.0
India	55.6	52.0	3.4	4.1	40.1
Indonesia	55.7	52.7	2.8	4.2	38.3
Brazil	62.5	42.1	4.0	4.9	17.7
Pakistan	63.3	59.2	4.1	3.9	33.7
Thailand	62.8	55.2	3.9	5.2	27.2
Mexico	61.4	51.9	4.1	4.9	42.1
Turkey	59.6	54.4	4.3	5.2	10.9
Philippines	59.2	54.8	3.3	3.8	44.8
South Korea	54.7	44.2	4.5	5.9	26.5
USSR	50.2%	42.9%	9.3%	11.9%	4.4%

*Totals include some countries not listed in table.
†Developed and developing regions as defined by the International Labour Office.
Sources: International Labour Office, *Economically Active Population, 1950-2025* and *Yearbook of Labour Statistics, 1988.*

during the later years of their work lives. As more workers in industrialized nations retire toward the close of the century, national health and pension taxes in these nations may rise as well. Unless these rising costs are offset by productivity gains, employers and nations that have older work forces may lose their competitive leadership in industries with standardized production technologies. This could be especially challenging for Japan, where the aging of the population is proceeding even more rapidly than in other industrialized nations.

One silver lining to this cloud of higher costs may be the higher rates of personal saving that come with older populations. As workers age,

Exhibit V.

Developed Countries Send More of Their Young to School

Country or Region	Percentage of Age Group in High School* 1986	Percentage of Age Group in College* 1986
OECD†	93.0%	39.0%
United States	95.0	59.0
Japan	96.0	29.0
Germany	72.0	30.0
United Kingdom	85.0	22.0
France	95.0	30.0
Italy	76.0	25.0
Spain	98.0	32.0
Canada	103.0	55.0
Australia	96.0	29.0
Sweden	83.0	37.0
Developing Regions†	40.0%	7.0%
China	42.0	2.0
India	35.0	9.0
Indonesia	41.0	7.0
Brazil	36.0	11.0
Pakistan	18.0	5.0
Thailand	29.0	20.0
Mexico	55.0	16.0
Egypt	66.0	21.0
Turkey	44.0	10.0
Philippines	68.0	38.0
South Korea	95.0	33.0
USSR	99.0%	22.0%

*Ratio of those enrolled to total school-age population. For high school, population base is typically age 13 to 17. For college population, age 20 to 24 is used. Gross enrollment level can exceed 100% if people from outside these ages are enrolled.

†Totals include some countries not listed in table.

Sources: United Nations Educational, Scientific, and Cultural Organization (UNESCO), *Statistical Yearbook, 1988;* U.S. Department of Education, National Center For Education Statistics, *Digest of Education Statistics, 1989.*

they tend to save a bigger chunk of their paychecks. This could increase the capital available for investment in industrialized countries and give them more money to buy productivity-enhancing equipment. (Of course, in a world of mobile capital, these funds could just as easily flow to the developing nations if economic conditions were more promising there.)

Wealth could be redistributed in another way too. As the number of retirees in industrialized countries rises, more of them are likely to cross national borders as tourists or immigrants. Traditionally, few retirees have settled outside their home countries. But cross-border retirements and travel are likely to burgeon in the 1990s: Japanese retiring to Hawaii, Americans receiving Social Security checks in Mexico, and English pensioners sunning themselves on the coast of Spain. As Algerians, Turks, and Mexicans return home bringing retirement checks with them, these flows could mirror the movements of young workers.

People worldwide will be increasingly well educated. The developing countries will produce a growing share of the world's high school and college graduates. Educational trends are hard to track because school and college systems differ so much from country to country and because the linkage between years of school and work skills is indirect and hard to document. Even the national data on years of education are often incomplete.

Still, the data reveal important developments. Based on the numbers of high school and college graduates, the world's work force is becoming better educated. In the decade and a half between 1970 and 1986, world high school enrollments grew by some 120 million students, or more than 76%. College enrollments more than doubled during the period—from 26 million to 58 million. This trend is likely to continue, as nations and individuals increasingly recognize the economic value of education. By the year 2000, it is likely that high school enrollment could grow by another 60%, reaching nearly 450 million, while college attendance could double again to top 115 million.

Today, higher percentages of children in industrialized nations attend high school and college. (See Exhibit V.) Most of them educate nearly all children through high school and typically further educate about one-third of college-age youths. (Germany and Italy are notable exceptions; only three-quarters of children between ages 12 and 17 go to secondary school.) Most of the developing nations have less than

Exhibit VI.

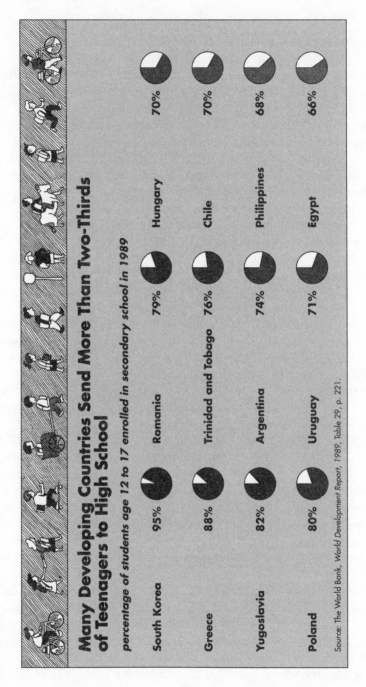

Many Developing Countries Send More Than Two-Thirds of Teenagers to High School

percentage of students age 12 to 17 enrolled in secondary school in 1989

South Korea	95%	Romania	79%	Hungary	70%
Greece	88%	Trinidad and Tobago	76%	Chile	70%
Yugoslavia	82%	Argentina	74%	Philippines	68%
Poland	80%	Uruguay	71%	Egypt	66%

Source: The World Bank, *World Development Report, 1989,* Table 29, p. 221.

half their young people in high school, and they seldom place more than one-fifth in college (although South Korea, Argentina, and the Philippines enroll more than one-third in college). (See Exhibit VI.)

But an important shift is under way: the developing world is producing a rapidly increasing share of the world's skilled human capital. This trend has been underway for some time and will accelerate through the turn of the century. In the decade and a half between 1970 and 1986, the United States, Canada, Europe, the Soviet Union, and Japan saw their share of world high school enrollees shrink from 44% to 30%. If current trends continue, their share is expected to drop to only 21% by the year 2000. (See Exhibit VII.)

U.S. high school students made up 9% of world enrollees in 1970 but only 5% in 1986. Not only is their relative number shrinking but also U.S. students are performing worse relative to the rest of the world. International standardized tests suggest that high school students from many other nations are now better prepared, at least in mathematics and science. (See Exhibit VIII.) In tests given to high school students worldwide during the mid-1980s, for instance, U.S. seniors ranked thirteenth among 13 nations in biology, twelfth in chemistry, and tenth in physics. The U.S. performance looks even weaker considering that only small fractions of American students took the tests, while greater percentages of non-U.S. students did.

The developed world is also losing ground when it comes to higher education. Between 1970 and 1985, the share of the world's college students from the United States, Canada, Europe, the Soviet Union, and Japan dropped from 77% to 51%. The share of college students in the developing world leaped from 23% to 49%, and these figures may be understatements because many students in Western universities are citizens of other countries and will return home when they graduate. By the year 2000, students from developing nations will make up three-fifths of all students.

It's true that in absolute numbers, the United States, the Soviet Union, and Japan are still the leading producers of college graduates of all kinds, but a growing number of the world's college graduates originate outside the traditionally highly educated countries. Four of the next six greatest sources of college graduates are developing countries: Brazil, China, the Philippines, and South Korea. Differences in the numbers of graduates are especially intriguing when sorted by discipline. China and Brazil rank third and fifth in numbers of science graduates, followed by Japan. For engineering graduates, Brazil,

Exhibit VII.

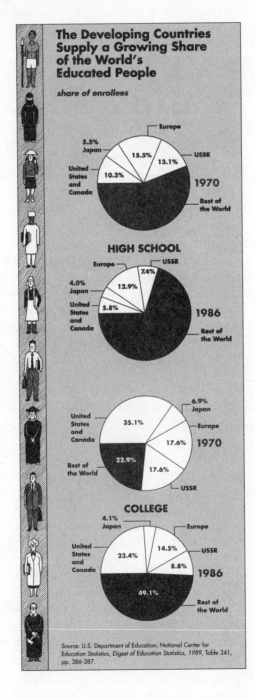

The Developing Countries Supply a Growing Share of the World's Educated People

share of enrollees

HIGH SCHOOL

1970 — Europe 15.5%, USSR 13.1%, 5.5% Japan, United States and Canada 10.3%, Rest of the World

1986 — USSR 7.4%, Europe, 12.9%, 4.0% Japan, United States and Canada 5.8%, Rest of the World

COLLEGE

1970 — 6.9% Japan, Europe 17.6%, USSR 17.6%, United States and Canada 35.1%, Rest of the World 22.9%

1986 — 4.1% Japan, Europe 14.5%, USSR 8.8%, United States and Canada 23.4%, Rest of the World 49.1%

Source: U.S. Department of Education, National Center for Education Statistics, *Digest of Education Statistics, 1989*, Table 341, pp. 386-387.

Exhibit VIII.

High School Students in Other Countries Outperform Americans in Science

*science test scores**

Country or Region	Biology	Chemistry	Physics
Singapore	66.8	66.1	54.9
England	63.4	69.5	58.3
Hungary	59.7	47.7	56.5
Poland	56.9	44.6	51.5
Norway	54.8	41.9	52.8
Finland	51.9	33.3	37.9
Hong Kong	50.8	64.4	59.3
Sweden	48.5	40.0	44.6
Australia	48.2	46.6	48.5
Japan	46.2	51.9	56.1
Canada	45.9	46.6	48.5
Italy	42.3	38.0	28.0
United States	37.9	37.7	45.5

*Scores normalized to a mean of 50, with a standard deviation of 10.

■ Developing countries.

Source: U.S. Department of Education, *Digest of Education Statistics, 1989*, Table 348, p. 391.

Exhibit IX.

Much of the World's Scientific Brain Power Comes from Developing Countries

thousands of college graduates in 1986

Country or Region	Total College Graduates	Scientists	Engineers	Ph.D.s
United States	979.5	180.7	77.1	394.3
USSR	839.5	61.7	352.3	na*
Japan	378.7	33.5	74.5	23.5
Brazil	244.6	34.1	20.0	8.9
China	227.7	44.7	72.7	14.2
Philippines†	212.0	26.3	23.4	na*
Germany	172.5	35.4	30.2	22.3
France	164.4	30.6	15.0	53.9
South Korea	155.0	16.9	21.9	20.7
United Kingdom	132.7	31.4	17.0	37.4
Canada	118.9	21.1	8.4	19.8
Mexico	112.8	20.4	25.3	8.0
Egypt	101.0	11.4	9.3	10.4

*Not available.   ■ Developing countries.
†Estimated.

Source: United Nations Educational, Scientific, and Cultural Organization (UNESCO), *Statistical Yearbook, 1988*, Tables 3-10; pp. 3-306.

China, Mexico, Korea, and the Philippines all place ahead of France and the United Kingdom. (See Exhibit IX.)

What makes the rising levels of education in developing countries especially significant is the link between education and economic growth. Those developing nations that educate large proportions of their young have achieved above average rates of growth and higher standards of living. Among the 42 nations labeled by the World Bank as "low income," only one, Sri Lanka, sends more than half of its high school-age children to school. Among those labeled "upper middle" or "high income" (excluding the oil producers), all but two send more than 60% of teenagers to school. Only Brazil and Portugal send less.

The Pressures to Emigrate

The link between the education levels of the work force and economic performance argues that some well-educated, middle-income nations may be poised for rapid growth in the 1990s. In Eastern Europe, for example, Poland, Hungary, and Czechoslovakia are especially well positioned for development because of their relatively well-educated work forces coupled with their relationships with other European countries. The Philippines, Egypt, Argentina, Peru, Cuba, and Mexico also have huge growth potential because they too have relatively well-educated work forces. But their fragile political and economic infrastructures and sometimes foolish economic policies make their development far less certain.

The tentative economic prospects of these well-educated nations illustrate the risks and opportunities facing countries whose educational systems outperform their economies. During the 1990s, workers who have acquired skills in school will be extremely valuable in the world labor markets. And if job opportunities are lacking in their native lands, better jobs will probably be only a plane ride away. Countries that fail to find a formula for growth can expect to become exporters of people. In Eastern Europe, for example, if the post-Communist rebuilding process stretches on for many years, hundreds of thousands—if not millions—of Poles, Czechs, and Hungarians will seek better opportunities in Western Europe or the United States. Similarly, if South America cannot find ways to restore investor confidence, the northward flow of economic refugees will accelerate.

Although most governments in industrial nations will resist these movements of people for social and political reasons, employers in the developed world are likely to find ways around government barriers.

The combination of slow work force growth, fewer women left to enter the work force, earlier retirements, and a shrinking share of high school and college graduates virtually guarantees that many industrialized nations will face labor shortages at various points during the economic cycles of the 1990s. When they do, a growing array of occupations and labor markets will become internationalized.

Not all workers are equally likely to emigrate—or equally likely to be welcomed elsewhere. The image of the labor force as a large pool of similar workers competing for jobs is inexact. There are actually many smaller labor pools, each defined by occupational skills. Patterns of immigration will vary, depending on the conditions of markets that are defined by specific skills.

Typically, unskilled workers—janitors, dishwashers, or laborers—are recruited locally. At higher skill levels, companies often search across states or regions. Among college graduates, national labor markets are more common: New York banks interview MBAs from San Francisco; Midwestern manufacturers hire engineers from both coasts. At the highest skill levels, the labor market has been international for many years. Bell Laboratories physicists, for example, come from universities in England or India as well as from Princeton or MIT. At Schering-Plough's research labs, the first language of biochemists is as likely to be Hindi, Japanese, or German as it is English.

When labor markets tighten and become even more specialized, however, many employers will expand the geography of their recruitment efforts. Recent trends in nursing and software design suggest the emerging patterns of the 1990s. As the shortage of nurses at U.S. hospitals became acute during the 1970s and 1980s, health care providers began to recruit in ever-widening circles. What was once a local labor market became regional, then national, and finally international. By the end of the 1980s, it was routine for New York hospitals to advertise in Dublin and Manila for skilled nurses. Similarly, in systems development, the shortage of engineers led rapidly growing companies to look to universities in England, India, and China to fill some of their U.S. job openings.

Government policies and corporate needs are likely to focus most on the immigration of younger, higher skilled workers filling specific occupational shortages. But while such flows of higher skilled workers will predominate, even unskilled jobs may become more internationalized in the 1990s. Indeed, during the 1970s and 1980s, some of the largest international movements of workers were relatively low-skilled workers immigrating to take jobs natives didn't want: Turks to Germany, Algerians to France, Mexicans to the United States. Although these movements of low-skilled workers generate explosive social and political tensions, the economic realities of the 1990s argue that the numbers will grow.

Gains from Trade in People

The globalization of labor is good for the world. It allows human capital to be deployed where it can be used most productively. Countries that recognize it as a positive trend and facilitate the flow of people will benefit most.

When workers move to a developed country, they become more productive because an established economic infrastructure can make better use of their time. (See Exhibit X.) A street corner vendor of tacos in Mexico City would be lucky to gross $50 for a day's work, while the same worker at a Taco Bell in Los Angeles might sell 10 to 50 times as much in a day. The higher output translates into higher wages. Even at minimum wage, the new Taco Bell employee will earn 10 times his or her former daily income.

For highly skilled workers, the effects are magnified. An engineer once relegated to clerical work in Bangkok may design a new computer system when employed by a Boston electronics company. A Filipino nurse can go from poverty to middle class by taking a job at a hospital in Atlanta. The positive impacts of immigration are visible in robust economies of Southern California and South Florida.

Immigration will be especially good for advanced nations with high levels of capital per worker but constrained labor. In particular, immigration may boost the economies of the United States, Canada, Germany, and other European nations.

The United States is likely to fare particularly well for a number of reasons. For one thing, its wages are among the world's highest, so they attract top talent. Also, political barriers have always been low, and opportunities for immigrants to advance are great. Further, its higher education system draws a large number of students from around the world. In 1987, U.S. universities granted to foreigners some 51% of doctorates in engineering, 48% in mathematics, 32% in business, and 29% in physical sciences. Many of these graduates return home, but many stay. Either way, they stimulate the U.S. econ-

Exhibit X.

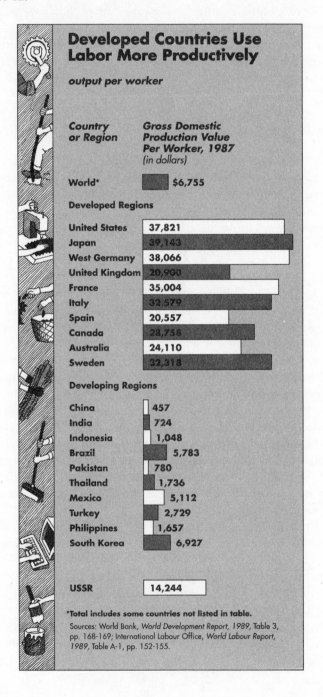

Developed Countries Use Labor More Productively

output per worker

Country or Region	Gross Domestic Production Value Per Worker, 1987 (in dollars)
World*	$6,755

Developed Regions

United States	37,821
Japan	39,143
West Germany	38,066
United Kingdom	20,900
France	35,004
Italy	32,579
Spain	20,557
Canada	28,758
Australia	24,110
Sweden	32,318

Developing Regions

China	457
India	724
Indonesia	1,048
Brazil	5,783
Pakistan	780
Thailand	1,736
Mexico	5,112
Turkey	2,729
Philippines	1,657
South Korea	6,927

| USSR | 14,244 |

*Total includes some countries not listed in table.

Sources: World Bank, *World Development Report, 1989*, Table 3, pp. 168-169; International Labour Office, *World Labour Report, 1989*, Table A-1, pp. 152-155.

omy—by enhancing trade relationships or by increasing the U.S. supply of human capital.

Australia, New Zealand, and some European nations—notably, Germany—are also likely to gain from the international flow of people. Historically, political and cultural obstacles have constrained emigration to Europe. But language and political barriers are weakening (English and German are becoming the languages of business), and the integration of formerly Communist states in Eastern Europe into the OECD trading regime suggests that Europe will increasingly welcome people who want to cross its borders. During the summer of 1990, for example, five nations in Western Europe agreed that they would eliminate all restrictions on the rights of their citizens to live and work anywhere within their five borders. In Germany, there has been a sharp political backlash against the guest worker program that allowed many Turkish workers into the country during the 1970s. Germany remains committed to preserving its ethnic identity and plans to tighten restrictions on immigration by non-Germans, but it continues to accept thousands of German-speaking people from Russia, Poland, and other East European countries. These workers are likely to strengthen the German economy during the 1990s.

While the politics of accepting more foreigners are unfavorable in virtually every industrialized nation (and may grow worse during the coming recession), the demographic and economic trends will create pressures in most nations to accept greater flows of people. Only Japan is likely to reject increased immigration, regardless of its looming labor shortages. Japan's enormous language and cultural barriers and its commitment to preserving its racial homogeneity virtually rule out the acceptance of many foreign workers. For the foreseeable future, Japanese economic growth will depend on native Japanese human resources. This may pose a stiff challenge for Japan because its work force is among the oldest in the world and its work force growth rate is among the lowest. One opportunity for Japan to pursue may lie in its female labor force: although a high proportion of Japanese women have paid jobs, many are underemployed and therefore not as productive as they could be. This may also be true for many—if not all—developed economies, but it seems to be especially true of Japan.

Leaders of developing nations often express concern that mass migration of their young people will harm their economies, but there is little evidence to support these fears. The large numbers of Korean, Taiwanese, and Chinese scientists and engineers who have emigrated to the United States do not seem to have had any appreciable impact on the economies at home. Indeed, many immigrants have returned home at some point in their careers, and the cross-fertilization seems to have boosted both economies. Nor have larger movements of less skilled workers harmed the economies left behind. Actually, the earnings sent home from Mexicans in the United States, Turkish guest workers in Germany, Algerians in France, and Egyptians throughout the Middle East have stimulated growth in labor-exporting countries.

A demonstration of the gains from trade in people occurred in Kuwait in 1990, when the gains were suddenly extinguished. When Iraq invaded, Kuwait's economy ground to an immediate and almost complete halt. Kuwait could no longer export oil, the occupying military force looted many businesses, but most important, the Asian and Middle Eastern workers who had made up two-thirds of the work force left for home. Hospitals lacked doctors and nurses, buses had no drivers, stores had no clerks. In the space of a few weeks, most of Kuwait's economy disappeared. Kuwait is not the only country to suffer. The huge repatriation of hundreds of thousands of Pakistani, Filipino, and Egyptian workers was equally traumatic for those nations. Not only did these workers and their families return to economies with few jobs available but their foreign earnings (a great part of which had been sent home from Kuwait) were also suddenly missing from the local economy. The gains from trade in people had been lost, and both the sending and the receiving nations were poorer because of it.

The developing countries can thrive despite massive emigration. The real test of whether they will realize their economic potential is how well they can combine their human capital with financial backing, sensible economic policies, and a sound business infrastructure. As always, they must win investors' confidence if they are to make any real progress.

From Globalization to Standardization

The globalization of labor is inevitable. The economic benefits from applying human resources most productively are too great to be resisted. At least some countries will lower the barriers to immigration, and at least some workers will be drawn by the opportunity to apply their training and improve their lives. But more likely, many countries will make immigration easier, and many workers will travel the globe. By the turn of the century, developing countries that have educated their young and adopted market-oriented policies will have advanced faster than those that have not. Developed countries that have accepted or sought foreign workers will be stronger for having done so. As the benefits become more obvious, the movement of workers will become freer.

The world will be changed as a result. As labor gradually becomes international, some national differences will fade. Needs and concerns will become more universal, and personnel policies and practices will standardize. As developing nations absorb women into the work force, for example, they are likely to share the industrialized world's concern about child care and demand for conveniences.

Two forces will drive workplace standardization: companies responding to global labor markets and governments negotiating trade agreements. For a global corporation, the notion of a single set of workplace standards will eventually become as irresistible as the idea of a single language for conducting business. Vacation policies that are established in Germany to attract top scientists will be hard to rescind when the employees are relocated to New Jersey; flexible hours of work that make sense in California will sooner or later become the norm in Madrid; health care deductibles and pension contributions designed for one nation will be modified so that workers in all nations enjoy the same treatment. Typical of most innovations in corporate personnel practices, the benefits of most importance to high-wage, highly valued employees (who will be the most often recruited internationally) will be standardized first.

Government efforts to harmonize workplace standards will accelerate these market-based responses. Currently, for example, officials from most EC countries are seeking to draft a single set of rules to govern workplaces throughout Europe, beginning in 1992. These will cover such things as wage and hour standards, employment rights, and worker safety. While the comprehensive European process is not likely to be repeated elsewhere, standardized working conditions and reciprocal work rules may become an element in many trade negotiations in the 1990s, particularly those relating to services. If Mexican and U.S. truck drivers were to be freely employed by companies on both sides of the border, for example, a U.S.-Mexico free trade agreement would need to cover driver licensing standards, hours of work, and fringe benefits.

Like the process of globalization of product and financial markets, the globalization of labor will be uneven and uncertain. Governments will play a greater role in world labor markets than in other markets, and governments often will be motivated by factors other than economic gain.

But for companies and countries that accept the trends, the 1990s and beyond can be a time of great opportunity. For countries seeking to maximize economic growth, strategies that develop and attract human capital can become powerful policy tools. For companies prepared to operate globally, willingness to compete for human resources on a worldwide basis can be a source of competitive advantage.

2
From Affirmative Action to Affirming Diversity

R. Roosevelt Thomas, Jr.

Sooner or later, affirmative action will die a natural death. Its achievements have been stupendous, but if we look at the premises that underlie it, we find assumptions and priorities that look increasingly shopworn. Thirty years ago, affirmative action was invented on the basis of these five appropriate premises:

1. Adult, white males make up something called the U.S. business mainstream.
2. The U.S. economic edifice is a solid, unchanging institution with more than enough space for everyone.
3. Women, blacks, immigrants, and other minorities should be allowed in as a matter of public policy and common decency.
4. Widespread racial, ethnic, and sexual prejudice keeps them out.
5. Legal and social coercion are necessary to bring about the change.

Today all five of these premises need revising. Over the past six years, I have tried to help some 15 companies learn how to achieve and manage diversity, and I have seen that the realities facing us are no longer the realities affirmative action was designed to fix.

To begin with, more than half the U.S. work force now consists of minorities, immigrants, and women, so white, native-born males, though undoubtedly still dominant, are themselves a statistical minority. In addition, white males will make up only 15% of the increase in the work force over the next ten years. The so-called mainstream is now almost as diverse as the society at large.

Second, while the edifice is still big enough for all, it no longer seems stable, massive, and invulnerable. In fact, American corporations are scrambling, doing their best to become more adaptable, to compete more successfully for markets and labor, foreign and domestic, and to attract all the talent they can find. (See the appendix for what a number of U.S. companies are doing to manage diversity.)

Third, women and minorities no longer need a boarding pass, they need an upgrade. The problem is not getting them in at the entry level; the problem is making better use of their potential at every level, especially in middle-management and leadership positions. This is no longer simply a question of common decency, it is a question of business survival.

Fourth, although prejudice is hardly dead, it has suffered some wounds that may eventually prove fatal. In the meantime, American businesses are now filled with progressive people—many of them minorities and women themselves—whose prejudices, where they still exist, are much too deeply suppressed to interfere with recruitment. The reason many companies are still wary of minorities and women has much more to do with education and perceived qualifications than with color or gender. Companies are worried about productivity and well aware that minorities and women represent a disproportionate share of the undertrained and undereducated.

Fifth, coercion is rarely needed at the recruitment stage. There are very few places in the United States today where you could dip a recruitment net and come up with nothing but white males. Getting hired is not the problem—women and blacks who are seen as having the necessary skills and energy can get *into* the work force relatively easily. It's later on that many of them plateau and lose their drive and quit or get fired. It's later on that their managers' inability to manage diversity hobbles them and the companies they work for.

In creating these changes, affirmative action had an essential role to play and played it very well. In many companies and communities it still plays that role. But affirmative action is an artificial, transitional intervention intended to give managers a chance to correct an imbalance, an injustice, a mistake. Once the numbers mistake has been corrected, I don't think affirmative action alone can cope with the remaining long-term task of creating a work setting geared to the upward mobility of *all* kinds of people, including white males. It is difficult for affirmative action to influence upward mobility even in the short run, primarily because it is perceived to conflict with the meritocracy we favor. For this reason, affirmative action is a red flag to every individual who feels unfairly passed over and a stigma for those who appear to be its beneficiaries.

Moreover, I doubt very much that individuals who reach top positions through affirmative action are effective models for younger members of their race or sex. What, after all, do they model? A black vice president who got her job through affirmative action is not necessarily a model of how to rise through the corporate meritocracy. She may be a model of how affirmative action can work for the people who find or put themselves in the right place at the right time.

If affirmative action in upward mobility meant that no person's competence and character would ever be overlooked or undervalued on account of race, sex, ethnicity, origins, or physical disability, affirmative action would be the very thing we need to let every corporate talent find its niche. But what affirmative action means in practice is an unnatural focus on one group, and what it means too often to too many employees is that someone is playing fast and loose with standards in order to favor that group. Unless we are to compromise our standards, a thing no competitive company can even contemplate, upward mobility for minorities and women should always be a question of pure competence and character unmuddled by accidents of birth.

And that is precisely why we have to learn to manage diversity—to move beyond affirmative action, not to repudiate it. Some of what I have to say may strike some readers—mostly those with an ax to grind—as directed at the majority white males who hold most of the decision-making posts in our economy. But I am speaking to all managers, not just white males, and I certainly don't mean to suggest that white males somehow stand outside diversity. White males are as odd and as normal as anyone else.

The Affirmative Action Cycle

If you are managing diverse employees, you should ask yourself this question: Am I fully tapping the potential capacities of everyone in my department? If the answer is no, you should ask yourself this follow-up: Is this failure hampering my ability to meet performance standards? The answer to this question will undoubtedly be yes.

Think of corporate management for a moment as an engine burning pure gasoline. What's now going into the tank is no longer just gas, it has an increasing percentage of, let's say, methanol. In the beginning, the engine will still work pretty well, but by and by it will start to sputter, and eventually it will stall. Unless we rebuild the engine, it will no longer burn the fuel we're feeding it. As the work force grows more and more diverse at the intake level, the talent pool we have to draw on for supervision and management will also grow increasingly diverse. So the question is: Can we burn this fuel? Can we get maximum corporate power from the diverse work force we're now drawing into the system?

Affirmative action gets blamed for failing to do things it never could do. Affirmative action gets the new fuel into the tank, the new people through the front door. Something else will have to get them into the driver's seat. That something else consists of enabling people, in this case minorities and women, to perform to their potential. This is what we now call managing diversity. Not appreciating or leveraging diversity, not even necessarily understanding it. Just managing diversity in such a way as to get from a heterogeneous work force the same productivity, commitment, quality, and profit that we got from the old homogeneous work force.

The correct question today is not "How are we doing on race relations?" or "Are we promoting enough minority people and women?" but rather "Given the diverse work force I've got, am I getting the productivity, does it work as smoothly, is morale as high, as if every person in the company was the same sex and race and nationality?" Most answers will be, "Well, no, of course not!" But why shouldn't the answer be, "You bet!"?

When we ask how we're doing on race relations, we inadvertently put our finger on what's wrong with the question and with the attitude that underlies affirmative action. So long as racial and gender equality is something we grant to minorities and women, there will be no racial and gender equality. What we must do is create an environment where no one is advantaged or disadvantaged, an environment where "we" is everyone. What the traditional approach to diversity did was to create a cycle of crisis, action, relaxation, and disappointment that companies repeated over and over again without ever achieving more than the barest particle of what they were after.

Affirmative action pictures the work force as a pipeline and reasons as follows: "If we can fill the pipeline with *qualified* minorities and women, we can solve our upward mobility problem. Once recruited, they will perform in accordance with our promotional criteria and move naturally up our regular developmental ladder. In the past, where minorities and women have failed to progress, they were simply unable to meet our performance standards. Recruiting qualified people will enable us to avoid special programs and reverse discrimination."

This pipeline perspective generates a self-perpetuating, self-defeating, recruitment-oriented cycle with six stages:

1. *Problem Recognition.* The first time through the cycle, the problem takes this form—We need more minorities and women in the pipeline. In later iterations, the problem is more likely to be defined as a need to retain and promote minorities and women.

2. *Intervention.* Management puts the company into what we may call an Affirmative Action Recruitment Mode. During the first cycle, the goal is to recruit minorities and women. Later, when the cycle is repeated a second or third time and the challenge has shifted to retention, development, and promotion, the goal is to recruit *qualified* minorities and women. Sometimes, managers indifferent or blind to possible accusations of reverse discrimination will institute special training, tracking, incentive, mentoring, or sponsoring programs for minorities and women.

3. *Great Expectations.* Large numbers of minorities and women have been recruited, and a select group has been promoted or recruited at a higher level to serve as highly visible role models for the newly recruited masses. The stage seems set for the natural progression of minorities and women up through the pipeline. Management leans back to enjoy the fruits of its labor.

4. *Frustration.* The anticipated natural progression fails to occur. Minorities and women see themselves plateauing prematurely. Management is upset (and embarrassed) by the failure of its affirmative action initiative and begins to resent the impatience of the new recruits and their unwillingness to give the company credit for trying to do the right thing. Depending on how high in the hierarchy they have plateaued, alienated minorities and women either leave the company or stagnate.

5. *Dormancy.* All remaining participants conspire tacitly to present a silent front to the outside world. Executives say nothing because they have no solutions. As for those women and minorities who stayed on, calling attention to affirmative action's failures might raise doubts about their qualifications. Do they deserve their jobs, or did they just happen to be in the right place at the time of an affirmative action

push? So no one complains, and if the company has a good public relations department, it may even wind up with a reputation as a good place for women and minorities to work.

If questioned publicly, management will say things like "Frankly, affirmative action is not currently an issue," or "Our numbers are okay," or "With respect to minority representation at the upper levels, management is aware of this remaining challenge."

In private and off the record, however, people say things like "Premature plateauing is a problem, and we don't know what to do," and "Our top people don't seem to be interested in finding a solution," and "There's plenty of racism and sexism around this place—whatever you may hear."

6. *Crisis*. Dormancy can continue indefinitely, but it is usually broken by a crisis of competitive pressure, governmental intervention, external pressure from a special interest group, or internal unrest. One company found that its pursuit of a Total Quality program was hampered by the alienation of minorities and women. Senior management at another corporation saw the growing importance of minorities in their customer base and decided they needed minority participation in their managerial ranks. In another case, growing expressions of discontent forced a break in the conspiracy of silence even after the company had received national recognition as a good place for minorities and women to work.

Whatever its cause, the crisis fosters a return to the Problem Recognition phase, and the cycle begins again. This time, management seeks to explain the shortcomings of the previous affirmative action push and usually concludes that the problem is recruitment. This assessment by a top executive is typical: "The managers I know are decent people. While they give priority to performance, I do not believe any of them deliberately block minorities or women who are qualified for promotion. On the contrary, I suspect they bend over backward to promote women and minorities who give some indication of being qualified."

"However, they believe we simply do not have the necessary talent within those groups, but because of the constant complaints they have heard about their deficiencies in affirmative action, they feel they face a no-win situation. If they do not promote, they are obstructionists. But if they promote people who are unqualified, they hurt performance and deny promotion to other employees unfairly. They can't win. The answer, in my mind, must be an ambitious new recruitment effort to bring in quality people."

And so the cycle repeats. Once again blacks, Hispanics, women, and immigrants are dropped into a previously homogeneous, all-white, all-Anglo, all-male, all native-born environment, and the burden of cultural change is placed on the newcomers. There will be new expectations and a new round of frustration, dormancy, crisis, and recruitment.

Ten Guidelines for Learning to Manage Diversity

The traditional American image of diversity has been assimilation: the melting pot, where ethnic and racial differences were standardized into a kind of American puree. Of course, the melting pot is only a metaphor. In real life, many ethnic and most racial groups retain their individuality and express it energetically. What we have is perhaps some kind of American mulligan stew; it is certainly no puree.

At the workplace, however, the melting pot has been more than a metaphor. Corporate success has demanded a good deal of conformity, and employees have voluntarily abandoned most of their ethnic distinctions at the company door.

Now those days are over. Today the melting pot is the wrong metaphor even in business, for three good reasons. First, if it ever was possible to melt down Scotsmen and Dutchmen and Frenchmen into an indistinguishable broth, you can't do the same with blacks, Asians, and women. Their differences don't melt so easily. Second, most people are no longer willing to be melted down, not even for eight hours a day—and it's a seller's market for skills. Third, the thrust of today's nonhierarchical, flexible, collaborative management requires a ten- or twentyfold increase in our tolerance for individuality.

So companies are faced with the problem of surviving in a fiercely competitive world with a work force that consists and will continue to consist of *unassimilated diversity*. And the engine will take a great deal of tinkering to burn that fuel.

What managers fear from diversity is a lowering of standards, a sense that "anything goes." Of course, standards must not suffer. In fact, competence counts more than ever. The goal is to manage diversity in such a way as to get from a diverse work force the same productivity we once got from a homogeneous work force, and to do it without artificial programs, standards—or barriers.

Managing diversity does not mean controlling or containing diversity, it means enabling every member of your work force to perform to his or her potential. It means getting from employees, first, everything we have a right to expect, and, second—if we do it well—everything they have to give. If the old homogeneous work force performed dependably at 80% of its capacity, then the first result means getting 80% from the new heterogeneous work force too. But the second result, the icing on the cake, the unexpected upside that diversity can perhaps give as a bonus, means 85% to 90% from everyone in the organization.

For the moment, however, let's concentrate on the basics of how to get satisfactory performance from the new diverse work force. There are few adequate models. So far, no large company I know of has succeeded in managing diversity to its own satisfaction. But any number have begun to try.

On the basis of their experience, here are my ten guidelines:

1. *Clarify Your Motivation.* A lot of executives are not sure why they should want to learn to manage diversity. Legal compliance seems like a good reason. So does community relations. Many executives believe they have a social and moral responsibility to employ minorities and women. Others want to placate an internal group or pacify an outside organization. None of these are bad reasons, but none of them are business reasons, and given the nature and scope of today's competitive challenges, I believe only business reasons will supply the necessary long-term motivation. In any case, it is the business reasons I want to focus on here.

In business terms, a diverse work force is not something your company ought to have; it's something your company does have, or soon will have. Learning to manage that diversity will make you more competitive.

2. *Clarify Your Vision.* When managers think about a diverse work force, what do they picture? Not publicly, but in the privacy of their minds?

One popular image is of minorities and women clustering on a relatively low plateau, with a few of them trickling up as they become assimilated into the prevailing culture. Of course, they enjoy good salaries and benefits, and most of them accept their status, appreciate the fact that they are doing better than they could do somewhere else, and are proud of the achievements of their race or sex. This is reactionary thinking, but it's a lot more common than you might suppose.

Another image is what we might call "heightened sensitivity." Members of the majority culture are sensitive to the demands of minorities and women for upward mobility and recognize the advantages of fully utilizing them. Minorities and women work at all levels of the corporation, but they are the recipients of generosity and know it. A few years of this second-class status drives most of them away and compromises the effectiveness of those that remain. Turnover is high.

Then there is the coexistence-compromise image. In the interests of corporate viability, white males agree to recognize minorities and women as equals. They bargain and negotiate their differences. But the win-lose aspect of the relationship preserves tensions, and the compromises reached are not always to the company's competitive advantage.

"Diversity and equal opportunity" is a big step up. It presupposes that the white male culture has given way to one that respects difference and individuality. The problem is that minorities and women will accept it readily as their operating image, but many white males, consciously or unconsciously, are likely to cling to a vision that leaves them in the driver's seat. A vision gap of this kind can be a difficulty.

In my view, the vision to hold in your own imagination and to try to communicate to all your managers and employees is an image of fully tapping the human resource potential of every member of the work force. This vision sidesteps the question of equality, ignores the tensions of coexistence, plays down the uncomfortable realities of difference, and focuses instead on individual enablement. It doesn't say, "Let *us* give *them* a chance." It assumes a diverse work force that includes us and them. It says, "Let's create an environment where everyone will do their best work."

Several years ago, an industrial plant in Atlanta with a highly diverse work force was threatened with closing unless productivity improved. To save their jobs, everyone put their shoulders to the wheel and achieved the results they needed to stay open. The senior operating manager was amazed.

For years he had seen minorities and women plateauing disproportionately at the lower levels of the organization, and he explained that fact away with two rationalizations. "They haven't been here that long," he told himself. And "This is the price we pay for being in compliance with the law."

When the threat of closure energized this whole group of people into a level of performance he had not imagined possible, he got one fleeting glimpse of people working up to their capacity. Once the crisis was over, everyone went back to the earlier status quo—white males driving and everyone else sitting back, looking on—but now there was a difference. Now, as he put it himself, he had been to the mountaintop. He knew that what he was getting from minorities and women was nowhere near what they were capable of giving. And he wanted it, crisis or no crisis, all the time.

3. *Expand Your Focus.* Managers usually see affirmative action and equal employment opportunity as centering on minorities and women, with very little to offer white males. The diversity I'm talking about includes not only race, gender, creed, and ethnicity but also age, background, education, function, and personality differences. The objective is not to assimilate minorities and women into a dominant white male culture but to create a dominant heterogeneous culture.

The culture that dominates the United States socially and politically is heterogeneous, and it works by giving its citizens the liberty to achieve their potential. Channeling that potential, once achieved, is an individual right but still a national concern. Something similar applies in the workplace, where the keys to success are individual ability and a corporate destination. Managing disparate talents to achieve common goals is what companies learned to do when they set their sights on, say, Total Quality. The secrets of managing diversity are much the same.

4. *Audit Your Corporate Culture.* If the goal is not to assimilate diversity into the dominant culture but rather to build a culture that can digest unassimilated diversity, then you had better start by figuring out what your present culture looks like. Since what we're talking about here is the body of unspoken and unexamined assumptions, values, and mythologies that make your world go round, this kind of cultural audit is impossible to conduct without outside help. It's a research activity, done mostly with in-depth interviews and a lot of listening at the water cooler. The operative corporate assumptions you have to identify and deal with are often inherited from the company's founder. "If we treat everyone as a member of the family, we will be successful" is not uncommon. Nor is its corollary "Father Knows Best."

Another widespread assumption, probably absorbed from American culture in general, is that "cream will rise to the top." In most companies, what passes for cream rising to the top is actually cream being pulled or pushed to the top by an informal system of mentoring and sponsorship.

Corporate culture is a kind of tree. Its roots are assumptions about the company and about the world. Its branches, leaves, and seeds are behavior. You can't change the leaves without changing the roots, and you can't grow peaches on an oak. Or rather, with the proper grafting, you can grow peaches on an oak, but they come out an awful lot like acorns—small and hard and not much fun to eat. So if you want to grow peaches, you have to make sure the tree's roots are peach friendly.

5. *Modify Your Assumptions.* The real problem with this corporate culture tree is that every time you go to make changes in the roots, you run into terrible opposition. Every culture, including corporate culture, has root guards that turn out in force every time you threaten a basic assumption.

Take the family assumption as an example. Viewing the corporation as a family suggests not only that father knows best; it also suggests that sons will inherit the business, that daughters should stick to doing the company dishes, and that if Uncle Deadwood doesn't perform, we'll put him in the chimney corner and feed him for another 30 years regardless. Each assumption has its constituency and its defenders. If we say to Uncle Deadwood, "Yes, you did good work for 10 years, but years 11 and 12 look pretty bleak; we think it's time we helped you find another chimney," shock waves will travel through the company as every family-oriented employee draws a sword to defend the sacred concept of guaranteed jobs.

But you have to try. A corporation that wants to create an environment with no advantages or disadvantages for any group cannot allow the family assumption to remain in place. It must be labeled dishonest mythology.

Sometimes the dishonesties are more blatant. When I asked a white male middle manager how promotions were handled in his company, he said, "You need leadership capability, bottom-line results, the ability to work with people, and compassion." Then he paused and smiled. "That's what they say. But down the hall there's a guy we call Captain Kickass. He's ruthless, mean-spirited, and he steps on people. That's the behavior they really value. Forget what they say."

In addition to the obvious issue of hypocrisy, this example also raises a question of equal opportunity. When I asked this young middle manager if he thought minorities and women could meet the Captain Kickass standard, he said he thought they probably could. But the opposite argument can certainly be made. Whether we're talking about blacks in an environment that is predominantly white, whites in one predominantly black, or women in one predominantly male, the majority culture will not readily condone such tactics from a member of a minority. So the corporation with the unspoken kickass performance standard has at least one criterion that will hamper the upward mobility of minorities and women.

Another destructive assumption is the melting pot I referred to earlier. The organization I'm arguing for respects differences rather than seeking to smooth them out. It is multicultural rather than culture blind, which has an important consequence: When we no longer force people to "belong" to a common ethnicity or culture, then the organization's leaders must work all the harder to define belonging in terms of a set of values and a sense of purpose that transcend the interests, desires, and preferences of any one group.

6. *Modify Your Systems.* The first purpose of examining and modifying assumptions is to modify systems. Promotion, mentoring, and sponsorship comprise one such system, and the unexamined cream-to-the-top assumption I mentioned earlier can tend to keep minorities and women from climbing the corporate ladder. After all, in many companies it is difficult to secure a promotion above a certain level without a personal advocate or sponsor. In the context of managing diversity, the question is not whether this system is maximally efficient but whether it works for all employees. Executives who only sponsor people like themselves are not making much of a contribution to the cause of getting the best from every employee.

Performance appraisal is another system where unexamined practices and patterns can have pernicious effects. For example, there are companies where official performance appraisals differ substantially from what is said informally, with the result that employees get their most accurate performance feedback through the grapevine. So if the grapevine is closed to minorities and women, they are left at a severe disadvantage. As one white manager observed, "If the blacks around here knew how they were really perceived, there would be a revolt." Maybe so. More important to your business, however, is the fact that without an accurate appraisal of performance, minority and women employees will find it difficult to correct or defend their alleged shortcomings.

7. *Modify Your Models.* The second purpose of modifying assumptions is to modify models of managerial and employee behavior. My own personal hobgoblin is one I call the Doer Model, often an outgrowth of the family assumption and of unchallenged paternalism. I have found the Doer Model alive and thriving in a dozen companies. It works like this.

Since father knows best, managers seek subordinates who will follow their lead and do as they do. If they can't find people exactly like themselves, they try to find people who aspire to be exactly like themselves. The goal is predictability and immediate responsiveness because the doer manager is not there to manage people but to do the business. In accounting departments, for example, doer managers do accounting, and subordinates are simply extensions of their hands and minds, sensitive to every signal and suggestion of managerial intent.

Doer managers take pride in this identity of purpose. "I wouldn't ask my people to do anything I wouldn't do myself," they say. "I roll up my sleeves and get in the trenches." Doer managers love to be in the trenches. It keeps them out of the line of fire.

But managers aren't supposed to be in the trenches, and accounting managers aren't supposed to do accounting. What they are supposed to do is create systems and a climate that allow accountants to do accounting, a climate that enables people to do what they've been charged to do. The right goal is doer subordinates, supported and empowered by managers who manage.

8. *Help Your People Pioneer.* Learning to manage diversity is a change process, and the managers involved are change agents. There is no single tried and tested "solution" to diversity and no fixed right way to manage it. Assuming the existence of a single or even a dominant barrier undervalues the importance of all the other barriers that face any company, including, potentially, prejudice, personality, community dynamics, culture, and the ups and downs of business itself.

While top executives articulate the new company policy and their commitment to it, middle managers—most or all of them still white males, remember—are placed in the tough position of having to cope with a forest of problems and simultaneously develop the minorities and women who represent their own competition for an increasingly limited number of promotions. What's more, every time they stumble they will themselves be labeled the major barriers to progress. These managers need help, they need a certain amount of sympathy, and, most of all, perhaps, they need to be told that they are pioneers and judged accordingly.

In one case, an ambitious young black woman was assigned to a white male manager, at his request, on the basis of her excellent company record. They looked forward to working together, and for the first three months, everything went well. But then their relationship began to deteriorate, and the harder they worked at patching it up, the worse it got. Both of them, along with their superiors, were surprised by the conflict and seemed puzzled as to its causes. Eventually, the black woman requested and obtained reassignment. But even though they escaped each other, both suffered a sense of failure severe enough to threaten their careers.

What could have been done to assist them? Well, empathy would not have hurt. But perspective would have been better yet. In their particular company and situation, these two people had placed themselves at the cutting edge of race and gender relations. They needed to know that mistakes at the cutting edge are different—and potentially more valuable—than mistakes elsewhere. Maybe they needed some kind of pioneer training. But at the very least they needed to be told that they were pioneers, that conflicts and failures came with the territory, and that they would be judged accordingly.

9. *Apply the Special Consideration Test.* I said earlier that affirmative action was an artificial, transitional, but necessary stage on the road to a truly diverse work force. Because of its artificial nature, affirmative action requires constant attention and drive to make it work. The point of learning once and for all how to manage diversity is that all that energy can be focused somewhere else.

There is a simple test to help you spot the diversity programs that are going to eat up enormous quantities of time and effort. Surprisingly, perhaps, it is the same test you might use to identify the programs and policies that created your problem in the first place. The test consists of one question: Does this program, policy, or principle give special consideration to one group? Will it contribute to everyone's success, or will it only produce an advantage for blacks or whites or women or men? Is it designed for *them* as opposed to *us*? Whenever the answer is yes, you're not yet on the road to managing diversity.

This does not rule out the possibility of addressing issues that relate to a single group. It only underlines the importance of determining that the issue you're addressing does not relate to other groups as well. For example, management in one company noticed that blacks were not moving up in the organization. Before instituting a special program to bring them along, managers conducted interviews to see if they could find the reason for the impasse. What blacks themselves reported was a problem with the quality of supervision. Further interviews showed that other employees too—including white males—were concerned about the quality of supervision and felt that little was being done to foster professional development. Correcting the situation eliminated a problem that affected everyone. In this case, a solution that focused only on blacks would have been out of place.

Had the problem consisted of prejudice, on the other hand, or some other barrier to blacks or minorities alone, a solution based on affirmative action would have been perfectly appropriate.

10. *Continue Affirmative Action.* Let me come full circle. The ability to

manage diversity is the ability to manage your company without unnatural advantage or disadvantage for any member of your diverse work force. The fact remains that you must first have a work force that is diverse at every level, and if you don't, you're going to need affirmative action to get from here to there.

The reason you then want to move beyond affirmative action to managing diversity is because affirmative action fails to deal with the root causes of prejudice and inequality and does little to develop the full potential of every man and woman in the company. In a country seeking competitive advantage in a global economy, the goal of managing diversity is to develop our capacity to accept, incorporate, and empower the diverse human talents of the most diverse nation on earth. It's our reality. We need to make it our strength.

Appendix

AVON: OUT OF THE NUMBERS GAME AND INTO DECISION MAKING

Like many other companies, Avon practiced affirmative action in the 1970s and was not pleased with the results. The company worked with employment agencies that specialized in finding qualified minority hires, and it cultivated contacts with black and minority organizations on college campuses. Avon wanted to see its customer base reflected in its work force, especially at the decision-making level. But while women moved up the corporate ladder fairly briskly—not so surprising in a company whose work force is mostly female—minorities did not. So in 1984, the company began to change its policies and practices.

"We really wanted to get out of the numbers game," says Marcia Worthing, the corporate vice president for human resources. "We felt it was more important to have five minority people tied into the decision-making process than ten who were just heads to count."

First, Avon initiated awareness training at all levels. "The key to recruiting, retaining, and promoting minorities is not the human resource department," says Worthing. "It's getting line management to buy into the idea. We had to do more than change behavior. We had to change attitudes."

Second, the company formed a Multicultural Participation Council that meets regularly to oversee the process of managing diversity. The group includes Avon's CEO and high-level employees from throughout the company.

Third, in conjunction with the American Institute for Managing Diversity, Avon developed a diversity training program. For several years, the company has sent racially and ethnically diverse groups of 25 managers at a time to Institute headquarters at Morehouse College in Atlanta, where they spend three weeks confronting their differences and learning to hear and avail themselves of viewpoints they initially disagreed with. "We came away disciples of diversity," says one company executive.

Fourth, the company helped three minority groups—blacks, Hispanics, and Asians—form networks that crisscrossed the corporation in all 50 states. Each network elects its own leaders and has an adviser from senior management. In addition, the networks have representatives on the Multicultural Participation Council, where they serve as a conduit for employee views on diversity issues facing management.

CORNING: "IT SIMPLY MAKES GOOD BUSINESS SENSE"

Corning characterizes its 1970s affirmative action program as a form of legal compliance. The law dictated affirmative action and morality required it, so the company did its best to hire minorities and women.

The ensuing cycle was classic: recruitment, confidence, disappointment, embarrassment, crisis, more recruitment. Talented women and blacks joined the company only to plateau or resign. Few reached upper management levels, and no one could say exactly why.

Then James R. Houghton took over as CEO in 1983 and made the diverse work force one of Corning's three top priorities, alongside Total Quality and a higher return on equity. His logic was twofold:

First of all, the company had higher attrition rates for minorities and women than for white males, which meant that investments in training and development were being wasted. Second, he believed that the Corning work force should more closely mirror the Corning customer base.

In order to break the cycle of recruitment and subsequent frustration, the company established two quality improvement teams headed by senior executives, one for black progress and one for women's progress. Mandatory awareness training was introduced for some

7,000 salaried employees—a day and a half for gender awareness, two-and-a-half days for racial awareness. One goal of the training is to identify unconscious company values that work against minorities and women. For example, a number of awareness groups reached the conclusion that working late had so much symbolic value that managers tended to look more at the quantity than at the quality of time spent on the job, with predictably negative effects on employees with dependent-care responsibilities.

The company also made an effort to improve communications by printing regular stories and articles about the diverse work force in its in-house newspaper and by publicizing employee success stories that emphasize diversity. It worked hard to identify and publicize promotion criteria. Career planning systems were introduced for all employees.

With regard to recruitment, Corning set up a nationwide scholarship program that provides renewable grants of $5,000 per year of college in exchange for a summer of paid work at some Corning installation. A majority of program participants have come to work for Corning full-time after graduation, and very few have left the company so far, though the program has been in place only four years.

The company also expanded its summer intern program, with an emphasis on minorities and women, and established formal recruiting contacts with campus groups like the Society of Women Engineers and the National Black MBA Association.

Corning sees its efforts to manage diversity not only as a social and moral issue but also as a question of efficiency and competitiveness. In the words of Mr. Houghton, "It simply makes good business sense."

DIGITAL: TURNING SOCIAL PRESSURES INTO COMPETITIVE ADVANTAGE

Like most other companies trying to respond to the federal legislation of the 1970s, Digital started off by focusing on numbers. By the early 1980s, however, company leaders could see it would take more than recruitment to make Digital the diverse workplace they wanted it to be. Equal Employment Opportunity (EEO) and affirmative action seemed too exclusive—too much "white males doing good deeds for minorities and women." The company wanted to move beyond these programs to the kind of environment where every employee could realize his or her potential, and Digital decided that meant an environment where individual differences were not tolerated but valued, even celebrated.

The resulting program and philosophy, called Valuing Differences, has two components:

First, the company helps people get in touch with their stereotypes and false assumptions through what Digital calls Core Groups. These voluntary groupings of eight to ten people work with company-trained facilitators whose job is to encourage discussion and self-development and, in the company's words, "to keep people safe" as they struggle with their prejudices. Digital also runs a voluntary two-day training program called "Understanding the Dynamics of Diversity," which thousands of Digital employees have now taken.

Second, the company has named a number of senior managers to various Cultural Boards of Directors and Valuing Differences Boards of Directors. These bodies promote openness to individual differences, encourage younger managers committed to the goal of diversity, and sponsor frequent celebrations of racial, gender, and ethnic differences such as Hispanic Heritage Week and Black History Month.

In addition to the Valuing Differences program, the company preserved its EEO and affirmative action functions. Valuing Differences focuses on personal and group development, EEO on legal issues, and affirmative action on systemic change. According to Alan Zimmerle, head of the Valuing Differences program, EEO and Valuing Differences are like two circles that touch but don't overlap—the first representing the legal need for diversity, the second the corporate desire for diversity. Affirmative action is a third circle that overlaps the other two and holds them together with policies and procedures.

Together, these three circles can transform legal and social pressures into the competitive advantage of a more effective work force, higher morale, and the reputation of being a better place to work. As Zimmerle puts it, "Digital wants to be the employer of choice. We want our pick of the talent that's out there."

PROCTER & GAMBLE: DISCOVERING COMPLEXITY AND VALUE IN DIVERSITY

Because Procter & Gamble fills its upper-level management positions only from within the company, it places a premium on recruiting the best available entry-level employees. Campus recruiting is pursued nationwide and year-round by line managers from all levels of the company. Among other things, the company has made a concerted—and successful—effort to find and hire talented minorities and women.

Finding first-rate hires is only one piece of the effort, however. There is still the challenge of moving diversity upward. As one top executive put it, "We know that we can only succeed as a company if we have an environment that makes it easy for all of us, not just some of us, to work to our potential."

In May 1988, P&G formed a Corporate Diversity Strategy Task Force to clarify the concept of diversity, define its importance for the company, and identify strategies for making progress toward successfully managing a diverse work force.

The task force, composed of men and women from every corner of the company, made two discoveries: First, diversity at P&G was far more complex than most people had supposed. In addition to race and gender, it included factors such as cultural heritage, personal background, and functional experience. Second, the company needed to expand its view of the value of differences.

The task force helped the company to see that learning to manage diversity would be a long-term process of organizational change. For example, P&G has offered voluntary diversity training at all levels since the 1970s, but the program has gradually broadened its emphasis on race and gender awareness to include the value of self-realization in a diverse environment. As retiring board chairman John Smale put it, "If we can tap the total contribution that everybody in our company has to offer, we will be better and more competitive in everything we do."

P&G is now conducting a thorough, continuing evaluation of all management programs to be sure that systems are working well for everyone. It has also carried out a corporate survey to get a better picture of the problems facing P&G employees who are balancing work and family responsibilities and to improve company programs in such areas as dependent care.

XEROX: THE DAILY EXPERIENCE OF GENUINE WORKPLACE DIVERSITY

Chairman David T. Kearns believes that a firm and resolute commitment to affirmative action is the first and most important step to work force diversity. "Xerox is committed to affirmative action," he says. "It is a corporate value, a management priority, and a formal business objective."

Xerox began recruiting minorities and women systematically as far back as the mid-1960s, and it pioneered such concepts as pivotal jobs (described later). The company's approach emphasizes behavior expectations as opposed to formal consciousness-raising programs because, as one Xerox executive put it, "It's just not realistic to think that a day and a half of training will change a person's thinking after 30 or 40 years."

On the assumption that attitude changes will grow from the daily experience of genuine workplace diversity, the Xerox Balanced Work Force Strategy sets goals for the number of minorities and women in each division and at every level. (For example, the goal for the top 300 executive-level jobs in one large division is 35% women by 1995, compared with 15% today.) "You *must* have a laboratory to work in," says Ted Payne, head of Xerox's Office of Affirmative Action and Equal Opportunity.

Minority and women's employee support groups have grown up in more than a dozen locations with the company's encouragement. But Xerox depends mainly on the three pieces of its balanced strategy to make diversity work.

First are the goals. Xerox sets recruitment and representation goals in accordance with federal guidelines and reviews them constantly to make sure they reflect work force demographics. Any company with a federal contract is required to make this effort. But Xerox then extends the guidelines by setting diversity goals for its upper level jobs and holding division and group managers accountable for reaching them.

The second piece is a focus on pivotal jobs, a policy Xerox adopted in the 1970s when it first noticed that minorities and women did not have the upward mobility the company wanted to see. By examining the backgrounds of top executives, Xerox was able to identify the key positions that all successful managers had held at lower levels and to set goals for getting minorities and women assigned to such jobs.

The third piece is an effort to concentrate managerial training not so much on managing diversity as on just plain managing people. What the company discovered when it began looking at managerial behavior toward minorities and women was that all too many managers didn't know enough about how to manage anyone, let alone people quite different from themselves.

PART

II

Racial Difference in the Workplace: How It Feels and What It Means

1

What It's Like to Be a Black Manager

Edward W. Jones, Jr.

Foreword

This author contends that most companies fail to recognize the crucial difference between recruiting blacks with executive potential and providing the much-needed organizational support to help them realize this potential. He cites his own experience in a large company to illustrate the type of lonely struggle that faces a black man in the absence of such support. Then he draws some lessons from this experience that should help management to overcome the subtle ramifications of racial differences within organizations.

Mr. Jones is the manager of an $11-million operating unit of a major company and is responsible for the supervision of 130 employees. After six years with the company, during which he rose from trainee to area manager, he attended the Harvard Business School, where he was graduated two years ago as a Baker Scholar.

When I was graduated from a predominantly black college, I was offered a job in one of the largest corporations in America. On reporting for work, I received a motivational speech from the personnel officer and acknowledged that I agreed with his opinion: the job was going to be challenging in its own right; however, the added burden of prejudice could make it unbearable. In a tone of bravado I said, "I promise you that I won't quit; you'll have to fire me."

At the time, I did not know how important that promise would become. For I was about to begin the most trying experience of my life—the rise to middle management in a white corporation. During those years, I found myself examining my actions, strategies, and emotional stability. I found myself trying desperately to separate fact from mental fiction. I found myself enveloped in almost unbearable emotional stress and internal conflict, trying to hold the job as a constant and evaluate my personal shortcomings with respect to it. At times I would look at myself in a mirror and wonder whether I had lost my mental balance. Somehow I always managed to answer positively, if not resolutely.

I think that my experiences should prove helpful to companies that are wrestling with the problem of how to move black employees from the entry level into positions of greater responsibility. I say this because the manner in which many companies are approaching the problem indicates to me that a number of well-intentioned efforts are doomed to failure.

Failure is likely because most companies merely substitute blacks in positions formerly filled by whites and then, acting as if the corporate environment is not color-sensitive, consider their obligation over. In short, U.S. business has failed to recognize the embryonic black manager's increased chances of failure due to the potentially negative impact of racially based prejudgments. Gaining acceptance in the organization, which the embryonic white manager takes for granted, can be a serious problem for his black counterpart.

The Job Offer

My story begins when I happened to bump into a recruiter who was talking to a friend of mine. On gathering that I was a college senior, the recruiter asked whether I had considered his company as an employer. I responded, "Are you kidding me—you don't have any black managers, do you?" He replied, "No, but that's why I'm here."

I did well in a subsequent interview procedure, and received an invitation for a company tour. Still skeptical, I accepted, feeling that I had nothing to lose. During a lunch discussion concerning the contemplated job and its requirements, I experienced my first reminder that I was black. After a strained silence, one of the executives at our table looked at me, smiled, and said, "Why is it that everyone likes Roy Campanella, but so many people dislike Jackie Robinson?"

I knew that this man was trying to be pleasant; yet I felt nothing but disgust at what seemed a ridiculous deterioration in the level of conversation. Here was the beginning of the games that I expected but dreaded playing. The question was demeaning and an insult to my intelligence. It was merely a rephrasing of the familiar patronizing comment, "One of my best friends is a negro." Most blacks recognize this type of statement as a thinly veiled attempt to hide bias. After all, if a person is unbiased, why does he make such a point of trying to prove it?

In the fragment of time between the question and my response, the tension within me grew. Were these people serious about a job offer? If so, what did they expect from me? I had no desire to be the corporate black in a glass office, but I did not wish to be abrasive or ungracious if the company was sincere about its desire to have an integrated organization.

There was no way to resolve these kinds of questions at that moment, so I gathered up my courage and replied, "Roy Campanella is a great baseball player. But off the field he is not an overwhelming intellectual challenge to anyone. Jackie Robinson is great both on and off the baseball field. He is very intelligent and therefore more of a threat than Roy Campanella. In fact, I'm sure that if he wanted to, he could outperform you in your job."

There was a stunned silence around the table, and from that point on until I arrived back at the employment office, I was sure that I had ended any changes of receiving a job offer.

I was wrong. I subsequently received an outstanding salary offer from the recruiter. But I had no intention of being this company's showcase black and asked seriously, "Why do you want me to work for you? Because of my ability or because you need a black?" I was reassured that ability was the "only" criterion, and one month later, after much introspection, I accepted the offer.

Initial Exposure

I entered the first formal training phase, in which I was the only black trainee in a department of over 8,000 employees. During this period, my tension increased as I was repeatedly called on to be the in-house expert on anything pertaining to civil rights. I was proud to be black and had many opinions about civil rights, but I did not feel qualified to give "the" black opinion. I developed the feeling that I was considered a black first and an individual second by many of the people I came into contact with. This feeling was exacerbated by the curious executive visitors to the training class who had to be introduced to everyone except me. Everyone knew my name, and I constantly had the feeling of being on stage.

The next phase of training was intended to prepare trainees for supervisory responsibilities. The tension of the trainee group had risen somewhat because of the loss of several trainees and the increased challenges facing us. In my own case, an increasing fear of failure began to impact on the other tensions that I felt from being "a speck of pepper in a sea of salt." The result of these tensions was that I began behaving with an air of bravado. I wasn't outwardly concerned or afraid, but I was inwardly terrified. This phase of training was also completed satisfactorily, at least in an official sense.

At the conclusion of the training, I received a "yes, but" type of appraisal. For example: "Mr. Jones doesn't take notes and seems to have trouble using the reference material, but he seems to be able to recall the material." This is the type of appraisal that says you've done satisfactorily, yet leaves a negative or dubious impression. I questioned the subjective inputs but dropped the matter without any vehement objections.

Prior to embarking on my first management assignment, I resolved to learn from this appraisal and to use more tact and talk less. These resolutions were re-emphasized by my adviser, who was an executive with responsibility for giving me counsel and acting as a sounding board. He also suggested that I relax my handshake and speak more softly.

On the Job

A warm welcome awaited me in the office where I was to complete my first assignment as a supervisor. I looked forward to going to work because I felt that subjectivity in appraisals would now be replaced by objectivity. Here was a situation in which I would either meet or fail to meet clearly defined numerical objectives.

There were no serious problems for three weeks, and I started to relax and just worry about the job. But then I had a conflict in my schedule. An urgent matter had to be taken care of in the office at the same time that I had an appointment elsewhere. I wrote a note to a supervisor who worked for another manager, asking him if he would be kind enough to follow up on the matter in the office for me.

I chose that particular supervisor because he had given me an embarrassingly warm welcome to the office and insisted that I "just ask" if there was anything at all that he could do to help me. I relied on the impersonality of the note because he was out on a coffee break and I had to leave immediately. The note was short and tactfully worded, and ended by giving my advance "thanks" for the requested help. Moreover, the office norms encouraged supervisory cooperation, so the fact that we worked under different managers did not seem to be a problem.

When I returned to the office, the manager I worked for called me in. He was visibly irritated. I sat down and he said, "Ed, you're rocking the boat." He stated that the supervisor I had asked for help had complained directly to the area manager that I was ordering him around and said he wasn't about to take any nonsense from a "new kid" in the office.

In a very calm voice, I explained what I had done and why I had done it. I then asked my manager, "What did I do wrong?" He looked at me and said, "I don't know, but whatever it is, cut it out. Stop rocking the boat." When I asked why the note wasn't produced to verify my statements, he said that it "wasn't available."

I left my manager's office totally perplexed. How could I correct my behavior if I didn't know what was wrong with it? I resolved that I had no choice except to be totally self-reliant, since one thing was obvious: what I had taken at face value as friendliness was potentially a fatal trap.

The feelings aroused in this incident were indicative of those I was to maintain for some time. While I felt a need for closeness, the only option open to me was self-reliance. I felt that my manager should support and defend me, but it was obvious that he was not willing to take such a stance. Worst of all, however, was my feeling of disappointment and the ensuing confusion due to my lack of guidance. I felt that if my manager was not willing to protect and defend me, he had an increased responsibility to give me guidance on how to avoid future explosions of a similar nature.

For some months I worked in that office without any additional explosions, although I was continually admonished not to "rock the boat." During a luncheon with the area manager one day, I remember, he said, "Ed, I've never seen a guy try so hard. If we tell you to tie your tie to the right, you sure try to do it. But why can't you be like Joe [another trainee the area manager supervised]? He doesn't seem to be having any problems."

THE APPRAISAL INCIDENT

I directed my energies and frustrations into my work, and my supervisory section improved in every measured area of performance until I led the unit. At the end of my first six months on the job, I was slated to go on active duty to fulfill my military requirements as a lieutenant in the Army. Shortly before I left, my manager stated, "Ed, you've done a tremendous job. You write your own appraisal." I wrote the appraisal, but was told to rewrite it because "it's not good enough." I rewrote the appraisal four times before he was satisfied that I was not being too modest. As I indicated earlier, I had resolved to be as unabrasive as possible, and, even though I had met or exceeded all my objectives, I was trying not to be pompous in critiquing my own performance.

Finally, on my next to last day on the job, my manager said, "Ed, this is a fine appraisal. I don't have time to get it typed before you go, but I'll submit this appraisal just as you have written it." With that, I went into the service, feeling that, finally, I had solved my problems.

Six months later, I took several days' leave from the Army to spend Christmas in the city with my family. On the afternoon of the day before Christmas, I decided to visit the personnel executive who had originally given me encouragement. So, wearing my officer's uniform, I stopped by his office.

After exchanging greetings and making small talk, I asked him if he had seen my appraisal. He answered, "yes," but when his face failed to reflect the look of satisfaction that I expected, I asked him if I could see it. The appraisal had been changed from the one that I had originally written to another "yes, but" appraisal. The numerical results said that I had met or exceeded all objectives, but under the section entitled "Development Program" the following paragraph had been inserted:

"Mr. Jones's biggest problem has been overcoming his own impulsiveness. He has on occasion, early in his tour, jumped too fast with the result that he has incurred some resentment. In these cases his objectives have been good, but his method has ruffled feathers."

I asked the personnel executive to interpret my overall rating. He answered, "Well, we can run the business with people with that rating." I then asked him to explain the various ratings possible, and it became clear that I had received the lowest acceptable rating that wouldn't require the company to fire me. I could not see how this could be, since I had exceeded all my objectives. I explained how I had written my own appraisal and that this appraisal had been rewritten. The personnel officer could not offer an explanation; he recommended that I speak to my old area manager, who had had the responsibility to review and approve my appraisal, and ask him why I had been treated in that manner.

A BLEAK CHRISTMAS

I tried to sort things out on my way to see my former area manager. My head was spinning, and I was disgusted. The appraisal was not just unfair—it was overtly dishonest. I thought of standing up in righteous indignation and appealing to higher authority in the company, but I had always resisted calling attention to my blackness by asking for special concessions and wanted to avoid creating a conflict situation if at all possible. While the 15-minute walk in the cold air calmed my anger, I still hadn't decided what I was going to do when I arrived at the area manager's office.

I walked into a scene that is typical of Christmas Eve in an office. People were everywhere, and discarded gift wrappings filled the wastebaskets. The area manager still had on the red Santa Claus suit. I looked around at the scene of merriment and decided that this was a poor time to "rock the boat."

The area manager greeted me warmly, exclaimed how great I looked, and offered to buy me a drink on his way home. I accepted, and with a feeling of disgust and disappointment, toasted to a Merry Christmas. I knew then that this situation was hopeless and there was little to be gained by raising a stink while we were alone. I had been naïve, and there was no way to prove that the appraisal had been changed.

I was a very lonely fellow that Christmas Eve. My feelings of a lack of closeness, support, and protection were renewed and amplified. It became obvious that no matter how much I achieved, how hard I worked, or how many personal adjustments I made, this system was trying to reject me.

I didn't know which way to turn, whom to trust, or who would be willing to listen. The personnel executive had told me to expect prejudice, but when he saw that I was being treated unfairly, he sent me off on my own.

"What do they expect?" I thought. "They know that I am bound to run into prejudice; yet no one lifts a finger when I am treated unfairly. Do they expect a person to be stupid enough to come right out and say, 'Get out, blackie; we don't want your type here'? This surely wouldn't happen—such overt behavior would endanger the offending person's career."

After the Christmas Eve incident, I went off to finish the remaining time in the Army. During that period, I tossed my work problems around in my mind, trying to find the right approach. The only answer I came up with was to stand fast, do my best, ask for no special favors, and refuse to quit voluntarily.

New Challenges

When I returned to the company, I was assigned as a supervisor in another area for five or six weeks, to do the same work as I had been doing prior to my departure for the military service. At the end of this uneventful refamiliarization period, I was reassigned as a manager in an area that had poor performance and was recognized as being one of the most difficult in the company. The fact that I would be responsible for one of three "manager units" in the area was exciting and I looked forward to this new challenge.

I walked into my new area manager's office with a smile and an extended hand, anxious to start off on the right foot and do a good job. After shaking hands, my new boss invited me to sit down while he told me about the job. He began by saying, "I hope you don't, but I am pretty sure you are going to fall flat on your face. When you do, my job is to kick you in the butt so hard that they'll have to take us both to the hospital."

I was shocked and angry. In the first place, my pride as a man said you don't have to take that kind of talk from anyone. I fought the temptation to say something like, "If you even raise your foot, you may well go to the hospital to have it put in a cast."

As I held back the anger, he continued, "I don't know anything about your previous performance, and I don't intend to try to find out. I'm going to evaluate you strictly on your performance for me."

The red lights went on in my mind. This guy was making too much of an issue about his lack of knowledge concerning my previous performance. Whom was he trying to kid? He had heard rumors and read my personnel records. I was starting off with two strikes against me. I looked at him and said, "I'll do my best."

MORE APPRAISAL TROUBLES

The area's results failed to improve, and John, the area manager, was replaced by a new boss, Ralph. Two weeks after Ralph arrived, he called me on the intercom and said, "Ed, John has your appraisal ready. Go down to see him in his new office. Don't worry about it; we'll talk when you get back." Ralph's words and tone of foreboding made me brace for the worst.

John ushered me into his office and began by telling me that I had been his worst problem. He then proceeded to read a list of every disagreement involving me that he was aware of. These ranged from corrective actions with clerks to resource-allocation discussions with my fellow managers. It was a strange appraisal session. John wound up crossing out half of the examples cited as I rebutted his statements. At the end of the appraisal he turned and said, "I've tried to be fair, Ed. I've tried not to be vindictive. But if someone were to ask how you're doing, I would have to say you've got room for improvement."

Discussions with Ralph, my new boss, followed as soon as I returned to my office. He advised me not to worry, that we would work out any problems. I told him that this was fine, but I also pointed out the subjectivity and dishonesty reflected in previous and current appraisals and the circumstances surrounding them.

I was bitter that a person who had just been relieved for ineffectiveness could be allowed to have such a resounding impact on my chances in the company. My predecessor had been promoted; I had improved on his results; but here I was, back in questionable status again.

THE TURNING POINT

About six weeks later, Ralph called me in and said, "Ed, I hope you make it on the job. But what are you going to do if you don't?"

At that moment, I felt as if the hands on the clock of life had reached 11:59. Time was running out very rapidly on me, and I saw myself against a wall, with my new boss about to deliver the coup de grâce. I felt that he was an honest and very capable person, but that circumstances had combined to give him the role of executioner. It seemed from his question that he was in the process of either wrestling with his own conscience or testing me to see how much resistance, if any,

I would put up when he delivered that fatal blow. After all, while I had not made an issue of my ill treatment thus far in my career, no matter how unjustly I felt I had been dealt with, he was smart enough to realize that this option was still open to me.

I looked at Ralph and any thought about trying to please him went out of my mind. Sitting up straight in my chair, I met his relaxed smile with a very stern face. "Why do you care what I do if I don't make it?" I asked coldly.

"I care about you as a person," he replied.

"It's not your job to be concerned about me as a person," I said. "Your job is to evaluate my performance results. But since you've asked, it will be rough if I am fired, because I have a family and responsibilities. However, that's not your concern. You make your decision; and when you do, I'll make my decision." With that statement I returned to my office.

Several weeks after this discussion, a vice president came around to the office to discuss objectives and job philosophy with the managers. I noted at the time that while he only spent 15 or 20 minutes with the other managers, he spent over an hour talking with me. After this visit, Ralph and I had numerous daily discussions. Then Ralph called me into his office to tell me he had written a new appraisal with an improved rating. I was thrilled. I was going to make it. Later, he told me that he was writing another appraisal, stating I not only would make it but also had promotional potential.

After Ralph had changed the first appraisal, my tensions began to decrease and my effectiveness began to increase proportionately. The looser and more confident I became, the more rapidly the results improved. My assignment under Ralph became very fulfilling, and one of the best years I've spent in the company ensued. Other assignments followed, each more challenging than the previous, and each was handled satisfactorily.

Lessons from Experience

My point in relating these experiences is not to show that I was persecuted or treated unfairly by people in a large corporation. In fact, after talking to friends in the company who knew me during the period just described, I am convinced that many of the lack-of-tact and rock-the-boat statements were true. I am also convinced, however, that the problems I experienced were not uniquely attributable to me or my personality and that it is important for companies to understand what caused them.

The manager to whom I reported on my very first assignment made some informal notes which help illustrate my conviction:

"I discussed each case with Ed. As might be expected, there is as much to be said in his defense as against him. He isn't all wrong in any one case. But the cumulative weight of all those unsolicited comments and complaints clearly shows that he is causing a lot of people to be unhappy, and I must see that it stops. I don't think it is a question of what he says and does or a question of objectives. It is a question of voice, manner, approach, method—or maybe timing. No matter what it is, he must correct whatever he does that upsets so many people."

These are not the words of a scheming bigot; they are the words of a man searching for an explanation to a phenomenon that neither he nor I understood at the time. I was not knowingly insensitive to other people or intent on antagonizing them. What this man and others failed to realize was that, being a black man in a unique position in a white company, I was extremely tense and ill at ease. Levels of sensitivity, polish, and tact which were foreign to me were now necessities of life. The world of white business presented me with an elaborate sociopolitical organization that required unfamiliar codes of behavior.

Abraham Zaleznik refers to this phenomenon in *The Human Dilemmas of Leadership*:

The anxiety experienced by the upwardly mobile individual largely comes from internal conflicts generated within his own personality. On the one hand, there is the driving and pervasive need to prove himself as assurance of his adequacy as a person; on the other hand, the standards for measuring his adequacy come from sources somewhat unfamiliar to him.[1]

My personal pride and sense of worth were driving me to succeed. Ironically, the more determined I was to succeed, the more abrasive I became and the more critical my feedback became. This in turn impelled me to try even harder and to be even more uptight. As a result, I was vulnerable to prejudgments of inability by my peers and superiors.

THE LENS OF COLOR

What most white people do not understand or accept is the fact that skin color has such a pervasive impact on every black person's life that it subordinates considerations of education or class. Skin color makes black people the most conspicuous minority in America, and all blacks, regardless of status, are subjected to prejudice. I personally was not as disadvantaged as many other blacks, but to some extent all blacks are products of separate schools, neighborhoods, and subcultures. In short, black and white people not only look different but also come from different environments which condition them differently and make understanding and honest communication difficult to achieve.

Many whites who find it easy to philosophically accept the fact that blacks will be rubbing shoulders with them experience antagonism when they realize that the difference between blacks and whites goes deeper than skin color. They have difficulty adjusting to the fact that blacks are different. It is critical that companies understand this point, for it indicates the need for increased guidance to help blacks adjust to an alien set of norms and behavioral requirements.

THE INFORMAL ORGANIZATION

One of the phenomena that develops in every corporation is a set of behavioral and personal norms that facilitates communication and aids cohesiveness. Moreover, because this "informal organization" is built on white norms, it can reinforce the black-white differences just mentioned and thus reject or destroy all but the most persistent blacks.

The informal organization operates at all levels in a corporation, and the norms become more rigid the higher one goes in the hierarchy. While this phenomenon promotes efficiency and unity, it is also restrictive and very selective. It can preclude promotion or lead to failure on the basis of "fit" rather than competence.

Chester Barnard recognized the existence of the informal organization in 1938. As he stated, "This question of fitness involves such matters as education, experience, age, sex, personal distinctions, prestige, race, nationality, faith. . . ."[2]

I believe that many of the problems I encountered were problems of fit with the informal organization. My peers and supervisors were unable to perceive me as being able to perform the job that the company hired me for. Their reaction to me was disbelief. I was out of the "place" normally filled by black people in the company; and since no black person had preceded me successfully, it was easy for my antagonists to believe I was inadequate.

I am not vacillating here from my previous statement that I was probably guilty of many of the subjective shortcomings noted in my appraisals. But I do feel that the difficulties I experienced were amplified by my lack of compatibility with the informal organization. Because of it, many of the people I had problems with could not differentiate between objective ability and performance and subjective dislike for me, or discomfort with me. I was filling an unfamiliar, and therefore uncomfortable, "space" in relation to them. Even in retrospect, I cannot fully differentiate between the problems attributable to me as a person, to me as a manager, or to me as a black man.

Toward Facilitating "Fit"

Because of the foregoing problems, I conclude that business has an obligation to even out the odds for blacks who have executive potential. I am not saying that all blacks must be pampered and sheltered rather than challenged. Nor am I advocating the development of "chosen" managers. All managers must accept the risk of failure in order to receive the satisfactions of achievement.

I do, however, advocate a leveling out of these problems of "fit" with the informal organization that operate against black managers. Here are the elements vital to this process:

Unquestionable top management involvement and commitment—The importance of this element is underscored by my discussions with the vice president who visited me during my crisis period. He disclosed that his objective was to see whether I was really as bad as he was being told. His conclusion from the visit was that he couldn't see any insurmountable problems with me. This high-level interest was the critical variable that gave me a fair chance. I was just lucky that this man had a personal sense of fair play and a desire to ensure equitable treatment.

But chance involvement is not enough. If a company is truly committed to equal opportunity, then it must set up reasoned and well thought-out plans for involvement of top management.

Direct two-way channels of communication between top management and black trainees—Without open channels of communication, a company cannot ensure that it will recognize the need for a neutral opinion or the intercession of a disinterested party if a black trainee is having problems.

Clear channels of communication will also enable top management to provide empathetic sources of counsel to help the new black trainee combat the potentially crippling paranoia that I encountered. I didn't know whom to trust; consequently, I trusted no one. The counsel of mature and proven black executives will also help mitigate this paranoia.

Appraisal of managers on their contributions to the company's equal opportunity objectives—The entire management team must be motivated to change any deep beliefs about who does and doesn't fit with regard to color. Accordingly, companies should use the appraisal system to make the welfare of the black trainee coincident with the well-being of his superior. Such action, of course, will probably receive considerable resistance from middle- and lower-level management. But managers are appraised on their ability to reach other important objectives; and, more significantly, the inclusion of this area in appraisals signals to everyone involved that a company is serious. Failure to take this step signals business as usual and adds to any credibility gap between the company and black employees.

The appraisal process also motivates the trainee's superior to "school" him on the realities of the political process in the corporation. Without this information, no one can survive in an organization. After upgrading my appraisal, Ralph began this process with me. The knowledge I gained proved to be invaluable in my subsequent decision making.

Avoid the temptation to create special showcase-black jobs. They will be eyed with suspicion by the black incumbents, and the sincerity of the company will be open to question. Blacks realize that only line jobs provide the experience and reality-testing which develop the confidence required in positions of greater responsibility.

Select assignments for the new black manager which are challenging, yet don't in themselves increase his chances of failure. My assignment with John was a poor choice. He was a top-rated area manager, but had a different job orientation and was struggling to learn his new responsibilities. So naturally he would resent any inexperienced manager being assigned to him. Moreover, the fact that he had never seen a successful black manager reinforced his belief that I could not do the job.

These basic steps need not be of a permanent nature, but they should be enacted until such time as the organizational norms accept blacks at all levels and in all types of jobs. The steps will help mitigate the fact that a black person in the organizational structure must not only carry the same load as a white person but also bear the burden attributable to prejudice and the machinations of the informal organization.

Conclusion

In relating and drawing on my own experiences, I have not been talking about trials and tribulations in an obviously bigoted company. At that time, my company employed a higher percentage of blacks than almost any other business, and this is still true today. I grant that there is still much to be done as far as the number and level of blacks in positions of authority are concerned, but I believe that my company has done better than most in the area of equal opportunity. Its positive efforts are evidenced by the progressive decision to sponsor my study at the Harvard Business School, so I would be prepared for greater levels of responsibility.

There are differences in detail and chronology, but the net effect of my experiences is similar to that of other blacks with whom I have discussed these matters. While prejudice exists in business, the U.S. norm against being prejudiced precludes an admission of guilt by the prejudiced party. Thus, in my own case, my first manager and John were more guilty of naïveté than bigotry—they could not recognize prejudice, since it would be a blow to their self-images. And this condition is prevalent in U.S. industry.

My experience points out that a moral commitment to equal opportunity is not enough. If a company fails to recognize that fantastic filters operate between the entry level and top management, this commitment is useless. Today, integration in organizations is at or near the entry level, and the threat of displacement or the discomfort of having to adjust to unfamiliar racial relationships is the greatest for lower and middle managers, for they are the people who will be most impacted by this process. Therefore, companies must take steps similar to the ones I have advocated if they hope to achieve true parity for blacks.

Equal job opportunity is more than putting a black man in a white man's job. The barriers must be removed, not just moved.

Notes

1. New York, Harper & Row, Publishers, 1966, p. III.
2. *The Functions of the Executive* (Cambridge, Harvard University Press, 1938), p. 224.

2
Black Managers: The Dream Deferred

Edward W. Jones, Jr.

In force for a generation, equal opportunity laws have brought blacks in large numbers into corporate managerial ranks. Starting from almost total exclusion, blacks now hold positions of responsibility, with prestige and income that our parents often thought impossible. Between 1977 and 1982 alone, according to the Bureau of Labor Statistics, the proportion of minority managers rose from 3.6% to 5.2%. EEO data from 1982 show that of all "officials and managers," 4.3% were blacks (including 1.6% black females) and 20.4%, white females. The companies that led this progress deserve commendation for their efforts in recruiting, hiring, and promoting not only blacks but also other minority members and women too.

Yet in the midst of this good news there is something ominous. In conversations with black managers, I hear expressions of disappointment, dismay, frustration, and anger because they have not gained acceptance on a par with their white peers. They find their careers stymied and they are increasingly disillusioned about their chances for ultimate success. They feel at best tolerated; they often feel ignored.

A sampling of headlines from the last few years underscores these perceptions: "Black Professionals Refashion Their Careers" (*New York Times*, November 29, 1985), "Many Blacks Jump Off The Corporate Ladder: Feeling Their Rise Limited" (*Wall Street Journal*, August 2, 1984), "Progress Report on the Black Executive: The Top Spots Are Still Elusive" (*Business Week*, February 20, 1984), "They Shall Overcome: Black managers soon learn that getting through the corporate door is only the first of their problems" (*Newsweek*, May 23, 1983),

"Job-Bias Alert: Roadblocks Out Of The Closet" (*Wall Street Journal*, May 17, 1982).

Little information exists about minority participation in the top rungs of America's largest companies. But two surveys of *Fortune* 1000 companies by the recruiting firm Korn Ferry International show that as of 1979 and 1985 these businesses have not made even a dent in moving minorities and women into the senior ranks. The 1979 survey of 1,708 senior executives cited three as being black, two Asian, two Hispanic, and eight female. The 1985 survey of 1,362 senior executives found four blacks, six Asians, three Hispanics, and 29 women. I think it's fair to say that this is almost no progress at all.

A CEO of a multibillion-dollar, multinational company framed the issue: "I'm concerned. The curve of progress has started to flatten more than it should relative to the effort we've made. I need to know how to be successful in moving up competent but diverse people who are not clones of those above them."

But not enough like him seem to be concerned. A 1983 survey of 785 business opinion leaders ranked affirmative action for minorities and women as twenty-third out of 25 human resource priorities, almost last.[1] Today, unlike the 1960s, equal opportunity is not an issue on the front burner of national or corporate concerns. For many reasons, the prevailing theme of fairness has been replaced by calls for protection of individual liberties and self-help. No one wants to listen to a bunch of complaining minorities. From many perspectives, the problem is seen as solved. It is yesteryear's issue.

My research for this article has convinced me that many of the top executives of our largest companies are committed to fairness and to promoting qualified minorities into positions of responsibility. As one white senior executive put it, "No thinking person would pick a white manager for promotion over a more qualified black manager." In most instances he's probably right. The problem is the influence of unconscious, unthinking criteria on the choice.

This article is based on three years of research, including hundreds of interviews of men, women, whites, blacks, and other minorities; of senior, middle, and junior managers; and of professionals in management, education, consulting, psychology, sociology, psychiatry, and medicine. They included more than 30 black executives, each earning at least $100,000, and more than 200 black managers, most MBAs.

My purpose here is to report on this research, to inform concerned executives of the issues as perceived by black managers. I am not trying to prove anything, only to report and to offer direct testimony on where black managers stand, the progress they have made, the problems that exist, the way blacks feel, and what seems difficult and unresolved.

"Color-Blind" Companies

There is a problem that the statistics don't reflect. Listen to four higher level black executives who have achieved some credibility and status in the business world:

"There was strong emphasis in the seventies for getting the right numbers of black managers. But now we're stagnating, as if the motivation was to get numbers, not create opportunity. I get the sense that companies have the numbers they think they need and now don't think anything more needs doing. Some companies are substituting numbers that represent the progress of white women and camouflaging and ignoring the lack of progress for black managers altogether. Many companies hired aggressive, self-motivated, high-achieving blacks who are now feeling deep frustration. Some have left, others stay but are fed up. Some can take more pain, others just throw up their hands and say to hell with it."

"When you work your way up, try to conform, and even job hop to other companies only to confront the same racial barriers—well, it's debilitating. I just don't want to go through that again."

"I went into corporate America to shoot for the top, just like my white classmates at business school. But the corporate expectation seemed to be that as a black I should accept something that satisfied some other need. Corporations are saying, 'We want you to be just a number in a seat representing a particular program. Stay in your place.' The psychological contract made by corporations is unfulfilled for black high achievers. We're dealing with a breach of contract."

"We can have all the credentials in the world, but that doesn't qualify us in the minds of many white people. They can train the hell out of us and we can do well, but they may still think of us as unqualified. Old biases, attitudes, and beliefs stack the cards against us."

These are typical statements black managers make in private. When you hear them over and over, you have to believe there's something very real about them. The myth is that companies are color-blind. "We

don't tolerate discrimination of any kind, and we've instituted procedures to make that a fact," is a typical comment by a white executive.
More accurately, discrimination is ever present but a taboo topic—for
blacks as well as whites. If you want to move up, you don't talk about
it.

When top executives talk about hiring at the lower end, it's not
taboo. Often it's actually obligatory for the sake of affirmative action.
But when a black middle manager thinks he (or she) has been held
back by a white boss because of race, he faces a tough choice. If he
remains silent, he is stigmatized by the boss's action and may find his
career pigeonholed. But if he speaks up, he is liable to be marked "too
sensitive, a troublemaker, not a team player" and lose in the long run
even if he proves unfairness.

So highly charged is this topic in corporations that I had to guarantee all interviewees anonymity. Candor might put companies at risk of
being embarrassed and careers of being ruined. One executive, noting
that blacks are few in his industry, declined to fill out a questionnaire
anonymously for fear he would be identified. One white consultant said
he lost a great deal of business after performing a survey for a large
company in which he reported that black managers were accurate
when they complained of unfair treatment. "They never called me
back after that," he told me, "and other companies I had dealt with
for years didn't call either. The word spread that I couldn't be trusted,
and I was blackballed."

ON A TREADMILL

Corporations and educational institutions have given thousands of
black managers the background to move up to more responsible positions. The corporate door is open, but access to the upper floors is
blocked. Ironically, companies that led in hiring the best prepared
blacks have the worst problem because their protégés' expectations of
success are proportionate to their preparation.

To expand on the impressions obtained in interviews, I conducted
two surveys of black MBAs. The first was a 23-page questionnaire
mailed to 305 alumni of the top five graduate business schools. I
received 107 back, without follow-up, for a response rate of 35%.
More than 98% of the respondents believe that corporations have not
achieved equal opportunity for black managers; 90% view the climate

of support as worse than for their white peers; and 84% think that considerations of race have a negative impact on ratings, pay, assignments, recognition, appraisals, and promotion. Some 98% agreed with a statement that subtle prejudice pervades their own companies, and more than half said the prejudice is overt. Less than 10% said their employers promote open discussion of racial issues.

In the survey I listed 15 words and phrases that persons I had interviewed used to describe the climate for blacks in their organizations. To elicit more information (though admittedly in an unscientific fashion: ten of the descriptions were negative and five positive), I asked respondents to select those that "best describe the organizational climate for black managers." The answers, in percentage of total respondents, were:

Indifferent	59%	Supportive	15%
Patronizing	41%	Positive	11%
Reluctant to accept blacks	40%	Open in its communication	10%
Encouraging	24%	Reactionary	10%
Psychologically unhealthy	21%	Negative	7%
		Untenable	7%
Unfulfilling	20%	Unwholesome	7%
Whites are resentful	20%	Trusting of blacks	4%

A number of respondents volunteered 18 other descriptions, of which 12 were negative. I included all 33 terms in an expanded question (contained in a shorter questionnaire) that I distributed at a meeting of some 200 black graduates of a variety of schools. I received 75 returns.

Getting the most mentions were these descriptions: supportive in words only (50%), lacks positive direction (41%), has a policy of tokenism (33%), reluctant to accept blacks (33%), and indifferent (33%). The favorable descriptions that received the most mentions were encouraging (17%) and positive (15%).

It doesn't matter whether, by some impossible objective standard, these people are right or wrong; what counts is how they feel. My findings contrast sharply, by the way, with opinions offered from 1979 through 1984 by some 5,000 white managers and other professionals in the data base of Opinion Research Corporation. Only 28% of them indicated they lack confidence in their employers' appraisal systems. In my first sample, 90% of the black MBAs declared that blacks are treated worse in appraisals than whites at the same levels.

Here are three illustrations of why black managers are frustrated and angry. First, however, a caveat. To condense into a few paragraphs events that transpired over a number of months may oversimplify them, but they do help clarify the attitude of black managers who feel rejected. The white executive who reads these accounts may think, "I'm sure there were other reasons for this. There must have been something about the person that made him unsuitable for more responsibility." But the people I interviewed and surveyed repeated the same kind of story time after time.

For more than ten years, John has held the number two post in his department in a large Midwestern chemical company. Some years ago, when his superior, a white, became ill, John filled in for him. After John's boss, who was a vice president, died of a heart attack two years ago, his skip-level boss, a senior vice president, named John acting department head while the company searched for a replacement. During the next 14 months, John repeatedly said he'd like the job and was qualified, but the senior VP said they wanted to start fresh. "We want to reorient the department," he would say, or "We didn't like the way the department was run; Wally was too involved in side issues." But each candidate who came along was less qualified than John.

Finally the company lured a white executive with all the right credentials away from a prime competitor at a salary much higher than John's boss had received. It was the first time the company had brought in an outsider at such a high level. John, who is still number two in the department, is convinced that top management simply did not want a black vice president. "I've searched and searched in my mind for the reason they didn't appoint me," he said when I interviewed him. "All the excuses don't apply to me. They were always critical of my boss, but not of me. I had good ideas for the department and was excited about the prospect of running it, but they never were interested. The reason always comes down to race. They wouldn't have treated a white manager this way."

Then there is Ron, a bright young administrator for a financial services company in California. In his second assignment, Ron accomplished in one year what his boss had said would take him three and was rewarded with a hefty raise and a transfer to a more difficult slot. There his group again decimated the plan, achieving sales levels in 18 months that the company had predicted would take three years. Again Ron was given praise, a raise, and a transfer—but no promotion.

Meanwhile, whites who had joined the company as trainees with Ron were promoted once and some of them twice. Ron was disillusioned. "My career is getting behind to the point I don't think I can catch up now," he told me. His color must have been a big factor in the way he had been treated, he claimed, because he had played according to all the rules, had outperformed his white peers, and had still come up short.

Bill's division was part of a company newly acquired by a large multinational enterprise located on the West Coast. Hired through a headhunter by the new parent, he was the first black manager in his division. Between the time Bill was appointed and the day he walked into his office, an executive who had opposed Bill's selection had been promoted and as a vice president was two steps above Bill as his boss's boss. Despite Bill's repeated requests, his immediate superior gave him no written objectives. But all of Bill's colleagues told him they liked his direction.

The only indication that race was even noticed was a comment from a sales manager whose performance Bill's division relied on: "I don't normally associate with blacks." Bill learned later that other managers were telling his boss that he was hard to work with and unclear in his plans. His boss did not confront Bill with these criticisms, just hinted at possible problems. Only later did Bill put them together into the indictment they really were.

After six months, out of the blue, he was put on probation. According to Bill's superior, the vice president said he "did not feel Bill could do the job" and suggested to him that Bill accept severance pay and look for other work. Bill decided to stick it out for pride's sake; he knew he could do the job. His work and educational records had proven him to be a winner.

During the following six months, his division performed ahead of plan. Bill was getting compliments from customers and colleagues. His boss assured him that he had proved his worth, and the probation would be lifted. It was. A few months later, Bill's boss finally agreed to set written objectives and scheduled a meeting with him. But when

Bill walked into his superior's office, he was surprised to see the VP there too. The purpose of the meeting was not to set objectives but to place Bill back on probation, or give him severance pay, because he did not "seem to be the right man." Bill left the company and started his own business.

It's noteworthy that Bill, Ron, and John all worked for "equal opportunity employers." Are these cases unusual? Listen to the testimony of a black I interviewed, a vice president of a large insurance company: "White executives at my level say they don't see race as a factor. This is contrary to my perceptions. When I say race, I refer to what is happening to all blacks. White executives choose to see these situations as issues of personal shortcomings. They say, 'We have to look at the possibility of upward mobility of blacks on an individual basis.' But when I look at it on an individual basis, I see all blacks being treated the same way. Therefore, I come to the conclusion that black managers are being treated as a group."

"COLORISM"

Racism is too highly charged a word for my theme. When some people think of *racist* they picture overt bigotry and hatred, the burning cross, the shout "nigger"—things our country has rejected by law. For black managers, what gives them a disadvantage is deep-seated attitudes that may not even be consciously held, much less manifest themselves in provable illegal behavior.

For this discussion I'll use the word *colorism* to mean an attitude, a predisposition to act in a certain manner because of a person's skin color. This means that people tend to act favorably toward those with skin color like theirs and unfavorably toward those with different skin color. Study after study shows that colorism exists among white Americans; whereas they generally have an automatically positive internal picture of other whites, they don't have one of blacks. It takes an effort to react positively toward blacks.[2]

A 1982 survey of Ivy League graduates, class of '57, helps explain colorism. For them "dumb" came to mind when they thought of blacks. Just 36% of the Princeton class, 47% at Yale, and 55% at Harvard agreed with the statement, "Blacks are as intelligent as whites."[3] These are graduates of three leading universities who are now approaching their 50s, the age of promotion into senior corporate positions. Though current data are unavailable, in the mid-1950s two-fifths of the American business elite were graduates of these three schools.[4]

All people possess stereotypes, which act like shorthand to avoid mental overload. We are products of all we have experienced directly or indirectly from infancy. Stereotypes will never be eliminated; the best we can do is bring people to a level of awareness to control their impact. Most of the time stereotypes are mere shadow images rooted in one's history and deep in the subconscious. But they are very powerful. For example, in controlled experiments the mere insertion of the word black into a sentence has resulted in people changing their responses to a statement.[5]

One reason for the power of stereotypes is their circularity. People seek to confirm their expectations and resist contradictory evidence, so we cling to beliefs and stereotypes become self-fulfilling.[6] If, for example, a white administrator makes a mistake, his boss is likely to tell him, "That's OK. Everybody's entitled to one goof." If, however, a black counterpart commits the same error, the boss thinks, "I knew he couldn't do it. The guy is incompetent." The stereotype reinforces itself.

While blatant bigotry is a problem in organizations, neutrality may be an even greater obstacle to blacks. While an estimated 15% of white Americans are extremely antiblack, 60% are more or less neutral and conform to socially approved behavior.[7] According to Joseph Feagin, a sociologist at the University of Texas at Austin, "Those managers and executives who are the biggest problem are not the overt racial bigots. They are people who see discrimination but remain neutral and do nothing about it. These are the people who let racially motivated behavior go unnoticed, unmentioned, or unpunished. These are the people who won't help."

Advancement in organizations obviously requires support from the top; and as they step through the maze of obstacles, aspirants try earnestly to pick up signals from those in power so they can tell which way the winds blow. Black managers feel obliged to use a color lens in interpreting those signals. A white male passed over for a choice assignment may wonder about his competence or even whether his style turned somebody off: "Was it my politics? My clothes? My laugh?" Blacks will ponder those things too, but the final question they must ask themselves is, "Was it my color?"

Of course, a decision about a promotion is a subjective thing. For blacks, colorism adds an extra layer of subjectivity. An outplacement consultant (white) who has worked for a number of the largest U.S.

corporations referred to "a double standard that boils down to this: the same qualities that are rewarded in white managers become the reason the black manager is disliked and penalized." A black personnel executive explained the double standard this way: "If you're aggressive then you're arrogant, but if you're not aggressive then you're not assertive. You try to be right in the middle, and that's impossible."

Studies show that senior executives are generally taller than average. Height is thus an advantage in moving up the corporate ladder—but not necessarily if you're black. "I was interviewing with a white vice president over cocktails for an opening in his organization," recalled one black executive. "I've always had a good track record and, as you can see, I'm not very large. After a few drinks he told me that he liked me, but if I were a big black guy with large muscles, he wouldn't even consider me for the job."

The corporate posture is that there is no race problem. Perhaps in the attitude of the person at the very top that's true, but not lower down. A black VP of a large East Coast bank said, "Our president talks about adhering to equal opportunity, and every year he sends out this letter saying he's firmly committed to equal opportunity. And I believe he's serious. But as the message gets to middle managers, it's lost." Another black manager put it this way, "The general may give the orders, but it's the sergeant who decides who gets liberty and who gets KP."

At the "sergeant's" level, competition is conditioned by colorism. "It's not a conspiracy, it's an understanding," said a black personnel director at a New England-based food distribution company. "Whites don't get together and say, 'Let's do it to this black guy.' That doesn't happen. Say Joe Blow, a black manager, is vying against ten white guys for a promotion to the assistant VP level. The ten white execs will behave in such a way as to hold Joe Blow back. They'll act independently of each other, possibly without any collusion. But given the opportunity to push Joe Blow ahead or hold Joe Blow back, they'll each hold him back."

Those who seek to step into upper management are playing a new and more complicated game. The stakes are higher and the rules are often less well defined, if they exist at all. So it is here in the middle management passage where the issue of prejudice is most acute.

To get ahead, a person depends on informal networks of cooperative relationships. Friendships, help from colleagues, customers, and superiors, and developmental assignments are the keys to success. Outsiders, or people treated as outsiders (no matter how talented or well trained), rarely do as well. Black managers feel they are treated as outsiders, and because of the distance that race produces they don't receive the benefit of these networks and relationships. Few win bosses as mentors. Moreover, they rarely get the vote of confidence from superiors that helps them to move up step-by-step and allows them to learn the business. These assignments would give them the expertise, exposure, and knowledge necessary for promotion to top posts.

What senior executives would support the promotion to their peer group of somebody they envision as stupid, lazy, dishonest, or preoccupied with sex (the prevailing racial throwbacks among whites about blacks)? This attitude permeates an entire organization because the corporate climate and culture reflect the unspoken beliefs of senior executives, and middle managers, desiring to be senior executives, conform to these norms. This statement by a black middle manager, a woman, illustrates the impact that a closed circle can have on blacks' aspirations:

"A black manager who worked for me deserved a merit raise. I came to the appraisal meeting with all the necessary documentation. There were three or four 40- to 50-year-old white men arguing for *their* people without any documentation. I was the only one supporting my manager, and I was the only one that saw him as eligible. I was overruled just by the sheer vote of it. It turned out to be a matter of 'Joe, you did a favor for me last week, so I'll support you in getting your person in this week. You owe me one, old buddy.'"

"You can try to legitimize the process by saying, 'We all got together and we went through a democratic process, so it was done fairly.' This process was democratic if by that you mean you have one vote in a group of buddies where everyone votes. But a lot of who gets what pay increase and who is put up for promotion is the underlying political buddy system. It's a matter of who believes in who, and each person's prejudices and beliefs come into play to decide the outcome."

A white consultant told me, "White managers aren't comfortable sponsoring black managers for promotion or high-visibility assignments. They fear ostracism from other whites." As a consequence, black executives are shunted into slots out of the mainstream. Here is the testimony of three of them, one from the pharmaceuticals industry, one from an insurance company, and a manufacturer:

"Too often black managers are channeled into The Relations, as I call them—the community relations, the industrial relations, the public relations, the personnel relations. These may be important functions, but they are not the gut functions that make the business grow or bring in revenues. And they're not the jobs that prepare an executive to be a CEO."

"The higher you go, the greater the acceptance of blacks for limited purposes, such as for all those programs that reach out to communities for various projects, the velvet ghetto jobs. And you become an expert on blacks. At my company, if an issue has anything to do with blacks, they come and ask me. On black purchasing they ask me. Hell, I don't have anything to do with purchasing, but because I'm black they think I ought to know something about it."

"White managers don't want to include black managers in the mainstream activities in corporations. Even blacks who have line responsibilities, to the extent that they can be pushed aside, are being pushed aside. They ask you to take a position of visible prominence not slated to the bottom line and give you financial rewards rather than leadership. It's all for outside appearance. But money doesn't relieve a poverty of satisfaction and spirit."

Pressure to Conform

"Business needs black executives with the courage and insight to help us understand issues involving equal opportunity," John deButts, former CEO of AT&T, once said. "They must tell us what we need to know, not just what they think we want to hear." But black managers are often afraid to risk their careers by speaking their minds.

In most organizations, conformity is an unwritten rule. If you don't conform, you can't be trusted—especially for higher positions. Black managers try to conform to the corporate values regarding race, and female managers, the values regarding women. If race is "not an issue," acceptance means you are expected to pretend race is not an issue. "A lot of black managers," one black executive told me, "are afraid that if they stand up and take an active role in some black concern, even though they believe it's the right issue, people will say, 'Oh, he's black and just standing up for blacks as any black would.'"

Moreover, some white managers become defensive if prejudice is mentioned. After all, it's un-American to be prejudiced, and who wants to be un-American? So white and black managers, fearful of confronting the issue, take part in a charade. "There is often less than total candor between blacks and whites at any level, and the higher up you go the more that is true," says psychiatrist Price Cobbs. "There is mutual patronizing and misreading, making blacks and whites unable to exchange ideas and express their feelings."

At each step up the organizational pyramid, of course, there are fewer positions. But the slots for minority members are even more limited. This creates an additional game—king (or queen) of the little hill—in which minority members and women compete against each other for the tiny number of near-top jobs available to them. And the first one who gets to the top of this smaller hill is sorely tempted to fend off, rather than help, other minority players.

Attempts by black managers to convince white superiors they are trustworthy, safe, and therefore acceptable manifest themselves in different ways. One black executive explained, "It might take the form of a manager not wanting a black secretary—not so much because he thinks the individual is unqualified, but because he's concerned about how his superiors and peers might perceive them. 'Hey,' they might say, 'that's a black operation over there, so it can't be too effective.'"

Here are some true stories that illustrate running a gauntlet:

Al, who aspired to the lower rungs of senior management, had to fill a vacancy in his organization. The most qualified candidate was another black manager, George. Al's company was an "equal opportunity employer," but he worried that if he promoted George he would be perceived as favoring blacks and therefore would be unacceptable as an executive. So he promoted a less qualified white candidate. George initiated a suit for discrimination, the company settled, and Al resigned.

Bob was an ambitious person who changed employers when passed over for promotion. After a year at his new job, he saw that white managers he thought to be inferior performers were being promoted above him. Actually, many of the company's black managers were becoming vocal about a perceived pattern of favoritism toward white managers, who were faring better on appraisals, assignments, promotions, and pay. So that his superiors would see him in a positive light, Bob didn't associate openly with other black managers—but he privately encouraged their efforts to speak up. They should be the "bad guys" while he played the "good guy" in the hope that at least one black might be the first to crack the color barrier at a high level.

In meetings with black managers, senior executives would say that they recognized that blacks were not moving up fast enough, but it takes time and the blacks should not be too pushy. Bob told the white executives, "I don't see why you're even meeting with those guys.

They're a bunch of complainers." Two months later, Bob was the first black to be promoted to the executive level.

Charlie, a junior executive, did not wear race on his sleeve but was straightforward and honest on the subject. One day several lower level black managers sought his advice on correcting what they saw as a pattern of discrimination stunting their careers. Charlie concluded that senior management ought to know about their concerns, and he agreed to arrange a meeting with top officers. Two days before the meeting, the president took Charlie aside in the executive dining room and said, "Charlie, I'm disappointed that you met with those people. I thought we could trust you."

Ellen, a politically astute black manager, noted that promotions for black managers in her organization diminished coincident with an increase in promotions for white females. Ellen skewed promotions in favor of white females and was a regular participant in meetings about women's issues. She would not promote black males because they were "undependable." Ellen was surprised when a white male declined a promotion because the black male who trained him "was more deserving."

The twist that colorism puts on the maneuvering of ambitious managers is not a new phenomenon. Jews and Italians (among Irish, and other ethnic newcomers in America) have tried to pass as less Jewish or less Italian than their Jewish or Italian colleagues. Obviously it is more difficult for blacks to overcome white executives' feelings about color, but they, like whites, will use what tactics they can to get ahead. But for blacks it's more than merely changing roles like changing hats. Adopting a white value system often means unconsciously devaluing other blacks—and ultimately themselves.

RACE AND SEX

Another phenomenon that black managers are talking about is "substituting the lesser evil." In their evident push to demonstrate progress toward equal opportunity, some companies are promoting white women in lieu of black men and women. Many of the black managers I interviewed mentioned this phenomenon. Of all the complex interracial issues, certainly the most controversial is the combination of race and sex. The white male-black female, black male-white female relationships are very sensitive matters. Here the most primitive feelings interact, and the stereotypes come boiling to the surface.

At higher levels of organizations, white women have problems in achieving acceptance that in some ways are like those of blacks. Even so, race poses the bigger barrier. According to Price Cobbs, the psychiatrist, "There will be far more white women in the old boys' club before there are large numbers of blacks—men or women."

Since white women comprise 40% of the U.S. population, compared with blacks' 12%, they naturally should move into positions of power in greater numbers than blacks. What seems to be happening, however, is the movement upward of white women at the expense of blacks—men and women. Black managers are concluding that senior executives who are uncomfortable promoting blacks into positions of trust and confidence—those positions that lead to the top jobs—feel less reluctant to promote white females to these posts. "It's as if there is a mind-set that says, 'We have a couple of women near the executive suite—we've done our job,' and they dismiss competent blacks," one black executive said. "It's corporate apartheid," said another.

If the comfort level is a big factor in an invitation to enter the executive suite, it is understandable that white women will get there before blacks. After all, the mothers, wives, and daughters of top officers are white women, and they deal with white women all their lives—but only rarely with black men and women. And they are likely to view white women as being more from their own social class than black men and women.

Stereotypes no doubt play a role here too. One study indicates that the higher the white male rises in the corporate hierarchy, the less likely he is to hold negative stereotypes about women but the more likely he is to hold negative stereotypes about blacks.[8]

Black women, of course, seemingly have to overcome issues of both race and sex. But these combined drawbacks may cause less resistance than that experienced by black men. A study of biracial groups concluded that black women are not perceived in the same sexual role as white women or in the same racial role as black men. Within a social context, black females are more readily accepted in roles of influence than black males. The author of the study reasoned that white society has historically allowed more assertive behavior from black women than black men because black women are considered to be less dangerous.[9]

If personal comfort levels are a main criterion for advancement, black women are less threatening and therefore more acceptable to white male executives and so will advance faster and farther than black men. Recently *Fortune* magazine found that "the figures for black men tell a disturbing story. From 1976 to 1984, black men lost ground relative to both white women and black women."[10]

BALANCING ACT

Most black managers feel that to satisfy the values and expectations of the white corporate hierarchy they must run a gauntlet of contradictory pressures. Running the gauntlet means smarting from the pain of prejudice even as white colleagues deny that your reality of race has any impact. It means maintaining excellent performance even when recognition is withheld.

It means being smart but not too smart. Being strong but not too strong. Being confident but not egotistical to the point of alienation. Being the butt of prejudice and not being unpleasant or abrasive. Being intelligent but not arrogant. Being honest but not paranoid. Being confident yet modest. It means seeking the trust and respect of fellow blacks and acceptance by whites. Speaking out on issues affecting blacks but not being perceived as a self-appointed missionary or a unifaceted manager expert only on black subjects. Being courageous but not too courageous in areas threatening to whites.

It means being a person who is black but not losing one's individuality by submersion into a class of "all blacks," as perceived by whites. Defining one's self while not contradicting the myriad definitions imposed by white colleagues. Being accepted as a leader for whites and not being seen as an Uncle Tom by blacks. Being a person who is black but also a person who is an authentic human being.

Some black managers are becoming psychological contortionists, struggling to play by the rules of this game. Feelings of self-worth and self-esteem are vital ingredients of mental health. High-achieving black managers are particularly vulnerable to depression if they strive for what white peers attain only to find that the objects of their desire are withheld. The knowledge that these goals should be attainable because of educational preparation and intellectual capability makes the conflict sharper and black managers that much more vulnerable to depression.[11] According to Price Cobbs, the level of outrage and indignation among black managers exceeds that of black Americans who are unemployed. Another psychiatrist I talked to adds: "Those black managers in the potentially greatest psychological trouble are the ones who try to deny their ethnicity by trying to be least black—in effect, trying to be white psychologically."

According to Abraham Zaleznik, a social psychologist at the Harvard Business School, if companies promote only those blacks "who are going along with the values of others, they are eliminating those blacks who have more courage, leadership potential, and a better sense of self worked out. This would be tragic because it would attack the very basis of building self-esteem based on an individual's unique capabilities."

Where to from Here?

The picture of frustration and pain that I have drawn is the reality for many, but certainly not all, black managers. I have stressed what is the predominant condition. Most black managers are convinced that their best is never seen as good enough, even when their best is better than the best of white colleagues. The barrier facing black managers is no less real than a closed door. But in the minds of many of their superiors, if people can't make it on their own, it must be their own fault.

I am not talking about the disadvantaged but about high achievers, those blacks who are most integrated into the fabric of our country's white-oriented culture. Yet because of colorism many of these best qualified managers are seen as unqualified "affirmative action hires." (Even so, affirmative action should not be a distasteful term—though it is in Washington these days. Its objective is to ensure that all qualified persons compete on a level playing field.)

What will be the outcome if many of America's best educated and best prepared blacks are not allowed to succeed, and if our country's leaders, including those in corporations, no longer care about this issue? Everyone may agree that "a mind is a terrible thing to waste," but are we not contradicting ourselves if we make waste matter of some of our best black managerial minds or relegate them to the scrap heap of human potential? How hypocritical will we appear in America if "equal opportunity" becomes primarily a white female slogan and the law is used to construct a system akin to corporate apartheid in which the positions of power and authority are nearly all held by whites? What will today's black managers say to their children if one day they ask, "Why don't I have the opportunity you had, and what did you try to do about it?"

Just as one cannot be a little bit pregnant, corporations cannot have a little bit of equal opportunity. There is unlimited opportunity, based on uniform rules, or equal opportunity does not exist. If, at a certain higher level, opportunity appears to peak because no blacks have ever been at such a level, blacks and whites may perceive that blacks could never—and therefore should never—be promoted there. They don't satisfy the "prototype" for an executive at that level, and therefore, among those who are competing for advancement, they are less appealing as candidates than their white competitors.

So their effectiveness as managers, even in their present roles, becomes an issue. Such a perception combines with ego adjustments of whites working for blacks (whites who may never have been subordinate to a black person before) to make effective leadership by a black much more difficult. Who wants to work for someone not seen as a winner? Or someone with a questionable future?

Will black managers ever be allowed to move up the organization and succeed in the old-fashioned way, by earning it? They must be allowed to fail as well as succeed. In other words, they must be treated the same as white managers.

The first step is to accept how deeply rooted our feelings are about race and color, then remove the taboo from candor on racial realities. We must open up communication and not deny or pretend. Corporations cannot manage attitudes, but they can manage behavior with accountability, rewards, and punishment, as in all other important areas of concern. What gets measured in business gets done, what is not measured is ignored.

The commitment must come from the top down—that of course is obvious. But more than sincerity is needed from the board of directors down through the management structure: commitment, example, and follow-through. Unless the CEO influences the corporate culture to counter the buddy system by compelling all managers to focus on competence and performance rather than comfort and fit, the in-place majority will merely perpetuate itself and the culture will continue to default to traditional racial etiquette and attitudes.

Equal opportunity will not be achieved by promoting one or two high-profile, "most acceptable" blacks into the executive suite, putting a black on a board of directors, or bringing in one or two "name" blacks from outside and bypassing middle management. A fair chance means that black managers can move ahead and still be genuine, that they don't have a psychological gauntlet imposed on them. Fairness means that successful black managers can be role models. A fair chance means that there can be black division heads of marketing, production, and strategic planning, as well as urban affairs and community relations. It also means that black executives can become part of the headquarters elite and report directly to the CEO, not only as vice presidents but as senior and executive vice presidents. It means black executives can be CEOs.

Where do we go from here? The answer lies in our vision for America: whether we want a land of opportunity for all Americans based on individual dignity and respect, or a land of advantage and disadvantage based on skin color. Whether we want a nation where competence and character will be the criteria for leadership, or whether color will ordain that Americans stay in a place determined in the minds and by the values of others. Senior corporate executives can help decide the outcome. Where do they choose to go from here?

Notes

1. Survey conducted in 1983 by Sirota and Alper Associates, New York.

2. See Faye Crosby, Steven Bromely, and Leonard Saxe, "Recent Unobtrusive Studies of Black and White Discrimination & Prejudice: A Literature Review," *Psychological Bulletin*, vol. 87, no. 3, 1980, p. 546.

3. *Wall Street Journal*, May 21, 1982.

4. Suzanne Keller, *Beyond the Ruling Class: Strategic Elites in Modern Society* (New York: Random House, 1953), p. 202.

5. William E. Sedlacek and Glenwood C. Brooks, Jr., "Measuring Racial Attitudes in a Situational Context," *Psychological Reports*, vol. 27, 1970, p. 971.

6. Mark Snyder, "Self-Fulfilling Stereotypes," *Psychology Today*, July 1982, p. 60.

7. Tom Pettigrew, "The Mental Health Impact," in *Impacts of Racism On White Americans*, eds. Benjamin P. Bowser and Raymond G. Hunt (Beverly Hills, Calif.: Sage, 1981), p. 116.

8. John Fernandez, *Racism and Sexism in Corporate Life* (Lexington, Mass.: Lexington Books, D.C. Heath, 1981), p. 80.

9. Kathryn Adams, "Aspects of Social Context As Determinants of Black Women's Resistance to Challenges," *Journal of Social Issues*, vol. 39, no. 3, 1983, p. 69.

10. Anne B. Fisher, "Good News, Bad News, and an Invisible Ceiling," *Fortune*, September 16, 1985, p. 29.

11. See Alexander Thomas and Samuel Sillen, *Racism and Psychiatry*, (Secaucus, N.J.: Citadel, 1972), p. 49.

3

Racial Remarks in the Workplace: Humor or Harassment?

Terry L. Leap and Larry R. Smeltzer

A black man employed by a Minnesota trucking company had racial slurs directed at him and was the target of graffiti written by fellow workers. A U.S. district court held that the trucking company violated Title VII of the Civil Rights Act of 1964 and ordered it to take affirmative action and disciplinary measures against offending employees. Furthermore, the court ordered the company to educate and sensitize its supervisors and managers in order to eliminate racial and national-origin hostility from the work environment.

The U.S. Court of Appeals (Fifth Circuit) reached a different decision in a case involving an offshore oil rig worker. Employee behavior that included "raw pranks, crude practical jokes," and oral racial abuse did not amount to harassment sufficient to support a black employee's claim that fellow workers forced him to quit his job on the rig. Few, if any, workers on the rig were spared; white as well as black employees were the target of obscene and racially derogatory remarks. The court ruled that in this instance the employer was not responsible for the actions of its employees.

These two cases exemplify situations faced with increasing frequency—and "solved" with some inconsistency—by the Equal Employment Opportunity Commission (EEOC) and the courts. Even so, this form of harassment is little understood, perhaps because it, unlike sexual harassment in organizations, has received scant attention in the legal arena and academic literature. But harassment along racial and ethnic lines has the potential to create disrupting tensions in the workplace.

What constitutes harassment is hard to say. The telling and sharing of crude jokes is commonplace in many organizational settings. Employees banter in racially derogatory terms during the normal course of their work. While such "humor" is perceived by some as being crude, vulgar, degrading, or inappropriate, to others it is just a form of hazing and perfectly harmless.

It is often difficult to determine whether an employer or supervisor who tolerates or condones such behavior is legally liable under civil rights legislation governing employment conditions. The courts, in trying to decide whether the conduct was appropriate, have often tried to evaluate the work environment and context in which slurs, epithets, and jokes were uttered. The appropriateness often depends on the legal and social distinction between harassment and hazing.

Our analysis of EEOC and court decisions reveals three categories of cases pertaining to racial and ethnic slurs in the workplace. We'll discuss each of these in turn.

1. *Flagrant violations.* Title VII of the Civil Rights Act says that no employer may discriminate against any person with respect to "terms, conditions, or privileges of employment, because of such individual's race." The EEOC has ruled that an employer must maintain a "working environment free of racial intimidation," which includes "positive action where positive action is necessary to redress or eliminate employee intimidation." Cases where a "concerted pattern of harassment" exists and where the racial slurs are "excessive and opprobrious"—to quote two judicial opinions—constitute violations of equal employment opportunity laws.

In one such case, that of the Minnesota trucker, not only was the black employee the object of racial slurs and graffiti, but also the tires on his auto were slashed and a foul-smelling substance was put in his shoes. Moreover, the court noted, his supervisors failed to take action to prevent the harassment and did not remove the graffiti from the walls and equipment. Another court case dealt with a civilian firefighter employed at a naval air station who, in addition to being subjected to a barrage of racially derogatory remarks, received threats of physical harm from fellow employees.

Both of these cases have several points in common:

> The use of racial epithets was continuous and abusive; there was no evidence that they were uttered merely in jest. On the contrary, they were intended to demean or threaten.

Management was aware of the behavior but failed to take corrective action against the culprits.

The offending supervisors and employees were ordered to undergo training in sensitivity in human relations and respect for diverse racial groups.

2. *Gray-area cases.* A second category consists of cases in which the racial slurs and epithets were less pervasive, were not directed at a certain employee, or were not necessarily deemed to be vicious or threatening.

An example is the case involving the black offshore oil rig worker, in which the appellate court held for the employer despite the frequent voicing of racial slurs and epithets. No individual was singled out for an inordinate amount of coarse treatment. In any case, the court observed "friendly and cordial" relations existing among employees.

A significant factor in determining whether discrimination exists, this court held, is the employee's perception of his environment. According to the testimony, the plaintiff "perceived these unpleasantries as part of the life on the rig," thereby "effectively laying to rest the suggestion that he was singled out because of his race." The court concluded that the worker "reasonably might have resigned because of offended sensibilities," but his fellow workers' behavior did not make the employer a violator of the law.

In another such case a car dealership was held to have violated Title VII by tolerating the repeated verbal abuse of a black trainee. The remarks were made in his presence, despite his objections. When he was fired, the company claimed excessive absenteeism as the reason, but the court concluded that the discharge was at least in part racially motivated.

3. *Isolated incidents.* Federal and state courts generally do not hold employers liable for situations in which there is no steady barrage of opprobrious racial comments leveled at minorities, in which the use of racial terms is limited to casual conversation, or in which such slurs reflect only individual attitudes and relationships.

In two cases, both involving police departments in southern cities, the respective federal district courts found that the use of derogatory racial names and jokes were either isolated events or did not have a significant bearing on other personnel actions affecting minority group members. In another situation, the Eighth Circuit Court found that a supervisor employed by a National Football League team did not violate Title VII because of several derogatory remarks about Italian-Americans made in conversation. Likewise, the New York Supreme Court held that an employer had not broken the state's human rights law when an "intemperate, crude, and anti-Semitic remark" was made in anger in an environment in which "no systematic exclusion or restriction or any evidence of persistent religious discrimination" had been demonstrated.

Although racial or ethnic remarks such as these do not infringe EEO laws per se, they may put the employer in a bad light. Many of these cases coincide with complaints about wrongful discharge or unfair job assignment. To bolster a charge of race discrimination, a plaintiff may cite incidents of derogatory remarks or jokes. One court held that racial slurs and epithets may help a plaintiff establish a prima facie case of discrimination. Once a prima facie case is established, the burden of proof shifts to the company, which then must show absence of discrimination.

What the EEOC and the courts appear to be saying in their rulings is that employers who perpetuate or condone a work environment where racially demeaning remarks are tolerated are more likely to violate Title VII than those in whose workplaces the remarks are either isolated events or reflect individual bigotry not supported or reinforced by the organizational culture. Factors such as the educational level of the company's labor force, the degree of stress associated with the job, job-related safety hazards, teamwork required among employees to ensure productivity and safety, and employer traditions all affect the organizational culture. They also may affect whether the EEOC and courts interpret incidents as racial harassment.

The coarse behavior of those on the oil rig may have served a useful purpose in combating boredom, reducing tension in a work environment bristling with safety hazards, and (in a bizarre way) creating a sense of camaraderie among nonprofessional and relatively unskilled employees who were forced to work close to each other and in isolation from the rest of society. (Nearly all the litigated cases to date dealing with racial slurs and epithets, incidentally, have involved nonprofessional and relatively unskilled workers.) Such was not the case with the trainee in the car dealership, who was forced to endure derogatory remarks that were inappropriate and unwarranted considering the nature of his job.

Where Does the Fun Stop?

How does harassment differ from hazing? Hazing is a ritual engaged in to determine whether new employees are trustworthy and able to stand up under stress and uncertainty. Employees who withstand the debasing experience receive "membership" in the work group as their reward. Hazing is usually carried out on an "equal opportunity" basis with sparing of few, if any, employees.

Harassment, of course, is more invidious. It involves singling out a person with the intention of discouraging the person's company or continued employment, or of creating an unpleasant or hostile environment.

Attempts at humor are also difficult to assess in determining what is and what is not racial or ethnic harassment. Next to jokes about sex, jokes directed at racial and ethnic groups make up the most popular form of humor. Individual perceptions of and reactions to attempts at humor, of course, vary widely. The victim of barbs, wanting to be considered a good sport, may pretend to be amused. Other victims may express displeasure or hurt feelings. Sometimes the target of an ethnic joke finds it funnier than the teller of the joke. The mayor of Hamtramck, a suburb of Detroit populated largely by people of Polish descent, demanded removal of a Polish joke book from a local newsstand only to find that it sold better in his community than anywhere else in the area.

From an organizational standpoint, humor and joking behavior may further group cohesiveness—as hazing often does. Joking can relieve tension or frustration, reduce boredom, reinforce status levels, establish roles, and provide a means for expression of feelings for which there is no socially acceptable outlet.

The telling of racial or ethnic jokes in the workplace does not violate Title VII or other fair employment laws unless two conditions prevail: the work environment is polluted with such behavior, and the employer (including supervisors) has implicitly or explicitly condoned widespread circulation of such jokes.

A written policy can go far in preventing racial and ethnic harassment, with all their destructive effects, from taking root. A general policy should support the dignity of each employee and forbid unnecessary forms of harassment and demeaning behavior. The policy should recognize the following:

Employees have the right to work in an environment free of undue personal harassment, stress, and interpersonal friction.

Certain types of racially motivated remarks and harassment are contrary to federal and state civil rights laws and can impose a legal liability on the employer as well as tarnish the organization's public image and damage employee morale.

Both supervisory and nonsupervisory personnel have an individual responsibility to desist from behavior that might offend the dignity and violate the personal and legal rights of others.

Supervisors are obliged to investigate incidents or complaints of racial harassment. Sanctions against offending employees should be imposed under the precepts of a progressive discipline policy.

When racial tensions and harassment are present in the workplace, management should consider using periodic race relations awareness training programs and counseling sessions to alert offending employees to the legal ramifications of their actions. Such programs can be used as part of the progressive discipline process just mentioned. Furthermore, these programs may reflect positively on management's effort to maintain a cordial work environment when the administrative enforcement agencies and courts examine an organization for signs of racial hostility.

PART

III

Women in the Workplace: New Ways to Think about Work

1
Two Women, Three Men on a Raft

Robert Schrank

The day was cold and gray. Under the pines that towered over their heads, 20 people assembled on the banks of the Rogue River in Oregon. They were members of a special group invited by Outward Bound to take a trip down the river on a raft. There would be five rafts, each holding four participants and one Outward Bound staff member. Raft No. 4 was the only one that had two women and three men. When the trip started, all that the participants knew was that there would be rapids with fearsome names; that each was responsible for doing his or her share of the cooking, tent pitching, ground clearing, supply hauling, and paddling; and that their teamwork or lack of it was what would make their trip a success or a failure. They knew nothing of each other, their Outward Bound staff member, or what a week on the river could really be like. This is one participant's story of how Raft No. 4 fared on the Rogue and what the experience taught him about the relationships between men and women at work.

One afternoon in June, I left the cloistered halls of the Ford Foundation and within 36 hours found myself standing on the pebbled banks of the Rogue River in Oregon with three other uncertain souls who had embarked on a week of "survival training" sponsored by Outward Bound. It was a cloudy, cold day, and as we pumped up our rubber raft and contemplated the Rogue, we also wondered about each other.

Before embarking on a Greyhound for the raft launching site, we had gathered the night before at the Medford Holiday Inn. That night, the Outward Bound staff had distributed individual camping gear and waterproof sleeping/storage bags to the 20 of us, almost all novices, and had given us a short briefing on the perils of going down the Rogue River on a raft.

As they explained the nature of the trip, the Outward Bound staffers reminded me of seasoned military men or safari leaders about to take a group of know-nothings into a world of lurking danger. Their talk was a kind of machismo jargon about "swells," rattlers, safety lines, portages, and pitons. Because they had known and conquered the dangers, it seemed they could talk of such things with assurance. This kind of "man talk" called to a primitive ear in us novices, and we began to perceive the grave dangers out there as evils to be overcome. In our minds, we planned to meet "Big Foot" the very next day, and we were secretly thrilled at the prospect.

If the Outward Bound staff briefing was designed to put us at ease, its effect, if anything, was the opposite. Hearing the detailed outline of what would be expected of us increased our anxiety. "You will work in teams as assigned to your raft," said Bill Boyd, the Northwest Outward Bound director, "and you will be responsible for running your raft, setting up camp each night, cooking every fourth meal for the whole gang, and taking care of all your personal needs."

The staff divided the 20 of us into four groups, each of which would remain together for the week on the raft. How we were grouped was never explained, but of the five rafts on the river, No. 4 was the only one that ended up with two women and three men. One of the men was a member of the Outward Bound staff, a counselor and guide who was considerably younger than his four charges.

The four of us on Raft No. 4 were all in our middle fifties. Each of us had experienced some modicum of success in his or her life, and Outward Bound had invited each of us in the hope that after a week of living on the Rogue River we would go back from that trip as Outward Bound supporters and promoters.

Outward Bound exists because of the surprising fact that during World War II fewer younger men survived being torpedoed on the Murmansk, Russia convoy run than older men. Dr. Kurt Hahn, C.B.E., an emigrant German educator living in England, had observed that the older men did things to help themselves survive, such as collecting rain water for drinking, building shelters in the lifeboats, catching and eating raw fish, and learning to care for each other.

Dr. Hahn found that many of the younger seamen, by contrast, tended to sit and wait for somebody to come and rescue them. If no one came, which was often the case, they died just sitting there. Dr. Hahn felt that these seamen must have lacked a certain self-confidence or an awareness that they could take action that would result in survival, and founded Outward Bound to help young people learn that they can take charge of their own survival and lives.

The worldwide organization has been operating in the United States for 14 years; its 35,000 graduates attest to its popularity. During this time, however, Outward Bound has evolved into more of a learning institution than a survival training organization. It now operates under a variety of different notions, one of them being that industrial man has lost and should regain the art of living with nature. The organization believes that the wilderness can teach people about themselves by providing a different backdrop against which they can gain insight into their day-to-day behavior.

This article is about what happened to two women and three men on a raft for a week on the Rogue River in Oregon.

On the River

Like most of the other 19 people on the trip, at the outset I had little or no idea of what to expect. I had participated in a few human growth encounter workshops, so I was prepared for, although again surprised at, how willingly people seem to accept the authority of a completely unknown group leader. Most people seem able to participate in all kinds of strange and, in many instances, new behaviors with no knowledge regarding the possible outcomes. This group was no exception. All of us had some notion of Outward Bound, but we knew nothing about each other, or our raft leader John, or the Rogue River.

Even though their preembarkation talk was filled with the machismo jargon I mentioned, the staff did not describe what we might actually expect to happen, nor did they talk about the many other river trips they had been on. I suppose the staff leaders assumed that the best way for a group of people to learn about themselves and each other is to let the experience talk to them directly.

The two women assigned to Raft No. 4 were named Marlene and Helen. Marlene was a recently divorced mother of five kids from Washington, whom a number of us had observed in her pink bikini in the Holiday Inn pool when we had arrived. Most of us acknowledged that because of that build we would love to have her along. Marlene used to wear her red ski suit at night and talked a lot about times she'd spent on the slopes. A top-notch skier, she said she divorced her husband because she was tired of making believe he was a better skier than she was.

Helen, a big blonde woman with a fierce sense of humor and a divorced mother of two grown boys, was at the time of our trip the president of the Fund Center in Denver, a coordinating body for local foundations, as well as a political activist. She and I became each other's clowns, and one night at a campfire she leaned over and asked me, "Bobbie, is this just another plaything of the bored rich, or can we really learn something out here in this Godforsaken wilderness?" I told her I wasn't sure but we ought to give it a chance, which we did.

One of the two other men was Bill, a very successful lawyer from Darien, Connecticut. He was the only one of the four passengers who was still happily married, since I too was divorced. Bill was a busy executive, but he managed to find time for hiking, skiing, and fishing. While Outward Bound took care of all our food requirements and most of our medical needs, Raft No. 4 had its own supply officer in Bill. His backpack was organized like a Civil War surgeon's field kit. He had all his changes of clothing scheduled, and when it rained, his extra plastic rainjacket kept me dry since mine leaked like a sieve. Though he and Marlene were obviously attracted to each other from the start, it was clear from his "happy family" talk that nothing was going to change, and it didn't.

The other man was John Rhodes, our heavily mustached, vigorous leader, in his early thirties, who saw himself as a teacher, educator, and trainer. As a progressive educator, John was overdedicated to the notion that no one can learn from anyone else since learning is a singular, unique experience. At night John slept away from the rest of us under a very fancy Abercrombie and Fitch drop cloth which was made to be strung up in many different ways. Trying a new fancy pitch, John would say to Bill and me, "Be imaginative in how you pitch your tarpaulin." As we had nothing but pieces of plastic as tarpaulins, we would greet John's injunction with amused silence.

The men and women of Raft No. 4 were a warm, friendly, outgoing bunch, each of whom helped create a nice supportive atmosphere.

When we arrived at the river, each was anxious to pitch in and do his or her part. The staff distributed the rafts, each of which had a small foot pump, and Bill and I, with instruction from John, proceeded to inflate ours. It was one of our first chores, and we did it with a machismo fervor that suggested either previous knowledge, or that it was man's work, or both. Marlene and Helen carried food bags, buckets, and ropes. It was a cold day, a gray mist hung over the towering Oregon pines, and I had a feeling that at least some of us, given a choice, would have opted for going back to the Holiday Inn.

There was a lot of forced joking and kidding, with which we attempted to overcome some of our anxieties—we were whistling in the dark.

John gave each of us a Mae West type life preserver and instructed us on how to use it. He told us, "You are not to go on the raft without it." Now with all of us bulging out of our Mae Wests, a Richter scale applied to anxiety would have registered eight or a full-scale breakdown. Postponing the inevitable, we shivered, fussed, and helped each other get adjusted to our life jackets. The trip down the Rogue was beginning to have a serious quality.

The rafts we used were small, about 10 feet long and 4 feet wide. The passengers sit on the inflated outer tube with their feet on the inside. Everyone is very close together with little or no room to move around. Also, unlike a boat, a raft has no keel or rudder mechanism, which means that it tends to roll and bobble around on top of the water. Unless the occupants work as a team and use their paddles in close coordination, it is very difficult to control.

While we were still on shore, John perched himself in the helmsman position at the back of the raft and said, "OK, I am going to teach you how to navigate the Rogue. When I say 'right turn,' the two people on the left side of the raft are to paddle forward and the two on the right are to backpaddle. When I say 'left turn,' the two people on the right are to paddle forward and the two on the left are to backpaddle. When I say 'forward,' I want everyone digging that paddle in like his life depended on it, and when I say 'backpaddle,' everyone paddle backward. When I say 'hold,' all paddles out of the water. Now you got it, or should we go over it again?" We pushed the raft out over the beach pebbles and paddled out into the Rogue, which at this point seemed like a nice pond. John barked his commands, and the team did just fine in the quiet water.

John told us that we were Raft No. 4 of five rafts, and it was important to everyone's safety that each raft maintain its position so that we could make periodic personnel checks to make sure no one was missing. John gave the command "forward," and because No. 3 raft was already far ahead of us and out of sight, Marlene, Helen, Bill, and I paddled vigorously.

As we proceeded down the river, John announced, "Each of you will take turns at being the helmsman." After some comment by

Helen, this term was quickly corrected to conform to the new nondiscriminatory linguistics, as well as for the EEOC, to "helmsperson." John said that this person would be in charge of the raft—steering from the stern and issuing the commands.

As John talked, my mind drifted. I was suddenly overwhelmed by the grandeur and beauty of this great wilderness river road we were traveling. In awe of the hugeness of the trees, I did not hear nor respond to a command. John, a very earnest fellow, was somewhat annoyed at my daydreaming and upbraided me saying, "Look, we all have to concentrate on our job or we will be in trouble." And then he explained the nature of the rapids up ahead.

He told us how to recognize a rapid's tongue (entrance), how to avoid "sleepers" (hidden rocks), and then how to ride the "haystacks" (the choppy waves that form at the outlet of the rapids) as you come through the rapids. He said that the most important art we would learn would be how to chop our paddles into the waves as we rode the haystacks. Since a raft has no seat belts, or even seats for that matter, unless you chop down hard the rough water can bounce you right out of it.

As we paddled through the still calm waters, trying to catch up with Raft No. 3, Helen began to complain that she was already getting tired. "I'm just not used to pushing a paddle, but I'm damn good at pushing a pencil," she said. I too was beginning to feel the strain of the paddle, but rather than admit it, I just laughed saying, "Why this is nothing, Helen. You should canoe the St. John in Maine. That would teach you." Bill chimed in with "Yeah, this is nothing compared to climbing Pike's Peak."

As we moved down the river a faint distant roar broke the silence of the forest. And as we drew nearer to it, our excitement grew bigger. One might have thought that rather than a 4-foot rapids, Niagara Falls lay dead ahead. I was relieved when, some distance before the rapids, John told us to head for the bank where we would go ashore and study the rapids. As a team we would then decide what kind of a course to take through them.

We had been on the river now for a few hours, and, as it would be many times during the trip, getting on dry land was a great relief. Life on a small rubber raft consists of sitting in ankle-deep cold water, anticipating a periodic refill over both the side of the raft and one's genitals. If there was not time to bail out, we would just sit in the cold water. And even if there were time we would still be soaking wet and cold from the hips down. Though this was our first chance to escape the cold water treatment, we quickly learned to look forward to such opportunities. The physical discomfort we felt together on the raft was overcoming our sense of being strangers; by the time we disembarked that first time, we were a band of fellow sufferers.

At that point on the river, the bank was very steep, so we had a tough climb up a high rock cliff to get a good look at the rapids. Just before the rapids, the river makes a sharp 90-degree bend creating an additional danger. The swiftly running river could pile the raft up on the bank or into a hidden rock. After considerable discussion, during which Bill and I tried to demonstrate to Helen and Marlene our previous if not superior knowledge of boating, we agreed on taking a left course into the tongue while at the same time trying to bear right to avoid being swept onto the bank.

Coming up and down the steep river bank Bill helped Marlene over the rocks, holding her elbow. A ways behind them Helen commented to me, "Honestly, Bob, Marlene isn't that helpless." As we climbed into the raft, Bill helped Marlene again, and I, smiling sheepishly, offered my arm to Helen. I said, holding the raft, "Well, if we go, we all go together, and may we all end up in the same hospital room." Sitting herself down, Helen said, "Who will notify next of kin since no one will be left." After they were seated, Bill and I huddled and agreed that if anything went wrong, he would look after Marlene and I would look after Helen.

Once back on the river, with John at the helm, we paddled into the rapid's tongue, where the raft picked up speed. Staying to the left but maintaining our right orientation, before we knew what had happened, we were roaring through the tongue, roller coasting through the haystacks, screaming with excitement. Flushed with our first real achievement, the raft awash with ice-cold water, we patted each other on the back on our first great success. While bailing out the raft we paid each other compliments and convinced ourselves that we could master the Rogue River.

But this was our first set of rapids, and while John assured us that we had done well, he also reminded us of the meaner rapids yet to come with such potent names as Mule Creek Canyon, Blossom Bar, Big Bend, Copper Canyon, and Grave Creek. My God, I thought, did we really have to go through all of those terrible places?

Life on the Rogue included many other things besides shooting rapids. We pitched tarpaulins every night, lugged supplies in and out of the raft, and became accustomed to the discomforts of having no running water and of being absolutely frozen after sitting in cold water for a whole day. Nothing cements a group together like collective misery, and the people of Raft No. 4 had a *real* concern for each other as mutually suffering humans.

Each raft carried a watertight supply bag of sleeping bags and personal clothing. The bag was strapped to the front of the raft and had to be carried to and fro every morning and night. When we tied up at our first campsite, Marlene and Helen each took an end and started to carry the bag from the raft up the bank. Bill ran after them yelling, "Hey, hold it. That's too heavy for you," and grabbed the bag. Throwing it over his shoulder, he said, "You shouldn't try to do that heavy stuff." Marlene smiled and said, "Bill, anytime, be my guest." Helen, who was a little annoyed, commented sarcastically, "Well, it's great to have these big, strong men around now, ain't it though?"

When we came off the raft at night, most everybody instantly undressed to put on dry clothes, caring not one fig for a leaf or modesty. But even though on the surface it looked as though the physical sex differences had disappeared, the emergency nature of things exerted a different pressure, forcing each of us to "do what you know best."

Bill and I, for example, would pitch the tarpaulins each night and haul water, while Marlene and Helen would make the beds, clean the ground, and arrange the sleeping bags. Our mutual concern was evident; it was a beautiful experience of caring for one's fellow sisters and brothers, and I loved it.

After pitching our plastic tarpaulins (which were not much bigger than queen-size beds) as protection against the rain, the four of us would wiggle into our sleeping bags for the night. The first night Helen said she thought we were "four wonderful people gone batty sleeping on the hard cold ground when they could all be in soft feather beds." We laughed and helped each other zip up, arranged sweaters as pillows, and made sure we were all protected. Raft No. 4 was a real team.

During the days, I was beginning to learn some basics about rafts and rapids. Once the raft starts down the river and enters a swiftly moving rapid, the helmsperson must give and the crew respond to commands in quick succession in order to avoid hidden rocks, suck holes, boulders, and other obstacles, which can either flip the raft over or pull it under, bouncing it back like a ball.

As we approached the second rapids, we again went ashore to "look over our approach." It was a bad situation as the rapids planed out over a very rocky riverbed. Helen suggested that we let John take the raft through while we watch. "Now, Bob," she said, "do we really care about this damn river? I don't care if we can squeak through these rocks or not. Hit your head on them or something and you could really get hurt." Bill, John, and I cheered us on.

When I became helmsperson, I discovered quickly how difficult it is to steer a raft. The helmsperson can have some effect on the direction in which the raft goes, and because Bill and I had some boating experience, we were at least familiar with the idea of using the paddle as a rudder. Neither Helen nor Marlene seemed to understand how to use a paddle that way, nor did they have the experience.

When one of the two women on our raft, more so Marlene than Helen, was the helmsperson, she would chant, "I can't do it; I can't do it." Each time they cried out neither Bill nor I would answer right away, but we would eventually try to convince them that they could. Typically, Marlene would say, "I don't know right from left. One of you guys do it; you're so much better."

At Copper Canyon we needed a "hard right" command. With Marlene at the helm, we got a "hard left" instead. Bill and I looked at each other in utter disgust.

He asked Marlene, "What's the matter, honey?"

She said, "I don't know right from left. You be the helmsperson."

He said, "Why don't we write on the back of your hands 'right' and 'left'?"

Bill was kidding, but the next thing I knew, they were doing it.

Helen was mad and said to me, "Is it really necessary to make a baby out of her?"

"No," I said, "of course not. But she really doesn't know right from left."

As Marlene would say, "I can't do it" Bill and I would say, "Of course you can do it. It's easy; you're doing just fine." All the time we were speaking, we were thinking, "Ye gods! When is she going to give up?" Each time either Marlene or Helen would be helmsperson, we'd have the same conversation; each time Bill's and my reassurances would be more and more halfhearted. Before long we weren't responding at all.

As the days wore on, Bill and I proceeded subtly but surely to take charge. The teamwork was unraveling. When we approached a tongue, if either Marlene or Helen were helmsperson, Bill and I would look at each other, and with very slight headshakes and grimaces we would indicate agreement that things were not going well at all. Once we had established that things were not going well, we then felt free to take our own corrective measures, such as trying to steer the raft from our forward paddle positions, an almost impossible thing to do. Not only is running the raft from the front not at all helpful to the person at the helm, but also if the helmsperson is not aware of the counter-forces, the raft can easily turn around like a carousel. The unaware helmsperson is then totally out of control. When that would happen, Marlene would say, "I just don't know what's wrong with me," and Helen would echo, "I don't know what's wrong with me either." Bill's and my disgust would mount.

Eventually, John became fed up with the inability of the bunch on Raft No. 4 to work together, which was mainly a result, he said, of the two "captains" in the front. As a last resort he ordered each one of us to give a single command that he or she would shout as needed. My command was "hold," Bill's command was "left," Marlene's was "right," and Helen's was "backpaddle." John's teaching objective was to get the four of us working together, or else. Needless to say, "or else" prevailed.

On the fifth day, Marlene was helmsperson. Bill and I were in the bow, silently anxious. Even voluble Helen was silent as the raft approached a fastmoving chute. At that time only a clear, concise, direct command and a rapid response would be of any use at all.

Instead of a "hard right" command, we had no command. Marlene froze, the raft slid up on a big boulder, and in an instant we flipped over like a flapjack on a griddle. The current was swift and swept the five of us away in different directions. As I splashed around in the cold water, cursing that "Goddamned dumb Marlene," I spotted Bill nearby. The two of us began together to look for Marlene and Helen, whom we found each grappling with paddles and gear they'd grabbed as the raft had gone over. We assured each other we were OK and expressed relief at finding each other.

Cold, wet, and shivering uncontrollably, we made our way out of the river. To warm us and to keep us moving, John chased us around the bank to get wood for a fire. He stuffed us with candies and other sweets to give us energy. As we stood around the fire, chilled and wet, unable to stop shaking, we talked about what had happened, and why.

There was mutiny in the air now and a consensus emerged. The four of us were furious at John and blamed him for our predicament. John retreated, but finally we were agreed that we would not have any more of this kind of thing. Regardless of John's wishes, anyone who did not want to be helmsperson could simply pass. Marlene was certain that she wanted no part of being at the helm, and Helen, though less sure, was happy to say, "Yeah, I just want to stay dry. Let you guys take the helm."

After becoming somewhat dry, sober, and a bit remorseful, the crew of Raft No. 4 returned to the river to resume our run down the Rogue. We had lost our No. 4 position, the other rafts having run past us. John was helmsperson. Helen and Marlene were settled into their backpaddle seats. Bill and I, miffed over our mishap, felt self-conscious and fell silent thinking of the inevitable joshing we'd receive from the other rafts.

We slowly overcame the tensions of our crisis, and as the trip came to an end, we were friends again; the fifth day was forgotten. As we climbed out of the raft for the last time, Marlene said, "Well, the next raft trip I take, it will be as a passenger and not as a crew member."

That last night on the Rogue, we celebrated with a big party. The women dressed up in improvised bangles and baubles. I was the maitre d', and none of us thought much about what really had happened on Raft No. 4.

Deliverance

What really happened on the river? Why did the raft flip over? Not until I was back in the comfort of my office did I begin to understand, and the realization of the truth was as shocking as any of the splashes of cold water had been on the Rogue. It became clear to me that not only had I been unhappy with a woman as helmsperson, but also that Bill and I had subconsciously, by habit, proceeded to undermine the women. When one of the other two men was in charge, I was comfortable, supportive, and worked to help him be a better helmsperson. When a woman was at the helm, I seemed to direct my activity at getting her replaced rapidly by one of the men.

A most revealing part of the raft experience, however, was not so much the power relationship between the sexes, which I think I understood, but how Bill and I unconsciously or automatically responded to protect our power from female encroachment. When the trip started, I knew that I might have some difficulty accepting a woman at the helm, but I did not realize that the threat would be so great that I would actually desire to see her fail. On that trip I did something new: I actively tried to sabotage Marlene's and Helen's efforts to lead.

Bill and I were unconsciously building on each woman's doubts about herself with negative reinforcement of her leadership role. The effect of our male, sabotaging behavior was to increase Helen's and Marlene's doubts about themselves as leaders. For each of them, their lifelong conditioning that a woman ought to be a passive sweet thing came into play, and they gave up the helm because men "do it better."

If the reader thinks males are just threatened in the outdoors, look what happens to us indoors. First there is the machismo business, which is a cultural way of granting power to males. To the macho male, it is his role to take care of the woman, particularly in the face of imminent danger, and, in the course of things, he should never yield any power. In most organizational settings the male need to be in charge in the presence of females may be subtle, which may make it harder to identify than on a raft on a swiftflowing river. If all the male readers of this article would write down just one way to undermine the budding woman executive, there would be quite a list.

Judging from firsthand experience and others' reports, I believe that what happened on Raft No. 4, Inc. occurs in most organizations when women enter positions of leadership. An exception might be organizations that have been run by women from their inception. Because organizations are usually designed as pyramids, the moving-up process entails squeezing someone else out. The higher up the pyramid, the more the squeeze. As women enter the squeezing, men are doubly threatened; first, the number of pyramid squeeze players is increasing; second, because the new players are women, our masculinity is on the block. The resentment of men toward women managers is also exacerbated by the shrunken job market.

As more women become managers in organizations, there will have to be a shift in power. The men who hold that power in fierce competition with each other will not expand the competition by encouraging women to become part of the battle without considerable changes in their own consciousness. In a wilderness setting, all decisions, either one's own or the group's, have immediate consequences, such as being dumped out of the raft. The rightness or wrongness of decisions in organizations is not so obvious since a decision may have no perceptible effects for days or even months. It is during this time lag that the male unconscious activity can occur to undermine the female.

Will women in administrative positions be supported, ignored, or subconsciously sabotaged by men who find their power threatened? As most experienced administrators know, a major problem in running an organization is directly related to the level of subordinate support. How should the organization go? Straight ahead, hold, turn left, or turn right? These decisions are judgments that may be tough, but the leader must make them; and unless they are supported by the subordinates, they might as well never have been made.

A command of "hard right" can be executed as hardhard, half-hard, and soft-hard, the last one being equal to just a facade of cooperation. That situation is the most dangerous one for the leader who presumes that orders are being executed, while in fact the raft is foundering. I suspect that one of the reasons that a woman has trouble is because the lack of support she receives from one man gets reinforced by others; it is a collective activity. Things might have been different on Raft No. 4 had we been willing to confront each other. It might have spoiled the fun, but we all might have learned something.

At first I thought there might not be much of an analogy between navigating a river and a big bureaucracy. Now I think there is. The requirements turn out to be different, and yet the same. The river is more easily understood: how it flows, its hydraulics, its sleepers, or its chutes, and women, like men, can learn these things. A big organization also has sleepers and chutes, but recognizing their existence is a far more political than intellectual task. Women trying to navigate most organizations may find them more complex than the Rogue, but they need to look for similar hazards. The sleepers and chutes will be vested groups of men, who, when their power is threatened, will pull any woman down for tinkering with their interests.

2
Coping with Comparable Worth

George P. Sape

Attacks on comparable worth come from every quarter these days. Government officials disparage the concept publicly. Business representatives charge that it will distort job markets, hamper competition, and unfairly redistribute wages. Even federal regulatory agencies seem to be backing away from any large-scale commitment to the idea of equal pay for comparable but dissimilar work.

Yet corporate executives who ignore comparable worth do a disservice to their companies and their employees. For one thing, basic questions of equity and fairness remain unresolved, however poorly the issue may be framed. And for another, the courts have made it clear that they will not tolerate sex-based wage discrimination by any employer, public or private.

Executives who see the logic of both law and equity will want to consider the course of action this author recommends. Drawing on both the judicial record and corporate experience, he urges managers to resist the temptation to view the problem as one that can be solved by raises alone. Instead they must examine all their company's compensation and employment practices to look for evidence of unsuspected discrimination.

In December 1983 the Federal District Court for the state of Washington awarded damages of $800 million to $1 billion to female state employees for sex-based wage discrimination. This ruling, decided under the theory of comparable worth, represents the largest damage award ever handed down under the equal employment laws. It also dramatizes the potential liability this area of the law holds for all employers.

In this case, *AFSCME* v. *State of Washington*, decided under Title VII of the Civil Rights Act of 1964, the court found that the state had deliberately underpaid women in female-dominated state jobs compared with what they were paid in male-dominated state jobs. The damages assessed by the court in this ruling, which affected approximately 15,000 state workers, represented the amount the court thought necessary to correct the current effects of past discrimination in the state's pay system. In addition, the state may have to adjust the women's salaries upward by as much as 30% to counter future discrimination. Even while the decision is on appeal, the state has begun to distribute immediate pay raises to those jobs that are furthest below the "comparable worth measurement line."

Although the damages have not been as dramatic, private employers, too, have been held liable for pay disparities. In *Taylor* v. *Charley Brothers Company*, for example, the court found widespread evidence of sexual discrimination within the company. Accordingly, it ordered the employer to raise the wages of its women warehouse employees so that they would be more equivalent to those given the men who did similar work.

If the *State of Washington* ruling survives further legal challenges, and if employers lose other comparable worth cases awaiting decision by the courts, the pressure to correct male-female pay disparities or face damaging lawsuits will mount. Even now, we can reasonably expect other suits that may have been dormant or under consideration over the past few years to be activated with renewed enthusiasm. Recently, for example, the American Nurses' Association filed an action against the state of Illinois with allegations similar to those that led to the Washington ruling. And similar suits on behalf of women state employees have also begun in Michigan, Hawaii, and California.

In addition, at least one state has acted voluntarily to redress civil service wage disparities uncovered in the course of a 1979 pay-practices study. In 1982 the Minnesota legislature changed its personnel law to require pay equity, established a process for correcting existing disparities, and ordered continuing supervision of state jobs and wages. In 1983 it voted to put $21.8 million into a separate fund for general wage adjustments, benefiting some 8,200 employees. So far the state has paid out about $13.1 million from that fund.

The U.S. Equal Employment Opportunity Commission, the agency responsible for examining allegations of wage-based discrimination involving federal laws, has a large number of comparable worth cases pending. Severely criticized by the House Committee on Government Operations in 1984 for failing to move more quickly, the commission has established a task force to evaluate its role in this area.

It is unlikely, however, that major actions will be forthcoming given the strong opposition to comparable worth voiced by various members of the Reagan administration. (While the staff at the EEOC has not openly attacked the concept, officials at the Department of Justice and the Council of Economic Advisers have been sharply critical, as has the chairman of the U.S. Commission on Civil Rights.) Thus the issue is likely to evolve through state actions, similar to those mentioned, and through lawsuits where pay disparity is a concern.

Evolution of Comparable Worth

The forces that are shaping the comparable worth or pay disparity issue are both structural and legal. Over time, however, employers' primary concerns are more likely to be their own compensation practices and employee-relations administration than the details of specific court rulings.

Wage comparability surfaced as a discrete issue within the broader framework of EEO concerns when women's activist groups realized that "equal pay for equal work," the traditional standard for determining pay discrimination, left some important sources of pay disparity unaddressed. This standard is set forth in the 1963 Equal Pay Act, which predates Title VII, and addresses wage disparity not as a civil rights matter but merely as one of a series of pay administration questions embodied in the Fair Labor Standards Act. Moreover, in adopting the Equal Pay Act, Congress specifically rejected the comparison of men's salaries with women's salaries when the jobs could not be shown to be equal or substantially equivalent.

As women's understanding of workplace discrimination evolved, their attention shifted from the problems of equal pay to the issue of comparable pay. This shift was premised on the realization that even though the Equal Pay Act was correcting pay rates in substantially equivalent jobs held by both men and women, such jobs represented only a portion of those women held. Most women-dominated jobs, in fact, had no equivalent male comparisons and were thus outside the scope of the Equal Pay Act.

Accordingly, women began to concentrate on female-dominated

jobs, which have no male-dominated equivalents against which direct salary comparisons can be made. So the issue of pay disparity widened from a focused concern with equal pay to an examination of job segregation in the workplace. This shift is critical because it means that the problem of wage disparity now potentially involves an organization's entire job structure, not just a few jobs that may be directly compared with each other. Discrimination remains an open question as long as certain jobs are held predominantly by women, and as long as those jobs are, by and large, lower paid.

By 1979 several studies had appeared suggesting that women continue to receive lower earnings because of a two-part act of discrimination: one, tacitly, if not overtly, employers support male-female job segregation, and two, they assign a lower value to jobs where women predominate. Women's advocates then began to focus on the way job worth is determined and to claim that the value given to female-dominated jobs does not represent their true worth, that it is not comparable to the value assigned other jobs in the organization filled predominantly by men.

SEARCHING FOR STANDARDS

Following hearings on this issue in 1980, the EEOC concluded that there was reason to believe that discrimination could have caused the disparities in wages between male and female jobs. But the commission was unable to agree on standards for addressing the problem. Rather than promulgate rules and regulations, therefore, it asked the National Academy of Sciences to study the question and suggest an approach. The academy's findings are inconclusive, however, and the EEOC to date has not developed a unified approach to wage comparability. In fact, congressional criticism notwithstanding, the EEOC's case-by-case approach is probably the only responsible course available given the absence of a uniform standard.

In the meantime, pay disparity has taken on greater definition in the courts. In an important case before the Supreme Court, for example, employer groups argued that since the Equal Pay Act precludes the comparison of dissimilar jobs, comparable worth advocates have no legal authority to challenge the issue. In 1982 the Supreme Court rejected the argument, however, and ruled instead in *The County of Washington* v. *Gunther* that the later-adopted and broader protections contained in Title VII of the Civil Rights Act could include legal challenges to rates of pay for dissimilar jobs when discrimination was claimed as the reason for the disparity. The court did not, however, embrace comparable worth as an appropriate response in such instances. It appeared to suggest that traditional EEO remedies might be more appropriate, as determined on a case-by-case basis.

This decision demonstrated that employers cannot automatically. insulate themselves from comparable worth challenges. But it said nothing about the kinds of standards to be applied in such cases. Rulings in parallel cases involving private employers, however, shed some light on this question.

In 1980 in *IUE* v. *Westinghouse Electric Corporation*, for example, the Federal Court of Appeals for the Third Judicial Circuit ruled that a union acting on behalf of its members could sue for pay adjustments if it could establish that an employer had knowingly set wage rates so that women were paid less than men for doing similar jobs. Because the dispute was settled out of court, the ruling never addressed the question of whether the company had underpaid women unlawfully. But it did establish an important legal principle that has yet to be fully developed in the courts, that is, the appropriate standard for proving the existence of a discriminatory pay disparity.

THE BURDEN OF PROOF

In the *Westinghouse* decision the court concluded that the "disparate impact" standard, which places the burden of proof on the employer and has traditionally been used to establish violations under Title VII, could be used only as a starting point for a pay disparity inquiry. Establishing the existence of a violation would require some demonstration that the employer had acted intentionally: inferences of discrimination drawn from statistical findings would not constitute sufficient proof.

This modification suggests that good faith reliance on well-established, racially or sexually neutral practices to set wages and salaries may insulate an employer from subsequent liability for pay disparity. Whether the courts will apply this standard broadly cannot be known, given the paucity of rulings in this area. But the few cases that have addressed this issue indicate that the courts may be willing to use this more favorable standard in pay disparity suits.

While the *Westinghouse* decision raises important issues for the development of pay equity, it does not provide much guidance for those who want to know how an employer's liability for sex-based wage discrimination might be determined. At about the same time, however, the Federal District Court for the Western District of Pennsylvania handed down a ruling in *Taylor* v. *Charley Brothers Company* that bears directly on this question.

In this case the employer was accused of illegal wage discrimination for paying women warehouse workers less than their male counterparts. The allegation stemmed from the fact that the company classified its warehouse employees into two departments by sex and used a different wage scale for each, even though the employees performed similar tasks.

To explain these pay practices, the company presented a variety of data including a job evaluation study that appeared to justify the wage differentials. But the plaintiffs had also commissioned an evaluation study, and it painted a different picture. On the basis of this second study, which the court found more accurate, some of the warehouse jobs were judged to be equal under the Equal Pay Act standard, while others were deemed comparable though not equal. Accordingly, the court ordered the company to equalize wages where appropriate and to adjust others upward so that the women's pay would be more "equivalent" to that received by the men.

What makes the *Charley Brothers* decision important is not the fact that the court rejected the employer's job evaluation study but rather the reasons for its action. The record is full of evidence indicating widespread and blatant sex discrimination in the company. And even though this evidence had no direct connection with the company's wage rates, it was noted repeatedly by the court. We can safely assume that it colored the credibility of the company's job evaluation and contributed to the court's finding of significant sex-based discrimination, manifest in part by the pay disparities.

As the *Charley Brothers* decision emphasizes, none of these initial cases makes it clear whether the courts were applying a comparable worth standard or whether their decisions were based on more traditional legal principles that prohibit various acts of discrimination, including those arising out of compensation-based actions. It was also unclear how the courts would treat the existing standards by which discrimination could be proved in the context of the various components that make up the comparable worth issue. In 1984, however, the Ninth Circuit Court of Appeals handed down a ruling in *Spaulding*

v. *University of Washington* that may signal an accepted judicial response to pay disparity issues. (This likelihood is enhanced by the fact that the Supreme Court denied review of the case and tacitly accepted the way in which it was resolved.)

The *Spaulding* case was brought by a group of nurses who claimed that they were the victims of illegal wage discrimination under both equal pay and comparable worth theories. To state their case, the plaintiffs compared various university jobs, including their own, in which women faculty members were paid less than men in different teaching posts. In addition, the plaintiffs claimed that the university's reliance on external market rates perpetuated historical sex-based discrimination.

In denying these arguments the appeals court seems to have accepted the loosely worded standard of proof set forth in the *Westinghouse* decision. The court rejected the plaintiffs' reliance on statistical evidence, ruling that the mere existence of a disparity does not establish discrimination. And it also rejected the plaintiffs' argument that the use of external market rates was a cause of discrimination, concluding instead that these rates were never meant to constitute a neutral employment policy. The court went on to state that the plaintiffs would have had to adduce more proof of discrimination than a disparity caused by external market forces. (As should be obvious, the court was not confronted with evidence of discrimination, such as that found in the *Charley Brothers* case, which would lead it to question the university's wage assignments.)

Thus both the *Spaulding* and *Westinghouse* decisions suggest that to prevail in a pay disparity allegation plaintiffs will have to demonstrate some specific and deliberate acts of discrimination and that the inference of discrimination drawn from the existence of disparities is not a sufficient meeting of that burden.

An Unavoidable Problem

Factors other than the law also ensure that pay disparity will be a key issue for corporate managers in the years ahead. Among them are certain critical workplace realities that affect most companies. First, de facto segregation still exists in most workplace environments. The pressure for equal employment brought to bear during the last 15 years has significantly altered neither sex stereotyping nor women's continuing self-selection of "women's jobs."

Second, women's already large presence in the work force will continue to rise. Women accounted for the majority of the labor force's growth in the last ten years, and the Bureau of Labor Statistics (BLS) projects that they will make up two-thirds of the new entrants between 1985 and 1995. Under the most conservative estimates, women will account for some 47% of the total work force by 1995. Third, women's earnings continue to lag behind those of men, even though they account for an ever-increasing share of the labor market. This earnings gap is cited by advocates of women's equality to demonstrate the continued existence of widespread wage discrimination.

BLS statistics, for example, show that in 1981 women earned 62 cents for every dollar earned by men, compared with 59 cents in 1970. Further, and more troubling, the gap in average starting salaries has widened over the past ten years, according to a study by Gordon W. Green, Jr., a labor economist with the Census Bureau. Whereas white women, on the average, could expect a starting salary that was 86% of a white male's in 1970, by 1980 the figure had dropped to 83%. Given the importance many compensation experts attach to starting salaries as a key determinant of future earnings, this finding may prove critical as the wage disparity issue evolves.

A rise in legal challenges is likewise inevitable as more and more women's advocacy groups come to believe that the current administration takes less interest in resolving EEO issues and that, as a consequence, employers are relaxing affirmative action efforts. Litigation in this area will also be spurred as some unions, seeking to expand their membership bases, assume an advocacy role on women's issues. (This factor is already evident in the *State of Washington* lawsuit and in recent actions by 9 to 5 Women Working, the public education and advocacy arm of the Service Employees International Union.)

Finally, with rising state-level litigation and interest in state government pay practices, pressure will continue to build for local legislation. Already, 15 states include some form of comparable worth standard in their pay statutes: Alaska, Arkansas, Georgia, Hawaii, Idaho, Kentucky, Maine, Maryland, Massachusetts, Nebraska, North Dakota, Oklahoma, South Dakota, Tennessee, and West Virginia. California, Montana, and Oregon have indicated that their fair employment practices laws allow them to inquire into comparable worth issues. And Minnesota has enacted legislation making equity compulsory for state employees' pay.

While much of this activity is haphazard and refers only to state payrolls, the questions and issues being debated are identical to those that confront private sector employers. So business executives must follow both the evolution of federal law and parallel developments at the state level.

What Managers Can Do

Before management initiatives for coping with pay disparity can be developed, the interaction of the three basic components that underlie liability must be understood. These are job segregation, pay disparities, and the presence of discrimination.

JOB SEGREGATION. Management must first ascertain whether any job segregation exists by identifying categories where women are in the large majority. While such job categories signal de facto segregation, they are not, by themselves, conclusive of any liability.

PAY DISPARITY. Once job segregation has been identified, employers must determine whether the women's jobs are lower paid than similar, but not identical, jobs held by men. In making this determination, managers should be careful to choose jobs that can be reasonably compared. A data entry operator's salary grade should be compared with a programmer's (assuming that the latter is a male-dominated job), for example, rather than with a marketing manager's.

Other comparisons should likewise be made on the basis of common, though not identical, elements such as employment in the same department, plant, or other facility. Some observers recommend an even broader approach, such as analyzing all salaries within a certain "band" of pay in the company and then determining whether sex may have played a role in the placement of employees in those bands.

PRESENCE OF DISCRIMINATION. Determining whether discrimination has caused pay disparities is the last and most difficult step in this process. Typically, some combination of history, the evolution of the job or job family, job evaluation (where used), and supply-and-demand considerations explains most salary differences. But none of these factors is immune to discrimination, and in the last analysis management may be able to ascribe only a portion of an existing wage gap to neutral sources that a court or outside agency would accept as nondiscriminatory. The remainder can therefore be presumed to be the result of discrimination and its elimination set as the attainment of comparable worth.

As the interaction of these three components demonstrates, the critical issue is not "comparable worth," as the term is commonly used, but rather the existence of unexplained pay disparity, with comparable worth the objective of any necessary corrective action. Second, and perhaps more important, analyzing and identifying the scope of the problem is more difficult than it may appear.

WHAT THE COURTS HAVE SAID

The problem with eliminating pay disparity is that usually no one element accounts for all the causes of possible discrimination. As a result, the courts have sought to examine an employer's conduct in evaluating pay discrimination charges rather than establish a general standard by which illegal pay disparity can be judged. An employer's efforts to identify and correct perceived pay inequities in its work force, then, are an important factor when the courts determine liability.

For example, in the *State of Washington* ruling the court examined the employer's conduct as well as the existence of pay disparities. As it happened, the state had conducted several internal studies that seemed to show its pay scales for predominantly women's jobs to be undervalued by its own standards. After identifying the disparity attributable to discrimination, however, the state failed to act on its own findings. Faced with this fact, the court could only conclude that the state was engaging in willful discrimination.

In contrast, another federal court, examining similar pay disparities in *Briggs* v. *City of Madison*, found that the Wisconsin city had gone to great lengths to ferret out possible discrimination in its pay systems. Concluding that the market value established from salary surveys for key benchmark jobs was the only factor accounting for the continued existence of the disparities and that this factor was beyond the city's control, the court rejected a finding of illegal discrimination.

The court's reasoning in the *Spaulding* decision reinforces the *City of Madison* ruling. Although the decisions differ slightly, both conclude that the use of external market wage data does not, by itself, constitute discrimination under the law, even if it results in pay disparities. These rulings, along with earlier decisions on the use of market data, suggest that employers are protected from wage-disparity liability so long as the information comes from bona fide salary surveys and has not been manipulated. (This assumes, of course, that the court also finds no evidence of intentional discrimination in other aspects of the employer's conduct.)

Between these extremes lie a series of practical problems for managers grappling with this issue. Chief among them are the legal risks that can flow from a proactive posture. These risks will vary depending on the actions a company's management undertakes. But employers must recognize the fact that any initiative that calls attention to internal inequities can create a liability-producing situation.

The worst example of this is, of course, the *State of Washington* case in which the employer's liability was drawn from its own initiatives. Clearly, it is foolhardy to neglect taking corrective action once potential problems have been found.

Legal problems may persist even where management is committed to remedial action because there is no clear-cut standard for judging pay-rate comparability. Attempts to solve disparity problems through wage adjustments alone may only aggravate the situation by introducing new liability through ill-conceived or improperly executed pay realignments.

HOW ONE COMPANY COPED

To understand how management can approach pay disparity from a broad-based perspective, let us consider what one large company in the chemical industry has done. Aware of pay disparity's growing prominence and the resolution of threshold legal issues in the Supreme Court's *Gunther* ruling, senior management concluded that it would be prudent to examine its internal pay relationships for areas that could lead to potential liability.

These managers believed that if such pay inequities existed, they would hurt employee morale and hamper employee relations and that the company probably had an implicit obligation under its affirmative action plan to address the issue. They were also concerned about the possibility of creating bigger problems down the line, given that the company's internal human resource projections showed a higher proportion of women workers at all levels during the next ten years.

The company ruled out massive wage readjustments from the start.

Its managers doubted that an across-the-board adjustment would solve the problem in the long run, even though it might provide some short-term relief. Wage and salary administrators were concerned that a large wage-scale adjustment would distort the company's competitive position in the wage market and unjustifiably disrupt its wage and salary program.

Thus the company rejected single-factor thinking at the outset. Instead its management marked out three areas for its inquiry: (1) organizational questions, (2) specific compensation-administration issues, and (3) an evaluation of existing EEO principles as they would apply to pay disparity. It appointed a management task force to evaluate each area and tie the findings together into a comprehensive action plan. It also concluded that the study should be initiated in response to a request from the company's legal department to protect the findings.

Task force members received assignments consistent with their area of expertise. Staff responsible for organizational issues, for example, were asked to identify female-dominated job groups and answer a series of questions about them: How long had the jobs been that way? Had their status or organizational placement changed over time? What were the conditions surrounding them?

The compensation staff was asked to conduct quantitative and qualitative evaluations of women's salaries across the entire company and within smaller units where meaningful comparisons between male- and female-dominant job groups could be made. It was asked to review job evaluation standards for bias and for inadvertent omissions that could be relevant to the women's jobs but would not apply to jobs held by men. And it was asked to examine salary policies and procedures, including the role of outside surveys in setting salaries, starting salary practices, and provisions for movement within and between salary grades.

The third segment of the task force studied some of the same factors as the other two, but it approached them from an EEO standpoint. It reviewed the job groups identified by the organization staff to determine whether rates of participation in these clusters had shifted over the years and what EEO-specific steps had been taken, consistent with the company's affirmative action plan, to change the makeup of both female-dominant and male-dominant job groups. The EEO staff also conducted an audit based on Equal Pay Act principles to ascertain whether pay disparities existed between men and women whose jobs involved substantially equivalent skills, effort, and responsibility.

By the time the task force completed its work, it had identified several potential problem areas:

1. Predominantly female job groups existed throughout the company, with particularly heavy concentrations in clerical work, electronic data processing, and some production jobs. In every instance these were the lower paying jobs in the organization, and all had been dominated by women since the passage of Title VII.

2. Modifications to the company's job evaluation plan, installed during the 1960s, had been small scale and few. Most involved adding new job titles and functions to keep up with technological advances. The task force felt that some of the determinants were outdated and that some could arguably be seen as discriminatory.

3. The pay audit revealed a significant number of women whose salaries were lower than the company's statistical salary model predicted. Ironically, promotions created most of these discrepancies because corporate policy on merit increases limited raises to a fixed percentage of the employee's current salary. So the women continued to fall behind in pay as they moved ahead in grade.

4. Efforts to break up female-dominated job clusters, such as seniority and pay-rate protection, special training programs, and one-time incentive payments, had produced few changes. They had, however, changed the composition of some job categories.

5. The company was relying heavily on third-party surveys to set its entry-level salaries, using several simultaneously to ensure the best possible fit with its job structure.

On the basis of the task force findings, management adopted a five-year plan to address these areas. The plan established an immediate review process for all women whose salaries were below grade and set in motion a study of the total cost of amending the company's merit increase policy to eliminate salary lags for rapidly advancing women and minorities.

It also provided for a reexamination of the standards applied to women's jobs, authorized reevaluations where necessary, and instituted an organizationwide review to determine whether some jobs could be combined with allied male-dominated positions to expand their functions and achieve a better male-female balance. At the same time, the plan called for continuing efforts to speed the promotion of women into higher paying, male-dominated jobs through existing affirmative action procedures.

In addition to these carefully documented steps, the company set up a series of ongoing audit procedures to get better, more current data on a broad range of job issues. It decided not to alter its participation in existing salary surveys, choosing instead to broaden the survey population for female-dominated jobs by seeking out male job holders who could fit within the survey's parameters.

This company's approach reflects a positive and comprehensive view of pay disparity. Its initiatives are clearly in step with the law as it is evolving, yet they neither overstate corporate objectives nor over-extend corporate resources. Moreover, while the plan commits the company to meaningful change, it does so in ways that are consistent with its established business practices.

Other executives may opt for different solutions consistent with their organizational needs. Managers bound by collective bargaining, for example, cannot initiate unilateral actions and will have to nego-tiate to get some changes they may want to make.

Nevertheless, there are several basic steps that all employers should consider given the direction of judicial decisions in this area.

Examine each element of the compensation system for controls on possible discrimination. Because pay systems contain many components that influence salary, the number of safeguards built into a compensation program to ensure EEO sensitivity will affect any subsequent findings of discrimination. Examples of safeguards include such items as EEO training on compensation issues for wage and salary administrators, periodic review by management of the salary decisions that affect male and female workers, and strong evidence that senior management oversees compensation programs with an eye toward their effect on corporate EEO policy. Management should also recognize that most compensation systems are neutral as they relate to discrimination and that their effects or application, therefore, are not self-correcting in areas where patterns of disparity may be found.

Review key job evaluation determinations for bias. Because many pay disparity cases can be traced to job evaluations, it is important to examine the factors considered relevant in a job's initial determination and in subsequent reevaluation. The focus of this examination should fall on those job elements in which "male values" were given more worth than "female values." Management should realize, however, that there is no perfect job evaluation plan and that it can probably more effectively audit and manipulate its current plan than try to install a new one.

Audit the impact of pay practices on men's and women's salaries on a regular basis. Most larger companies can accomplish this by developing a corporatewide statistical model of the pay program and running a regression against all incumbents. Management should examine any statistically significant findings to ensure that factors other than sex can account for the disparity. For smaller populations the same result can be obtained by examining the distribution of men and women within set salary bands without the aid of a computer.

Work to eliminate job segregation. Since this is a long-term proposition, employers should carefully document all attempts to move female incumbents to other, better paying, male-dominated jobs. Rejection by female incumbents of attempts by management to move them to male-dominated, better paying jobs is particularly important in this regard.

Take corrective action. Employers who identify potentially discrimination-based pay disparities should begin to take corrective action. This does not mean an immediate adjustment of 100 cents on the dollar for all employees affected, but rather a commitment over the longer term to eliminate unjustifiable disparities. Good-faith efforts to address internal disparity problems and work toward their elimination will not obviate the possibility of a lawsuit. But on the basis of the case law to date, they can reduce an employer's liability if a complaint reaches the courts.

3
Women as a Business Imperative

Felice N. Schwartz

Memo to: Peter Anderson

President, Chairman, and Chief Executive Officer, Topform Corporation
From: Felice N. Schwartz, President, Catalyst
Re: Women as a Business Imperative

A year ago, you asked me to analyze how Topform deals with its women and to advise you about your policies. Since then I have studied your company and talked at length with your top managers in order to arrive at a clear understanding of Topform's treatment of women.

You believe, I know, that you have made strides toward offering women equal opportunity. However, you think your efforts haven't been appreciated. The women who stand to profit most from your help don't seem grateful. You worry about the perplexingly high turnover of women within your managerial ranks, but, at the same time, you express annoyance at the messy details of modern double-gender business life, such as maternity leave and sexual harassment in the workplace. These problems seem distracting at best and, at worst, are obstacles to accomplishing your most important objectives: to make better products and to run a more profitable company.

Even though you value candor, you won't like what you're about to hear. If you are like most CEOs, you will want me to say that everything is all right, that the policies you've implemented have already made yours a family-friendly company. You will receive no such reassurances. In fact, my view is virtually the opposite: you must make a radical change now, not take more incremental, ad hoc steps. I must challenge you, not reassure you.

It is imperative that you help women advance in your company—and not just for their sake but for the sake of Topform as well. Moreover, the atmosphere of your company, which you regard as tolerant and welcoming to all employees, is actually corrosive to women. But if you accept this challenge and make a radical change in your treatment of women, you can effect tremendous improvement in your bottom line.

You and your peers who lead the most powerful companies in the United States are missing a huge opportunity. In fact, because you fundamentally misunderstand how to manage and motivate one-half of your human resources, you tap only a fraction of their capacity. One reason you continue to ignore these problems is that a conspiracy of silence precludes discussing the matter openly. You don't voice your concerns for fear of litigation, and you are joined in this conspiracy of silence by women who don't want to be seen as different from men. You pretend that everything is all right. But you cannot fix a problem that you tacitly avoid talking about.

Your company is not alone. Women encounter unpleasant, even harsh circumstances at *most* companies in our nation, even if CEOs and managers consider themselves enlightened, thoughtful, and compassionate people. Actually, Topform is better than many other companies. But the fact that you are neither alone nor the worst offender should not console you. You still need to change.

The solution is not merely instituting some "feel good" policies. The solution is fundamental change. It is a revolution in thought and action that will have a terrific impact, an impact that can be measured in dollars and cents.

What, for example, might be the economic power of this radical policy change? Imagine for a moment that you were not considering human resources policies but were instead attending a presentation from your R&D shop about a spectacular new product. This product, which has been under development for years, is now nearing completion. If its introduction succeeds—and you believe that it will—your revenues will skyrocket. Wouldn't you react impatiently after that meeting ended, eager to get cracking? *Treating women as a business imperative is the equivalent of a unique R&D product for which there is a huge demand.* It promises to be the most important "new product launch" you and your company could implement. Making a radical change and accepting the women's imperative is the right thing to do; but, more important, it makes good economic sense.

U.S. Companies: From Zero to Five

You asked me to evaluate Topform. As you know, I travel all over the country, visiting and discussing these issues with hundreds of top executives yearly. These site visits and discussions have given me an empirical basis for comparing your company with many others.

From your vice president of human resources, I learned that almost half of all Topform employees are women. In fact, 40% of your exempt employees and 7% of your vice presidents are female. These percentages compare favorably with national averages. But simply counting women employees, vice presidents, or board members is not an effective way to appraise corporate performance. Both of us realize that setting arbitrary numerical objectives can produce spurious accounting, which in turn produces false reassurances, while chronic underlying problems go unaddressed. Attempting to measure complicated personnel questions by using only the blunt instrument of the adding machine is a mistake. As subtle as these issues are, and as difficult as it may be to translate them into cold mathematics, it helps nonetheless to look at them critically. Consequently, I have developed a simple but effective rating system that runs from zero to five to gauge how motivated companies are to accept the women's imperative as a *business* imperative.

At the low end, *Zeros* are companies that are dead to the issue of developing women. They simply don't care. These companies make no effort to recruit, train, or promote women. Executives at Zero companies work with blinders on. They are even blasé about the law. They get sued, repeatedly in some cases, but apparently accept the costs of settling those suits as just another annoying part of doing business— their way.

Next are the companies that simply want to keep ahead of the law. They are *Ones*. They track numbers and fill out Equal Employment Opportunity Commission forms, but they don't take any initiative in leveling the playing field for women or addressing the needs of working parents, which are still, unfortunately, the needs of working women. According to one study, for instance, a third of U.S. companies have done virtually nothing that is not legally mandated to help their employees cope with family problems. By my standards, those companies are Ones.

Twos are companies that want to do what is fair and right. The Twos have formulated two or three specific policies for child care, part-time clerical jobs, or unpaid maternity leave—but those who work at the company still feel it is a man's world. Twos give little thought to women's upward mobility or to removing the obstacles to women's productivity. Deep down, the men who run these companies believe that women should not be part of the real action. They go through the motions of improving women's situations, but they have not come to terms with their deeply rooted preconceptions.

There are only a few employers who can legitimately say, "We are doing well by women," even in a limited sense, on family and work issues or leadership development. Those companies that do I call *Threes*. For example, newspaper giant Gannett, where there is a passion to develop women, is a Three. (In fact, the former publisher of Gannett's successful *USA Today*, Cathleen Black, is a woman.) The Federal National Mortgage Association, which increased the number of women employees from 4% in 1981 to 26% in 1988, is another Three. IBM, which built on Thomas Watson's respect for the individual, and Corning, which has a strategic plan for change, are both Threes.

Fours are mythical companies where one day the playing field will be leveled for everyone. No one is there yet, but some companies such as Xerox are at least trying to get there. Companies at the Four level would be truly responsive to women. These would be companies managed by men and women who have examined their own preconceptions and shaken off those vestiges of old-fashioned, outdated thinking that prevent progress.

Fives are off today's charts. The Five level is a place where the playing field itself starts off flat for both men and women. This exemplary vision includes an ideal, egalitarian environment, where the whole management structure is not a power-oriented hierarchy of ascending status at all but a jungle gym with lateral sidebars and many-leveled challenges, with help and rewards available for employees at every step. Becoming a Five will represent the ultimate achievement, and it will yield the ultimate payoff.

Right now, most companies stand at levels One or Two. Their executives ardently believe that they are "OK on women," that the policies they've adopted are appropriately enlightened. Of course, they don't think they are on the cutting edge—but, then again, they don't want to be ahead of the curve.

They are complacent—and they are in danger.

Your company, like many others, is stuck at Two.

Eight Costs of Where Women Are

Here is another way to view the problem. Imagine that your corporate management group takes the form of a pyramid. (Whether or not Topform's structure should be a pyramid or a different shape is an interesting question by itself but not one we will discuss at the moment.) In 1960, virtually all of the white-collar employees in your company—and in the management ranks of almost all companies in the United States—were men. Today more than a third of your managers—370 out of 1,000—are women. That represents improvement.

This improvement was almost inevitable, of course, given the changing demographics of the country. There simply are not enough capable men available today to fill all of the managerial jobs. Your human resources director can tell you that the nation's labor pool isn't growing fast enough to keep up with management demand. Family size contracted from an average of almost four children per family in the 1950s to fewer than two children per family from the mid-1970s to today. The new generation of college graduates—52% female—from which you recruit your future managers is much smaller than anticipated. This age group is actually only half the expected size based on demographic predictions that assumed the baby boom would continue.

Of course, the current downturn, as well as mergers, restructurings, and job consolidations, has had a crushing impact on the lives of those managers who have lost their jobs. This pain and despair is experienced by both men and women. We should acknowledge and sympathize with those who are suffering. However, this dismal period will end, and we must regain our competitive position in the world economy. To do so, we must mobilize our talent. Women are not part of the problem, they are part of the solution.

There are already women executives today throughout U.S. business. As a matter of fact, about 37% of your managers are women. That's progress, of a sort. But consider where most of these women are: in jobs at the bottom of your team's pyramid.

Picture the company pyramid in your mind's eye again. It is a geometric truth that if you divide any pyramid into four slices of equal height, the top slice will contain 1.5% of its volume, the next slice will contain 11%, the third slice will contain 29.5%, and the bottom layer will contain 58%.

Now note that out of 1,000 managers at Topform, 15 are in the pyramid's top slice, the corporate pinnacle where all of your other ambitious staffers set their sights. In the second slice are 110 of your managers, with 295 on the third level, and 580 on the bottom. The pyramid's bottom slice contains the entry-level management jobs where promising junior people as well as competent but unexceptional older managers are found.

When we analyze where Topform's women are, we find that their distribution is typical of the pattern for Two companies in the United States. Half of your entry-level managers on the lowest level are women. Fewer than one-quarter of the jobs in the next level up are held by women. Of the managers on the second tier, only 10% are women. And only 1 of your 15 highest ranking managers is a woman.

What is wrong with this picture? Over the last decade, you have led an effort to recruit bright, promising men and women to join Topform's management ranks, as most U.S. companies have done. You have searched for talent in the best undergraduate and business schools in the land, schools in which there are more women in attendance every year. You yourself have told me that the women at Topform are as strong in basic leadership traits like intelligence, energy, and analytical ability as the men because your standards are exacting and you expect to hire only the best people. And yet women languish after you hire them.

If women are as smart, capable, and eager to exercise their skills as men are, all of which you say you believe, then why are the highest two levels in your company almost exclusively male domains? Ignore the matter of what is right or wrong. What does that segregation, intended or not, cost you? How are you hurt?

1. *You're not mobilizing your best people at the top.* Any successful business today is only as good as its senior management team. Traditionally, the most prestigious corporations (like yours) and the top professional companies have confined their hiring to the top 10% of potential management employees. In the past, that meant selective recruiting of the highest ranked available men who could be found at elite business schools. However, today women have displaced men in these schools. Women now earn 55% of all undergraduate accounting degrees and 35% of MBAs. So if you attempt to depend solely on male graduates from the top 10% of the best schools in the country, you will drastically reduce the pool from which you draw.

2. *You're not maintaining quality at every level.* Today the marketplace offers little leeway for managerial error. The nation's leadership needs are growing rapidly both in quantity and in quality—and doing so faster than the work force itself is growing. Competition has become

global and more intense. International corporations vie with one another in every sizable industry and in every market that offers promise. Products grow more sophisticated each day. Technology grows
more complex. Managers have to be very, very good.

Now that a significant number of women are in management, you
can concentrate on enhancing the quality of your people at every level
by identifying and promoting the best women instead of benignly
ignoring them after you hire them. In fact, one of the United States's
greatest assets in international competition is its pool of qualified
female managers. Recognition of the contribution that U.S. women
can make to business success, whatever this country's current shortcomings, gives the United States a terrific advantage in competing
against some of its toughest competitors like Japan. In that nation,
women have barely gained token entrée into lower management circles. Japanese salarymen already seem to be working at peak capacity,
which leaves little room for ratcheting up the intensity they already
bring to their jobs.

Thank goodness women are available for consideration as part of
the talent pool in the United States. But unless you actively draw from
the entire universe of people with high potential, *including* women
candidates, you will hurt your company and yourself. If you fail to
draw, train, and advance women candidates, you will neither hone
this national advantage, nor will you compete successfully in the
United States or beyond.

3. *You're treating a big portion of your employees as dead weight.* There is
a psychological lag between Topform's decision to employ women and
your will to use them. You accept women as workers, but in your
mind, they really have not entered the mainstream of business. Not
only are most of the women in your managerial ranks situated at the
bottom of the pyramid but they have also been shunted off to the
sides. In your mind, women are ancillary. Is it possible that you still
think as bosses did 30 years ago? Do you secretly think that men
belong in business, while women create problems? Are you hiring,
training, and advancing women only to ensure mere adequacy? Does
adequate female managerial representation mean doing just enough
to quell women's restlessness, avoid the wrath and litigation of
women employees, satisfy the corporate conscience, and develop a
few high performers for show? Do you pay lip service to equality
between the sexes while unconsciously sabotaging that equality?

If nearly half of your managers are women who are discounted in
this way, then you're dragging a very heavy anchor.

4. *You're putting a lid on the contribution individual women can make.* You stifle people when you make them report to less talented bosses. Many female managers, who occupy the sides and bottom of the organizational chart, are working for men who are less talented than they are. Thus their talent and vision are constrained by the limitations of the underqualified men to whom they report.

A person who works for someone less competent is stunted and thwarted by that relationship. The capable but underappreciated subordinate soon realizes that recognition for effort is not commensurate with output and that the rewards of her work are not sufficient. It is enervating to work for a boss whom one does not respect. The results are predictable: the more talented subordinate throttles down, begins to cut back, produces less, or leaves altogether.

Inequity and injustice of this kind have real fiscal costs. The company suffers from decreased productivity and inefficiency. These problems are compounded when they are systemic; for instance, when it is clear to all of the women managers in an organization that women are victimized by consistently insensitive treatment and by relegation to second-class managerial citizenship. Add to this already punishing environment the effects of inadvertent sexist behavior. To be sure, not all sexist behavior is overt, such as a pinch at the watercooler, an off-color joke that is intended to throw the woman who hears it off-guard, or much worse, pernicious sexual harassment. Some of it is tacit, unspoken, and attitudinal. Most of it is unconscious. Regardless, for many women, working means encountering a series of hurdles and tests. The problem is exacerbated at the upper levels of the company hierarchy, where negative experiences become more intense because women are fewer and more isolated.

With each step backward, women are further debilitated, and attrition among your highest potential women increases. This may, in fact, explain the relative overrepresentation of talented women entrepreneurs. Some of the best women set out to work for themselves in a supportive environment of their own creation where talent can be recognized and rewarded.

5. *You're undervaluing promising people who wish to take a role in family caregiving.* Very simply, if you see commitment to your company as the inverse of employees' commitment to their families, you're creating a false and damaging dichotomy for judging employee potential. Worse, this division of commitments perpetuates the prejudice that it is not possible to combine career and family. As a consequence, business loses good people who would bring the same high standards to their

work that they bring to their families—if given the choice *not* to make a choice between work and home.

It is almost second nature to think of child and elder care as "women's work," domestic issues, matters that have nothing to do with the rough-and-tumble business world. Revenues, margins, rates of return, market share—these are supposed to be the primary concerns of business. Making things and selling things are business concerns. But rearing children is a women's issue. Because women haven't been assimilated fully into business, child care isn't considered a business issue, nor is flexibility thought to be an important company priority.

No one can deny that since women have entered the nation's work force in vast numbers, there is no longer a solid family-support structure at home. Only 16% of full-time workers go home to a nonworking spouse, according to the Bureau of Labor Statistics. In two-career couples, neither parent can expect that the other will automatically tend to the needs of their children. Since high-quality, affordable day care is rare, many working parents are permanently anxious about their children. And as the population ages, these working parents are often responsible for their own elderly parents too.

But the clock will not go backward. If all of the United States's working women were to return home to cook and clean tomorrow, businesses would disintegrate. U.S. business depends on women. Companies may not use them as well as they should, but they depend on women employees no less.

The result? When companies don't offer child care and flexibility in scheduling work as matters of course, these companies suffer along with their deprived workers. And those individuals who drop out may be some of the most responsible employees, those in the company who could bring the same uncompromising standards to their performance in the workplace that they do to the rearing of their children.

6. *You're wasting recruiting and training money.* On average, college-educated women postpone the birth of their first child until they are 31 years old. If a woman joins your company after her college graduation, Topform makes a decade-long commitment to her training and development. If she leaves you when her child is born—because your culture retards her career growth, or because parental-leave provisions and family support are inadequate—you fail to amortize that ten-year investment. It is worse for you, of course, if she leaves Topform to work for a competitor and puts her experience to work against you.

Ironically, wherever she goes, the unhappy cycle continues because chances are good you'll replace her with another woman who may not work out at all and will in any case need training and development for years before she (or a male counterpart, for that matter) can perform on par with the original woman you lost. Then, when the replacement has a baby—which is also probable—the whole cycle begins again.

7. *You're failing to create beacons for the best women entering the workplace.* You know that women constitute an increasing proportion of a shrinking work force, and you believe that Topform needs all the help it can get. But do you view hiring women as a last resort? If so, that is shortsighted.

Companies that do not take pains to develop and retain able women will continue to feel the absence of women at higher levels in the future, when all talent will be scarcer. The smartest women graduating from the best schools will scout out their employment prospects, searching for the right beacons. They will conclude, reasonably enough, that companies that advance few women to the upper tiers are less attractive than those that have already demonstrated they value women. Companies that fail to develop women for leadership positions now will be forced to settle later for women who are not as qualified. Nonetheless, half of your management pyramid will be women in the future. If you attract only those woman who are second tier, you will lose a competitive advantage.

8. *You could be capitalizing on a tremendous opportunity.* Women can lead your company to new profitability.

When you expand the pool from which you draw your top management, you will see greater talent at every level of the enterprise. In an information economy, an economy of ideas, an economy of knowledge, nothing is more important than the thinking skills of your people and their capacity to make smart, timely decisions. Better decisions lead to enhanced productivity, improved pricing and packaging, and more ingenious innovations. You need to attract—and win— the commitment of managers with those skills. The best way to win their commitment to Topform is to demonstrate your commitment to them. You can earn the loyalty of the women in your organization at a time when loyalty is a vanishing U.S. corporate virtue. By providing flexibility, you will retain good women through the childbearing years just as they become most useful to the company. And a solid cadre of women at the senior levels will serve as role models and mentors to junior women as they rise.

This new approach will appeal to your stockholders, more than half of whom are women, both for economic reasons and reasons of principle. Your public image will improve, which is not an insignificant issue. Today companies compete through their values as well as their products. Customers want to know what a company stands for. When a company can demonstrate that it has moved aggressively in the way in which it recruits, trains, promotes, rewards, and values women, it will not only attract the brightest women, it will speak directly to the millions of women and men who care deeply about this issue. A company's reputation for good human values is as valuable an asset as capital equipment. When your customers, clients, and employees realize that you value women as a central resource rather than inadvertently perpetuating a system that defeats them, a new, positive cycle will be born to replace the old, unhappy, expensive one.

Women are not going to go home again. The clock ticks forward, not back. So you can either force women and men who wish to participate in family life to make some very unpleasant choices, or you and your company can change. You can insist that women play by men's rules, and as a result, they will fail. Similarly, you can insist that men follow in their father's footsteps and focus their energies on careers, limiting severely their participation in their children's lives. You can require women and men to give up the dream of having children. Or you can urge those who have children to turn them over to full-time surrogate care. And some of your employees will leave Topform to work elsewhere or to start businesses of their own that give them more flexibility and career satisfaction.

Or you can do everything possible to support families while clearing away the barriers to women's—and men's—progress.

Four Actions for Change

The biggest obstacle to corporate change is the reluctance of leaders to see the need for it. When you accept the notion that women should be full participants in the management of your company, when you are ready to consider changing, you'll find that implementing a solution is neither difficult nor expensive. *The restraints that now hold women back can be loosened easily, and these problems will be swiftly remedied.*

There are four actions you should take to ensure that the women you employ will function as effectively as the men. The first is to acknowledge the fundamental difference between women and men, the biological fact of maternity. The second is to provide flexibility for women and men who want it. Third is to provide women who already have basic leadership traits with the special additional management skills and tools that are vital to excellent performance. The last action you can take is to improve the corporate environment by removing barriers that exist for women but not for men.

ACKNOWLEDGE MATERNITY.   End the conspiracy of silence in which leaders as well as workers pretend that they think the biological differences between the sexes do not exist. Of all women, 85% have babies. Giving birth is a uniquely female experience. These are facts. But they are facts that companies don't handle well.

We should distinguish pregnancy, childbirth, and disability from parenting. Maternity, when defined as childbearing, is predictable and finite. It is good practical policy to acknowledge this natural process and to help women as they move through it. You can manage maternity so that it takes a small fraction of current costs in productivity and attrition.

There's no denying the physical and emotional impact of pregnancy. Yet most women find pregnancy an experience of heightened energy and happy anticipation. Within the last few decades, the average woman has changed her pattern from one of leaving work at the end of the first trimester to working right up until the month, if not the week or day, of delivery. What discourages pregnant women are the attitudes of other people in the workplace. The supervisor and colleagues of the mother-to-be tend to discount her and see her condition as something negative rather than the plus it is. At best today, a pregnant woman's condition is ignored. At worst, she is forced to hide her pregnancy as long as possible and to avoid natural coping responses such as walking around at intervals during long meetings, elevating her feet when seated, or wearing comfortable clothes.

You should formulate clear, comprehensive disability and maternity-leave policies—as differentiated from a parental-leave policy—that will enable you to retain your best women. Do not require an unequivocal statement of intentions from the mother-to-be before the baby is born. Wise, self-interested companies will allow women to return to work when they are ready, when child-care arrangements are in place, and permit those women to have flexible schedules that will help them be productive. It is my belief that most women will opt to return early on part-time schedules. Thus paid maternity leave is not an issue—and a modest fraction of the expense of that forgone paid leave could be used to subsidize the part-time return of low-income women.

Finally, work coverage when the woman is on leave must be jointly planned by both the employee and her manager. Encourage frank talk. When you help women employees with maternity rather than punish them, you'll inspire their confidence and be rewarded with candor that permits you to plan accordingly. The fact that women have babies doesn't alter their commitment to a job or the quality of their work—except when maternity goes unacknowledged, unplanned for, and unmanaged.

PROVIDE FLEXIBILITY.   Begin by accepting that parenthood is linked to business and that intact families include two parents. Note that there is no evidence that men are less nurturing than women. Just a few years ago, talk of "co-parenting" would have taxed the patience of male senior managers, so advocates of shared parental responsibility had to tackle maternity first. Now we can talk openly.

A small percentage of men and women are singularly career-focused, while a small number are entirely family-focused. But the vast majority of men and women want to combine family and career, and they want to switch their main focus of attention from time to time throughout their lives. Here is the main point: these men and women require flexibility in order to be productive at work and to be active, responsible parents.

Now that women are in the work force, children have a business impact. Today you must accept parenthood as a part of doing business. You can reduce its cost by consciously disregarding the traditional roles of men and women. The result will be that you, the employer, will get the best, most committed workers and that children will get the best, most committed parents. Moreover, the net return to the employer when husbands and wives share parenting will be greater. When women are forced to be primary caregivers, their productivity and their careers become stunted because they cannot come to work early or stay late. However, when parenting is shared, either parent can be home with the children and both parents are free to make a serious, sustained commitment to their employers, their careers, and their children.

Permit parents to cut back to half-time (at prorated pay) and then reenter the competition for senior management jobs, partnerships, or tenure if they choose. Let new fathers take paternity leaves in sequence with their wives. Encourage and legitimize the growing desire of men to take an active role in parenting. Since some women choose to spend five or six years with young children, don't shoot yourself in the foot by denying them reentry and the chance to move up when they return. It is crusty tradition that makes us think that the thirties are the prime career years. When these women return refreshed, guilt-free, and ready to go at full throttle, they can produce for 25 or 30 more strong years.

Let parents (and other executives) work at home. New technology—personal computers, fax machines, modems, and so on—makes working at home practical. Take advantage of the freedom this technology affords. And, finally, learn how to measure real *productivity* instead of counting hours spent in the office.

PROVIDE TRAINING.   Helping women maximize their potential helps not only them but also your company. You recruit only the best managerial candidates, good men and women, from a pool that is both diminishing in total number and increasingly female (51% of all master's degrees, for instance, now go to women). But don't stop at simply avoiding discrimination in hiring. Recognize that women face a tougher challenge than men do after they join your male-oriented company.

Women are newcomers to the male world of business. Their socialization does not prepare them for this new world. Some men view them as temporary, uninvited guests whom they treat insensitively and accept grudgingly, if at all. Often women are penalized for lacking aggressive instincts, but, contradictorily, they are scorned for being too aggressive. So you must help your promising women with training and education that includes behavioral advice. Permit them to display the qualities that are traditionally inculcated in men: competitiveness, aggressiveness, risk-taking, and long-term, dependable commitment to a career.

Fortunately for women, the work world has become increasingly information-oriented, which means that supposedly innate feminine skills in communication and sensitivity are at a premium. But if you need managers to act authoritatively, give women permission to be as tough and aggressive as you need them to be; you'll find they respond accordingly. Watch women managers grow after they become comfortable in the workplace.

IMPROVE THE ENVIRONMENT.   Removing the barriers that obstruct women entails first accepting the premise that women belong in the work force—and then eliminating the corrosive atmosphere that pervades most companies. The glass ceiling is not a physical barrier erected by nefarious CEOs. Rather, it is an attitudinal hurdle consisting of largely unconscious stereotypes and preconceptions. So make men aware of negative behavior. Sensitize your male managers to the new demographic realities and the practical reasons for proper conduct between the sexes at work. Eradicate sexual harassment.

Next, coach women as you do men, and accept in women the behavior that usually characterizes successful men. Assign them to line jobs that will tax and teach them. At the same time, don't feel betrayed when women plateau or drop out; instead, ask yourself whether conditions in your company forced them out. And don't worry about raising women's expectations too much by announcing your intention to change. If you don't raise expectations, women will despair that the status quo will never change.

My hope is that Topform and all U.S. companies will work to integrate the lives of their employees, permitting work and family to fit smoothly together instead of conflicting with one another. When work supplies energy to the home, and home revitalizes life on the job, each half joins to make a vibrant whole. If, on the other hand, the status quo does not change, bitterness and frustration will grow.

Can we achieve this ideal? We have come so far since the revolution began 30 years ago, when women began pouring into the work force. Further movement, accelerated movement, is not only logical but also eminently practical.

But it is not inevitable. If the status quo goes unchallenged, many more women will leave corporations and professions to become entrepreneurs. Men who remain at these corporations will be forced to work harder. They will suffer from fatigue, frustration, diminished productivity, and further estrangement from their families. The women who continue working and remain primarily responsible for home management and child care won't be able to compete for leadership positions.

Most likely, if unchallenged, the pace of change will be just fast enough to perpetuate the conspiracy of silence. In that case, we'll remain where we are now, where it is not working. Everybody knows it, but nobody is talking about it.

I believe the process of change must begin with CEOs who now cling to an image of the past that tells them women should be home rearing children. They think women's careers burn out prematurely because work is not really as important to them as it is to men. They believe there always will be enough high-performing males to replenish their ranks.

But CEOs will change because business is quintessentially realistic. Senior executives will see the many changes in the workplace that have already succeeded and the many changes that are still necessary. And they will cast aside their stereotypes and preconceptions.

The logjam impeding women's forward movement will be broken by a top-level acknowledgment that the status quo is unacceptable. As this movement accelerates, we should see more women and men break with traditional sex roles. We should see more self-determinate women. Men will grow more comfortable inside the home, and this too will have positive ramifications. Couples may be able to build partnerships that preclude feelings of exploitation and anger. Families will grow stronger.

But the best news I can offer is this prediction: your company will gain tremendous financial benefits when you accept your responsibility to women and working parents.

PART
IV

AIDS in the Workplace: The Organizational and Individual Experiences

1

Uncommon Decency: Pacific Bell Responds to AIDS

David L. Kirp

Sitting nervously in the public health clinic that Friday before Labor Day in 1986, awaiting word on his AIDS test, Pacific Bell repairman Dave Goodenough already half knew what he would be told: he had AIDS. He'd suspected as much for seven months, ever since he first noticed the markings on his chest. His doctor dismissed them as bruises picked up at work, but when the purplish markings started showing up all over his body, Goodenough sought another opinion. It had taken the second doctor only moments to identify the symptoms as "KS"—Kaposi's sarcoma, a type of cancer frequently associated with AIDS—and the test results confirmed that diagnosis.

Suspicions of AIDS are one thing, certainty something very different. "I was wiped out," Goodenough recalls. As he began to sort out the implications of the news, one question kept recurring: Would he—could he—go back to work?

Goodenough had been with Pacific for a decade, and working meant a lot to him. He liked what he did and liked the crew he worked with; he appreciated the fact that he didn't have to hide his homosexuality. Back in Ohio, Goodenough had been sacked from a probation officer's job when word leaked out he was gay. But San Francisco was different. And even though the phone company had a reputation as a bastion of mid-America, operating with a rule book as thick as a phone directory, by the late 1970s Pacific had just begun learning how to cope with the reality that a sizable number of its employees were gay.

To Goodenough, confirmation of AIDS only reinforced how important it was to him to stay on the job. "If I left the job," he recalls thinking, "it would be like putting a limit on the amount of time I have to live." His friend Tim O'Hara, a long-time Communication Workers of America steward and a spokesman for gay concerns in the union, encouraged Goodenough not to quit—and to tell company officials that he had AIDS.

Initially, Goodenough resisted this last bit of advice. "I won't let anybody know," he insisted. But a few days later he changed his mind. "I can't hold something like this inside," he decided. "It'd be like being in the closet all over again."

On Goodenough's behalf, O'Hara went to Chuck Woodman, supervisor of the 750 people in Operations who keep the phone system in San Francisco up and running. Woodman's response was, "We'll do everything we need to do to keep Dave working," and he called Goodenough's immediate superior to enlist his support. Later that week, Goodenough phoned Woodman to thank him. "You could hear in his tone of voice how much Chuck cared," Goodenough remembers. "What he said kept me going. He told me, 'You've always got a job here.'"

Chuck Woodman hadn't always been so concerned about people with AIDS. To his subordinates Woodman had a reputation as a tough guy, a self-described redneck whose heroes included John Wayne and George Patton. A devout Mormon, father of 8, and grandfather of 20, Woodman's attitude about AIDS began to change in 1985 when he was transferred to San Francisco. He remembers how he was affected by a funeral for a worker who had died of AIDS.

"As I listened to that minister talking about how angry it made him that people with AIDS were shunned, I began to feel some of that anger," Woodman says. "The whole moral question of homosexuality got put aside."

To learn more, Woodman turned to Tim O'Hara, whom he knew and liked. With O'Hara's assistance, Woodman got a thorough education on AIDS. Information brought understanding, and understanding gradually eased the fear. After that first funeral, Woodman started asking questions. "What can we do for the people with AIDS on the job?" he wondered.

"They need to keep working," O'Hara answered. "It gives them a reason to stay alive."

Woodman began talking with supervisors and visiting workers with AIDS when they were too sick to work. Out of those talks with Woodman and Michael Eriksen, the company's director of preventative medicine and health education, came Pacific's first steps toward dealing with AIDS in the workplace: an AIDS Education Task Force, with company nurses and volunteering union members trained by the San Francisco AIDS Foundation giving presentations in offices and company garages all around the city. Woodman's bosses in the Pacific hierarchy were pleased with his AIDS initiatives. But peers who knew him from his earlier days were stunned. "I got maybe half a dozen calls from guys around the state. 'What are you doing, Woodman,' they'd say, 'do you love those gay guys?' I told them, 'Until you've walked in these tracks, you can't understand. You start buying in when it's someone you know.' And here's something. Each of those guys called me back later to say, 'I've got someone with AIDS. Now what do I do?'"

Chuck Woodman talks about AIDS as a managerial challenge, the toughest in his nearly 40 years at Pacific. "When I look at where I was and where I am now, AIDS has had a bigger impact on my thinking about people than anything I've come up against."

This comment about the impact of AIDS is no hyperbole; that isn't Woodman's style. And Woodman's remark applies not just to himself, not even just to Pacific, but to business generally. Just as AIDS has already changed American society, it will reshape American corporations.

That is not the conventional wisdom. To most managers, AIDS is a medical and social epidemic of still-unknown dimensions—the federal Centers for Disease Control conservatively estimate that 1.5 million Americans now carry the AIDS virus and that by 1991 every county in the United States will have at least one AIDS case. Much less common is a managerial awareness that American business must reckon with AIDS. Managers in general regard AIDS as a problem not for workers but for homosexuals and drug users and their promiscuous sexual partners, as a disease that attacks people outside the office and factory walls.

Such denial, however understandable, doesn't fit the facts. Among 273 companies responding to a 1987 American Society for Personnel Administration survey, one-third acknowledged having workers with AIDS. This was more than triple the percentage reported two years earlier and a figure that will steadily grow, if only because of AIDS's long incubation period (it can take seven years or more for symptoms to develop). Furthermore, those numbers represent only the most direct impact of AIDS, and this is not necessarily its most important dimension to the corporation.

AIDS molds behavior in many ways. In the worst, usually hushed-up incidents, employees afraid of AIDS-carrying coworkers have walked off the job. More common are dances of avoidance—workers refusing to share tools or even sit in the cafeteria with a stricken coworker. And then there is a very different reaction—grief at the loss of a friend and colleague. In a society where, for many, the workplace isn't merely the source of a paycheck but also a source of community, where fellow workers are also friends, there is simply no way for business to wall out AIDS.

How does a company respond to something as alien as AIDS? The best answer, as Pacific learned, is to recognize AIDS as a legitimate part of the corporate environment and to tailor a response that is of a piece with all that the company stands for and is doing. Pacific's reaction to AIDS was affected by the fact that the utility is headquartered in San Francisco—with its large gay community—and that telecommunications is a highly regulated industry. Nevertheless, the remarkable turnaround of this unlikely innovator tells an instructive tale for every major U.S. corporation.

Three years after AIDS was first identified, in 1984, Pacific's preventative medicine and health education director, Michael Eriksen, began hearing stories about Pacific employees worried about getting AIDS on the job. There was the coin collector who refused to touch the phone booths in the predominantly gay Castro district of San Francisco. One Los Angeles crew balked at installing phones in the offices of the L.A. AIDS Foundation, and another San Francisco crew insisted on being issued head-to-toe covering before installing phones in General Hospital's AIDS ward. And there was the lineman who refused to use the truck of a fellow employee, rumored to have died of AIDS, until it was sterilized.

As the number of crisis phone calls mounted, Eriksen resolved to determine the dimensions of Pacific's AIDS problem, to conscript other activists in shaping a plan—and to act. Later, one colleague recalled, "Eriksen became our AIDS guru." Bearded, mid-thirties, casual, fresh out of a Johns Hopkins Ph.D. program, Eriksen had been hired several years earlier to move the company toward a "wellness" approach. Already he had developed an in-house program to help employees quit smoking and to enable women to spot the first signs of breast cancer. Eriksen brought an activist's impatience to Pacific. In a company where going by the book is the instinctive response of lifetime employees, he equated going through corporate channels with death by memo.

Eriksen's work on AIDS began with the facts. He reviewed the company's 1984 death certificates and turned up 20 employees who had died of the disease. This meant that, after cancer, AIDS was the most frequent cause of death among active Pacific employees. Pacific officials, who hadn't considered AIDS a workplace issue, were startled; but the data made sense, since the nearly 70,000 employees and 250,000 people in Pacific's larger "family" were concentrated in San Francisco and Los Angeles, two cities with a high incidence of AIDS cases.

Moreover, Eriksen knew that the figure of 20 was decidedly conservative since it excluded workers who had gone on the permanent disability rolls before dying and cases where the doctor had not specified AIDS on the death certificate as the cause of death. In the general population, the number of AIDS cases was doubling every year; this meant Pacific was seeing just the beginning of the epidemic. Add those deaths among the company's work force to the stories of Pacific workers' fears about encountering AIDS while serving customers, and something had to be done. But what, and by whom?

If AIDS had been a garden-variety disease, tracing the path of corporate response would be easy. Policy would have been designed by the company's human resources division, with the medical director, Ralph Alexander, having the final say. But because AIDS was new and frightening, it demanded the kind of cross-the-boundaries effort that is hard for a company to marshal on any issue, let alone on a subject so loaded with bias, contention, and misinformation.

The corporate medical group needed to sift prevailing medical wisdom—but that was just the start. The human resources division, drawing on corporate-safety and labor-relations experts, had to determine how AIDS would be treated in the workplace—whether prospective employees would be screened for the virus, whether workers with AIDS could continue on the job—and what benefits to offer people with AIDS. Potentially every manager in the company needed help in handling workplace fears, and not just in San Francisco and in Los Angeles. Phone operators in California's decidedly unswinging Central Valley had no personal fears about contracting AIDS, but expressed real concern for their children. And because the AIDS issue was so hot, whatever the company did was potentially news—that made the corporate communications division a player as well.

Urged on by Michael Eriksen, the lawyers and medics and corporate-safety staffers determined that workers with AIDS would be treated like anyone with a life-threatening illness. The culture of the phone company, with its strong emphasis on two-way commitment and loyalty, kept Pacific from seriously considering the option of revoking the medical coverage of employees with AIDS—a policy that some companies followed. Jim Henderson, the company's executive director of human resources policy and services, says bluntly, "People with AIDS are sick. We don't fire sick people."

This policy was not only humane but also affordable, a vital consideration for any business. Reviewing the company's 20 AIDS-related deaths, Michael Eriksen estimated that the lifetime cost of medical treatment for an AIDS patient ran about $30,000, about the same as costs for treating other life-threatening illnesses such as cancer. To Pacific, whose escalating health costs were subject to review by California's Public Utilities Commission, that news was reassuring.

In practice, AIDS forced the company to make much-needed reforms that went beyond this one disease. For example, Pacific was already searching for ways to reduce reliance on hospitalization. The company sought less expensive alternatives, and its sick workers considered less impersonal ones. Both preferred new options, like at-home or hospice care, which offered more personal settings and attention at reduced costs. These quickly became part of corporate health coverage. Pacific's capacity for individual case management also needed strengthening so it could better determine—on a case-by-case basis—which regimen of care made best sense. Moreover, since many drugs used to treat AIDS patients were most readily available by mail, the company extended its health plan to cover mail-order drugs.

None of these innovations applied to AIDS alone. Indeed, business organizations like the Washington Business Group on Health have preached for years that case management is the best way for a company to tame the costs of catastrophic diseases. But AIDS treatment demonstrated the efficacy of the approach. One Southeastern public utility, relying heavily on hospitalization for AIDS patients, reported that its first eight AIDS cases cost the company $1 million—almost four times Pacific's per-patient cost. At Pacific, AIDS was a catalyst for reshaping many employee health benefits. The resulting package offered better treatment at markedly lower costs.

Pacific was drawing from its own traditions in defining benefits for employees with AIDS. But in dealing with workers' fears about being exposed to AIDS through casual contact, Pacific had to determine entirely new responses.

The accounts that Eriksen and Jean Taylor, director of employee counseling, had collected—installers shunning customers, workers avoiding AIDS-stricken associates—hinted at a dangerous level of anxiety in the field. And those employees' misgivings mirrored feelings in the society. In 1984, when AIDS fears had first begun to surface at Pacific, far less was known about the disease than today, and uncertainty left ample room for fearfulness and misinformation.

Managers had to wrestle with difficult questions. How would Pacific allay its employees' worries and thereby ensure that an AIDS incident didn't escalate into a fiasco? How could it protect the confidentiality of disclosures about AIDS while attending to the concerns of employees with the disease? What changes were needed in Pacific's detailed rule book to help managers deal with the special needs of employees with AIDS?

The way Pacific handled the 1985 case of the phone installer who refused an assignment in San Francisco's Castro district suggests the delicacy of the issue and the need for new and nonpunitive approaches—educational approaches—to win over frightened workers. When the balking phone installer was suspended, he went to Shop Steward Tim O'Hara. But instead of lodging a grievance, O'Hara struck a deal. The worker would return to the job and a joint union-management AIDS education program would begin immediately at the site. The idea was feasible because Pacific and its union had developed an unusually cooperative and nonadversarial relationship during the last contract talks.

O'Hara's evenhanded approach respected the workers' fears and met the needs of the company's customers. Meanwhile, the shop steward put together a list of 30 volunteering workers, whose lifestyles ran the gamut from the most traditional heterosexual middle American to the openly gay. If other workers were ever unwilling to make an installation where there was an AIDS victim, this squad was ready to handle the job. Here again, preparation and education worked: no supervisor has ever had to turn to O'Hara's list.

But despite early agreement on nondiscrimination as the broad company policy, corporate AIDS education at Pacific did not advance beyond crisis intervention. Yes, several hundred employees did show up in April 1985 at the company's headquarters downtown for a question-and-answer session with Michael Eriksen and a San Francisco AIDS Foundation representative. But that was a one-time occasion. For all the other employees—the San Francisco work crews who wouldn't dream of coming all the way downtown; the 7,200 backroom personnel working in "San Remote," a Pentagon-like fortress 35 miles outside the city in suburban San Ramon; the employees in Los

Angeles and throughout California and Nevada—there was essentially no AIDS education.

Within Pacific's medical department, there was disagreement about the adequacy of the company's approach thus far. The dispute reflected deep differences in perspective between the classic medical approach and the newer views of wellness specialists.

For longtime medical director Ralph Alexander—a consistently conservative official who believed that, as an M.D., he should have the last say—what Pacific was doing sufficed. In discussions with other divisions, Alexander regularly stressed the need to keep a sense of proportion when responding to AIDS, which he viewed as a relatively minor health concern for the company. "There's danger of offending a hell of a lot of people," said Alexander. It was better, he argued, for the company to devote more attention to heart disease and cancer, far bigger killers and diseases that wouldn't "raise eyebrows."

Wellness specialist Michael Eriksen saw matters differently. AIDS, he believed, deserved special attention because it was new and unnerving. He began to hook up with other like-minded colleagues, most of them mid-level managers involved in communications both inside and outside the company. These middle-level policy entrepreneurs believed that acting decisively on AIDS was the right thing to do; moreover, such a stance would benefit the company. It was these middle managers who took the lead in shaping Pacific's response to AIDS, exercising leadership from below.

One opening salvo was an article on AIDS that slipped into Pacific's newspaper, *Update*, moving the issue higher on the corporate agenda. In early 1985, Eriksen had suggested to *Update* Editor Diane Olberg that she run an AIDS story; coincidentally, the organizers of the company's blood drive made the same request. They were troubled by reports of workers refusing to donate blood for fear that they could get AIDS—reports that showed the workers' generally low level of knowledge about the disease. Higher-ups would balk at the idea of an article on AIDS, Olberg knew, insisting that this was really just a San Francisco issue. But sensing the importance of the topic, Olberg went ahead on her own.

That first article focused entirely on the facts about AIDS in the workplace, avoiding the sensitive matter of company policy. It appeared on July 22, 1985—the same day Rock Hudson went public with the fact that he had AIDS—and demand for that issue of *Update* was unprecedented. The newspaper had to run reprints. To corporate tea-leaf readers, the coverage said that AIDS was something Pacific cared about; the strong employee response showed that AIDS was something employees cared about, and that paved the way for other AIDS-related stories. This reaction and the increasing demand for AIDS education sessions in the field sent another message up the corporate ladder: informing those who were healthy but worried might be as important to Pacific as ministering to those with the disease.

On March 20, 1986, the conference room at Levi Strauss's downtown San Francisco headquarters was packed. Over 230 managers from 100 companies were there for the first-ever conference on "AIDS in the Workplace." The demand so exceeded the organizers' expectations that 100 would-be participants had to be turned away. Reporters from leading daily newspapers were in the audience and TV crews from as far away as France recorded the event.

It came as no surprise to California executives that Levi Strauss had a big part in organizing this conference. The company had a long history of social activism, and CEO Bob Haas had personally acquired a reputation for dealing forthrightly with AIDS. Back in 1982, when several Levi employees told him that they were nervous about distributing AIDS information leaflets on company property, Haas had responded by stationing himself in the headquarters lobby, handing out leaflets to passersby.

But sharing the spotlight with Levi Strauss was Pacific—and this *was* surprising, for here was a company that usually made itself invisible on provocative topics. The corporation's name was prominent among the conference sponsors because the Pacific Telesis Foundation (established by Pacific's parent) had underwritten—and in conjunction with the San Francisco AIDS Foundation, Pacific's corporate TV group had produced—the first AIDS video aimed at U.S. business.

First screened at a breakfast session attended by 20 CEOs and then shown at the conference, "An Epidemic of Fear" pulled no punches: in telling detail it presented the panic, the medical evidence, the emotional tugs. Present on camera was Todd Shuttlesworth, who had been fired from his job by Broward County, Florida when he was diagnosed with AIDS. Shuttlesworth's case served to remind managers how expensive a wrongheaded AIDS policy could be to a business; after his dismissal Shuttlesworth had taken his employer to court and secured a six-figure settlement.

Outsiders weren't the only ones surprised at Pacific's prominent visibility. Some high-ranking Pacific officials were amazed and decidedly uncomfortable about this unusual corporate position. It was appropriate for the company to treat its AIDS-stricken workers decently, they agreed. But to link AIDS with the corporation in the public mind was entirely different: that would associate Pacific with gays, drugs, and contagion, potentially driving away prospective employees, conceivably scaring creditors and customers who depended on the company's stability. There was every reason for the company to avoid sticking its neck out, said the advocates of a low corporate profile.

But Pacific did stick its neck out with AIDS-related decisions—decisions that in part reflected the company's determination to change its corporate culture to fit its new competitive realities. Gradually but steadily, Pacific went beyond the nondiscrimination policies that suited the old character of the company to real leadership that helped define the company Pacific was becoming.

Pacific Telesis Group is a holding company for Pacific Bell, the regional phone company that accounts for over 90% of the entire business's revenue and PacTel Corporation, which manages the company's diversified businesses. When it was launched after the 1984 AT&T breakup, many viewed Pacific as the weakest of the Baby Bells. "Of all the Bell regional holding companies, Pacific Telephone holds the most risk for investors," declared the *New York Times*. "The company's record of poor earnings and its long-running feud with the California Public Utilities Commission make it a risky investment at best."

Like other AT&T offspring, Pacific had to learn how to respond to the discipline of the marketplace. And in California, the company found itself in the nation's most hotly contested, fiercely competitive telecommunications markets. Other Bell companies, including NYNEX and Southwestern Bell, as well as a host of new entrants, were all clamoring for a piece of the action, advertising heavily to an urbanized population with a reputation for buying whatever is new.

To respond to these changed conditions, Pacific had to meet three challenges: to be financially successful where smart investors were betting against Pacific's likely financial performance; to create an innovative and forward-looking organization, where tradition dictated that long-standing employees had to mold themselves until they gradually developed "Bell-shaped heads"; and to adopt corporate positions responsive to new constituencies that were socially conscious, where the company had always been seen as socially and politically backward. Together these challenges called on Pacific to redefine itself. It was under these conditions that AIDS became a measure of the company's transformation—and a vehicle for it. And it did so at a time when the company's efforts at change consistently misfired, reminding managers just how difficult large-scale change really is.

In its enthusiasm to demonstrate its newfound competitive hustle, for example, Pacific launched aggressive marketing campaigns. But what came to light were dubious sales tactics, like selling unneeded phone services to non-English-speaking customers who didn't understand what they were buying. Morale suffered among employees who didn't expect the phone company to behave like a used car dealership.

Pacific's effort at organizational transformation also ran into problems. To become more innovative, top management realized, the company would need to shake up its rigidly hierarchical structure, a steep pyramid with 14 precisely delineated levels. The problem was, how to change?

Looking for direction, Pacific contracted with an outside consultant for $40 million worth of leadership-development and personal-growth training. The system was called Kroning, after Charles Krone, the consultant who developed the training material. It backfired. Instead of opening up communication, it sharpened divisions between the "in" group, who claimed to fathom Kroning, and everyone else in the company. Instead of easing relations with the Public Utilities Commission, the controversial corporate expenditure triggered a "cease and desist" recommendation from the Commission's advocacy arm. Instead of improving Pacific's public image, the fiasco yielded a harvest of journalistic ridicule.

A big part of becoming competitive was learning about the state's shifting political environment—and that meant becoming more socially conscious. Historically, Pacific's idea of responsiveness was to join all the Rotary Clubs in California. While that approach might have worked in the 1950s, in the 1980s California's shifting coalitions of interest groups—blacks, Hispanics, consumer-oriented organizations—increasingly wielded political power. Pacific had long treated these groups as if they were the enemy. Now, however, these same groups were major purchasers of telecommunications services, and they had the ear of the most aggressive state Public Utilities Commission in the country. For the phone company to prosper on its own, it somehow had to co-opt these groups—to reach a mutually workable level of understanding and accommodation.

Steve Coulter, Pacific's director of consumer affairs, had the job of handling these troubling concerns. Coulter was a former Nevada legislator in his mid-thirties, a man who had made a political career out of enlisting constituencies to his cause. His collegial style and political savvy enabled him to get away with being a corporate guerrilla warrior. "A 'no' from above isn't necessarily the end of things," Coulter explains. "I'd ask 'Where's the block?' Then I'd go look for allies."

Working under Jim Moberg, then the vice president for corporate communications, Coulter had been devising company approaches to such new issues as minority procurement and multilingual services. Coulter was also involved in negotiations over minority hiring and procurement with the NAACP and HACER, a consortium of some of California's major Hispanic groups organized by Pacific. To Coulter, a visible Pacific presence on AIDS was appropriate: it was politically astute, operationally important, and morally right. In collaboration with Michael Eriksen and other allies, Coulter became a leading advocate for an AIDS policy inside Pacific.

The politics were particularly interesting. Pacific had long been in open warfare with San Francisco's affluent and influential gay community, and the company badly needed to mend its fences. In the early 1970s, Jim Henderson, now executive director of human resources policy and services, had helped draft the company's policy on homosexuals. Back then, Henderson recalls, "Some managers were afraid that gay activists would show up to work wearing dresses." In 1973, those fears prompted Pacific to adopt a policy against employing "manifest homosexuals." In practice, this rule meant that anyone who publicly acknowledged his or her homosexuality couldn't get a job with the phone company.

Although Pacific formally revoked its "manifest homosexuals" policy in 1976, it wasn't until 1986 that the then-defunct policy's earlier existence came to light. By then, Pacific had tangled with the City of San Francisco, refusing to subscribe to a city ordinance barring discrimination against homosexuals. In 1979, the company lost an employee-discrimination lawsuit in the California Supreme Court, which ruled that the state's human rights law prohibited public utilities from refusing to hire gays. Shortly before a trial for damages was scheduled to begin, Pacific lawyers produced a previously undisclosed 1973 job application that confirmed the company's former antihomosexual policy. In December 1986, the company negotiated a $3 million settlement, the biggest ever in a gay discrimination case.

All this recent history—the disclosures of shoddy business practices, the troubles with Kroning, the acknowledged need to reach out to outsiders, the mishandling of the gay community—was artfully deployed by those within Pacific who pushed to make AIDS a visible corporate concern.

Eriksen provided the substantive information on AIDS, Coulter spoke mostly of politics and positioning. What Pacific needed, he argued to his bosses, was a winner, an issue on which the company could do well by doing good. AIDS could be the issue. Confronted with considerable internal opposition, it took all of Coulter's political experience and lots of help from other insiders to carry the day.

In March 1985, at a meeting of San Francisco's Business Leadership Task Force, Levi Strauss CEO Bob Haas raised the AIDS issue for the CEOs to discuss. The group's agenda already covered items like the role of the elderly worker and health-care cost containment. It was time, Haas said, to put AIDS on the list. Everyone else in the room, top officers from Wells Fargo, Chevron, Bank of America, and McKesson—and Pacific—said nothing, as if they could make something very embarrassing go away by being quiet.

Yet despite the CEOs' initial unease, AIDS did not disappear from the agenda. Haas continued to push the matter. So did Leslie Luttgens, organizer of the Leadership Task Force, who served on the boards of several important local foundations and blue-chip corporations, including Pacific. A one-time president of the United Way, Luttgens combined a strong commitment to social causes with a persuasive but diplomatic style. She had learned about AIDS as an overseer of the University of California-San Francisco Medical School; now she was convinced that trouble in the workplace was inevitable if businesses continued to deny the scary reality of the disease. After Haas made his proposal to the CEO group, Luttgens spent the next few months talking up the need to promote AIDS education, imparting a sense of urgency that kept the issue alive.

Making the rounds about this time was a request from the San Francisco AIDS Foundation asking for corporate financial support for an AIDS education video. Pacific Telesis Foundation officials expressed considerable interest in funding the video; the in-house filmmakers added their enthusiasm for actually producing it. But at the top of corporate communications, Jim Moberg was unpersuaded. For advice, Moberg turned to Pacific's medical director, Ralph Alexander—and what he heard was conservative medical and corporate policy. According to Alexander, Pacific's role on industrial health issues was as a "national weather vane—and that's why we need to be doubly cautious about having a public profile."

Steve Coulter, like Mike Eriksen, equated caution with timidity. An AIDS video was clearly needed by businesses. Moreover, as Coulter argued in a memo to Alexander, getting the phone company publicly involved in AIDS education might just bolster its position in the pending gay discrimination lawsuit. Such a stance might provide some sorely needed good publicity. It was responsive to the AIDS-related concerns of other stakeholder groups including the NAACP, which, as Coulter pointed out, identified AIDS as a top national health priority. It could also improve relations with California's Congressman Henry Waxman, a powerhouse in telecommunications policy who was historically no friend of Pacific's and the congressmember most knowledgeable about AIDS.

As a savvy corporate politician, Coulter knew that he could not realistically expect Moberg to reverse his decision against the video project. The idea had to be repackaged, and that meant reviving the notion of Leadership Task Force involvement. Perhaps if the AIDS video proposal appeared in a different guise from a different sponsor, the answer would be different. Working with Michael Eriksen and the AIDS Foundation, Coulter sharpened the video proposal, waiting for another chance to bring up the matter with Moberg.

The occasion came on the eve of a December 1985 meeting of the Leadership Task Force. Coulter had been designated to sit in for Moberg as Pacific's representative at the session. On the table was a plan put forth by Leslie Luttgens for an "AIDS in the Workplace" conference. Hoping that he could now deliver Pacific's support for the AIDS video, Coulter phoned Moberg in New York, where Pacific had just signed a statement of mutual cooperation with the NAACP. Coulter's pitch to his boss noted the internal support for the AIDS video— from Luttgens, corporate TV, and the Foundation—as well as the endorsement of enterprises like Bank of America, Chevron, and Levi Strauss. "I need to be able to say, 'We have $25,000 on the table,'" Coulter argued.

Jim Moberg, euphoric after his successful NAACP negotiation, gave his cautious go-ahead—"as long as we don't seek publicity and don't stand alone." Leslie Luttgens's quiet advocacy had reassured him that AIDS activism was not a far-out idea; after all, here was a Pacific board member offering encouragement and a degree of protection if things misfired.

Then Moberg took up the matter with his fellow VPs, who had questions of their own. "Anytime you do something different from what's normal in the business community," Moberg says, "questions will be raised: 'Why only us?'" Some of these officers wondered aloud whether AIDS wasn't just a passing phenomenon, but Moberg set them straight. "In the end, they accepted the proposal on faith . . . it was enough that someone they trusted advocated it." Now AIDS had become something "owned" by corporate Pacific—not just by some of its more enterprising staffers.

With that corporate approval, Coulter's group went to work. In less than three months, they prepared the video and an inch-thick managers' workbook on AIDS and organized and publicized the conference.

The reaction to the March 1986 gathering was more enthusiastic than even Steve Coulter could have hoped for. Pacific, a company that lately had seen little but media brickbats, was now getting raves; a company known for its habit of avoiding social issues had gone out front, to considerable applause. The thank-you letters and the press clips circulated inside the company. At the next meeting of the Pacific board, Leslie Luttgens made a point of noting that the AIDS video that Pacific had produced was being aired nationally on PBS, as well as in France and Japan.

There was one internal casualty of the struggle to promote AIDS education: Michael Eriksen was abruptly fired by Ralph Alexander immediately after the AIDS conference. "I no longer have any need for you," the medical director had told Eriksen. There had been continuing disagreements between the two men. For his part, Alexander says, "Some programs he was supposed to run didn't work out."

The loss of Eriksen was deeply troubling to his colleagues, who had relied on his expertise. But his loss at this point was sustainable. There was product and momentum. With the video in hand and the AIDS Education Task Force functioning, the internal education efforts began to pick up. Success led to success. Responding to a request from the union that Pacific require AIDS education, Operations Vice President Lee Cox sent a letter to all supervisors, not insisting but recommending that they show the video as part of an AIDS education session.

Producing the video pushed Pacific into the public arena on AIDS. What came next was even further removed from corporate tradition and even more dangerous: taking a public position on a statewide AIDS ballot proposition.

An organization led by political extremist Lyndon LaRouche, whose motto, "Spread panic, not AIDS," became the rallying cry for a cause, had garnered enough signatures to force a statewide vote on a measure—Proposition 64—that, if passed by the electorate in the November 1986 election, would turn panic into law. The implications of the badly drafted measure were that thousands of workers who had AIDS could be fired, hundreds of students who carried the virus could be removed from school and college; moreover, people with AIDS could be quarantined. It appealed to people's emotions and played on their fears— yet had the simple allure of seeming to offer voters their chance to do something to protect themselves from the dread AIDS virus.

Most of California's chief public figures—politicians, church leaders, educators—opposed the measure. Steve Coulter wanted Pacific to add its voice to the opposition. Yet the huge number of signatures—it took nearly half a million to qualify the measure for the ballot—testified to the proposition's popular appeal. And some of the state's leading political conservatives voiced their strong support for the measure.

Like most companies, Pacific seldom took a stand on any ballot measure that did not directly affect its business. This political principle gave the company an easy and clear dividing line and protected it from needlessly making enemies over extraneous issues. Instead, Pacific preferred to exert its political influence through quieter relationships between lobbyists and lawmakers in the state capital. On the ballot measure, Pacific's lobbyists in Sacramento adamantly urged the company to remain mute.

For months, the debate over Propositon 64 continued inside Pacific. The conservatives from government relations and human resources insisted that opposing the measure would only earn Pacific powerful political enemies. The corporate communications activists countered that silence would put Pacific in league with those who proposed quarantining AIDS carriers and would also offend key external stakeholders, who might then "find additional avenues to criticize the company."

The stalemate was finally broken at the officers' level. Art Latno and Gary McBee, the two top external-affairs officials, determined that the company would publicly urge the defeat of Proposition 64. McBee, who had come to know the human cost of AIDS when a member of his staff died from the disease, became a strong voice for taking on LaRouche. "Given our internal position on AIDS," he says, "it would have been unconscionable for us not to oppose Prop. 64." The officers authorized a $5,000 corporate contribution to the campaign, the biggest single donation from any California business.

The stance was different—a decided shift from business as usual. Yet it reflected a fact of life about the shifting relationship between business and politics. In California—and increasingly across the country—voters are deciding more and more significant policy questions, rather than leaving matters to the elected officials. If a company wants to have a say on those matters, it must go public.

In the November 1986 election, California's voters resoundingly rejected Proposition 64. Although some Sacramento lawmakers grumbled at Pacific's lobbyists, the feared retaliation never occurred; and when LaRouche put the same measure on the ballot in June 1988, Pacific officials opposed it without thinking twice.

But the real test of how far Pacific had come on the issue took place in November 1988, when Proposition 102 hit the ballot. This was no kooky extremists' handiwork but a proposal authored by GOP Congressman William Dannemeyer that would essentially abolish anonymous AIDS testing. While leading public health figures opposed the measure, fearing that its reporting requirements would drive those at risk for AIDS underground, the proposition did not threaten quarantining. It had modest support among doctors—and, more important, an endorsement from the popular Republican governor, George Deukmejian. Pacific risked political wrath—facing down a barrage of appeals from Dannemeyer—by opposing the measure. McBee again championed that position. The proposition was defeated.

Now there were other constituencies enlisting Pacific in their efforts to combat AIDS. Prompted by Lynn Jimenez in corporate communications, Pacific spent nearly $100,000 in 1987 to promote a Spanish-language AIDS *videonovela*. This venture too had its risks, for the story line dealt candidly with homosexuality and drug use, two topics anathema to the conservative Hispanic community. But HACER, the coalition of Hispanic groups, urged the company to go ahead—despite the opposition of religious and political leaders in the community. The videonovela was yet another success story, with local TV stations reporting larger than usual audiences. Pacific Telesis Foundation proceeded with its plans to underwrite a dubbed-into-English version.

In 1988, Pacific and the Foundation received a presidential citation for their AIDS initiative. And there was more recognition: the *Wall Street Journal*, *Newsweek*, and *Business Week* lauded the company as enlightened; Sam Puckett and Alan Emery's book, *Managing AIDS in the Workplace*, called it a "role model for the rest of the nation" (along with other companies, including Dayton-Hudson, Bank of America, Digital Equipment Corporation, and Westinghouse). AIDS policy had become a winner inside Pacific. And more begat more, with new corporate enthusiasts for AIDS education emerging. "People love favorable recognition," points out Terry Mulready, Moberg's successor as corporate communications vice president. The company produced a video aimed at families, "Talking to Your Family About AIDS," and planned a video for the black community. The making of AIDS policy had taken on a life of its own.

On a sunny Wednesday afternoon in July 1988, 11 Pacific employees with the AIDS virus gather in the medical department's conference room for their weekly support group session. Three-piece suits sit amicably alongside flannel shirts. Janice Dragotta, a counselor who spends about a quarter of her company time on AIDS, encourages group members to check in.

As the talk moves around the table, members share information on drug treatments, describe their medical condition, offer advice, complain about a benefits nurse "who went to Auschwitz U," dish up tales of life in the gay bars, commiserate with those who tell how exhausted the preceding Sunday's group-sponsored picnic left them. There is an edgy humor, gallows humor, in the talk. One man, off to visit his parents in Ohio, imagines the local headlines if he were to die—Gay Comes Home To Die—and his mother's reaction: "How can you do this to us—again?" The employees also talk about the strength they draw from the group, about how it helps to have a place to discuss questions that arise on the job, conflicts with colleagues, and guilt about not being able to work as hard as they once could.

Until recently, no one at Pacific would have imagined such a group on company premises and on company time. "When I first proposed it in 1985, there were no takers," says Dragotta. Employees with AIDS were afraid to come forward. "At the time I started doing AIDS education," counselor Jean Taylor recalls, "an embarrassed official buttonholed me and said, 'Do anything you want, Jean, just don't talk about condoms.'" Now everything related to AIDS is open to discussion. Union Steward Tim O'Hara, relying on a poll detailing workers' interests, is pushing the idea of a corporate-produced video on the correct use of condoms. The concern that some employees might be offended by frank talk about sex is receding.

In organizing discussions of safe sexual practices or running AIDS support groups, Pacific, like any company, has to walk a fine line. AIDS is still encased in moral debate, but discussions of private morality have no place in the business setting. What is relevant are sound business practices and sensible personal precautions. The AIDS support group is both a humane gesture and an appropriate business move. Taylor says, "We started seeing people with the AIDS virus, and those who were well but worried, going out on disability. These groups are a way to help people stay productive, a way for people to begin processing their own grief."

New evidence of Pacific's support for AIDS education is clear not only in these groups but also throughout the organization. At the second annual AIDS Walk, a citywide fund-raising event in July 1988, over 400 Pacific employees sporting company T-shirts walked together under the company's banner. Elsewhere in the company, AIDS-related causes have become almost as familiar and noncontroversial as the United Way. At Pacific Telesis Foundation, the staff has made AIDS causes a top priority for charitable giving.

Still, there remain important and unresolved AIDS issues on Pacific's agenda. AIDS education is not a part of an overall corporatewide strategy. Whether employees ever see the AIDS video or get to talk through their concerns about AIDS depends entirely on whether a supervisor volunteers to organize such a session. This bottom-up approach means that, where such education is least needed—in San Francisco and Los Angeles, two cities where public knowledge about the disease is high—it is most likely to be provided. But elsewhere in California, in the fortress at San Ramon and the outposts beyond, where a majority of phone company workers are employed, many managers still treat AIDS as someone else's problem.

Those supervisors who phoned their colleague Chuck Woodman, asking how to handle an AIDS case on their work force, may still regard it as just a once-in-a-career concern; and their workers are still unwilling to talk openly about AIDS. "Whenever I get an AIDS call from Fresno," says counselor Jean Taylor at San Francisco headquarters, "it's always like Deep Throat, and it's always, 'Someone I know was wondering. . . .'"

For Pacific, an AIDS education effort pitched to the varying concerns of its employees is not only enlightened practice. It is sound business. Pacific may be among the companies with the most AIDS cases in the country. As those numbers continue to mount—and they will—the work force problem will become more critical. Already, Chuck Woodman has some 25 workers with AIDS, requiring regular shuffling of his 750-person roster. According to company sources, a 1987 estimate prepared by medical director Ralph Alexander—but never made public—indicated that as few as 200 and as many as 2,000 employees might be infected with the AIDS virus.

There is little that the company can do for these employees with

AIDS that it isn't already doing—treating them just as it would treat anyone with a life-threatening illness—but it can do more to slow the spread of the disease. If Pacific can strengthen and expand the scope of its in-house AIDS education, intelligently implementing a program that will reach a quarter-of-a-million lives, then this unlikely corporate pioneer will continue to enlighten others coming to terms with AIDS.

Across the country, the corporate time clock of AIDS policy has run quickly if unevenly, with wide variations in responses reported. According to the 1987 American Society for Personnel Administration survey, some companies persist in punishing workers with AIDS, firing them or limiting their health benefits. A majority of companies offer no AIDS education and have no contingency plans for handling employees refusing to work with an AIDS victim. Barely one business in ten has a written AIDS policy. As discouraging as these data are, they probably exaggerate the degree of corporate responsiveness, since companies that deny the corporate reality of AIDS are unlikely to answer such a survey.

On the other side of the ledger, since the landmark 1986 Bay Area "AIDS in the Workplace" conference, there have been dozens of similar conferences across the country. In February 1988, 30 prominent corporations—among them, IBM, Warner-Lambert, Time Inc., Chemical Bank, Johnson & Johnson—endorsed an AIDS "bill of rights," ensuring that employees with AIDS would receive evenhanded treatment.

For the CEOs in Knoxville or Kansas City still wondering whether their companies should deal with AIDS, the answer should be plain: there is little choice. Nor can handling AIDS be just the province of corporate doctors or human resources specialists. Everyone has a stake in this boundary-crossing issue—that's one of the things that makes AIDS both so hard to manage and so important.

There is considerable help available to businesses. The groundbreaking experience at Pacific is instructive, AIDS educational materials are now widely marketed, and groups like the Red Cross and local AIDS organizations can assist. But to confront AIDS intelligently means having a new look at a wide range of business practices. It means rethinking a company's approach to medical benefits. Those issues Pacific found readily manageable several years ago have become tougher now because recent scientific advances have reshaped the equation. Medication like the antiviral drug AZT is now prolonging the productive lives of workers, but at a cost—one insurance company estimates that AIDS-related illnesses will make up between 2% and 5% of all group-health claims by 1991.

Devising an AIDS policy also means reexamining the company's approach to wellness education, its concern for prevention, and its willingness to talk about once-forbidden subjects like sex. It means rethinking relations between employer and employee, rethinking relations among units within the company, rethinking the boundaries between the company and the public domain.

The outcome of that reanalysis will likely reach far beyond AIDS education to produce a telling portrait of the corporation. For American business, as for Americans generally, AIDS is something like a mirror that, unwillingly and unexpectedly, we have come upon. The meaning of Chuck Woodman's, and Pacific's, odyssey is this: in our reactions to AIDS, something of significance about ourselves and about the character of our enterprises is revealed.

2
Nothing Prepared Me to Manage Aids

Gary E. Banas

The trouble with almost everything I read about AIDS or AIDS in the workplace is that it's too cut and dried. Popular advice to managers is strikingly unhelpful because it always seems to involve choices that are neat and easy. Confidentiality, equity, and accommodation are among the prescribed managerial practices, but these words describe a world very distant from the world of real people doing real work in real organizations.

I know, because in the course of less than four years, two of my subordinates developed AIDS. One after the other, I saw two men and the people they supervised suffer through AIDS and its inevitable consequences: debility, denial, impaired performance, and death for the men themselves, deteriorating productivity and morale for their subordinates. Nothing I thought I'd learned from pamphlets and seminars prepared me for either ordeal. For that matter, the first ordeal did not prepare me for the second.

My whole reason for writing this article, including the parts that don't reflect particularly well on myself, is to make this one point: Don't let anyone kid you, when you confront AIDS in the workplace, you will face untenable choices that seem to pit your obligation to humanity against your obligation to your organization. Contrary to popular opinion, you will almost certainly fall short in both areas.

Most of my early education in the proper managerial approach to AIDS occurred while I was personnel officer for the southwestern district of the Comptroller of the Currency. I attended and even organized AIDS awareness seminars, and I stayed conscientiously abreast of

AIDS literature. By the mid-1980s, I reckoned myself one of the nation's leading personnel directors in the effort to recognize and respond to AIDS as an emerging workplace issue. In early 1987, I moved to our New York office as director for administration, and it was here that I came face to face with the disease for the first time.

In spring of that year, one of my mid-level supervisors, a capable manager whom I'll call Frank—and whose job I won't identify too closely—began showing signs of serious illness. He was losing a great deal of weight. He was also beginning to miss work, and his absences grew longer and more frequent. At first, he'd call in the morning to say he was sick, or he'd leave early in the afternoon for a doctor's appointment or because he felt ill. Within a few weeks, he was out sick for days at a time. In addition, he became short-tempered with his staff and began avoiding me altogether. More important, the quality and timeliness of his work rapidly declined. His required reports were often late or incomplete, and he was often unavailable or unprepared for essential meetings.

Before he became ill, Frank was candid about his homosexuality. He would jokingly volunteer to others, for example, that he belonged to a high-risk group for AIDS. Yet now he was very guarded about his medical condition. Since I had known him only a few months before his illness came on, I could understand his reluctance to confide in me. But all of us could see that he was sick.

After more than a month—and several attempts to get him to tell me what was wrong—Frank went to the hospital for the first time. When I visited him, he told me he was suffering from a rare form of tuberculosis. He also said he was responding to medication and assured me he would soon recover his full health.

Two weeks later, he did come back to work but told me his diagnosis had changed. He was now taking medication for intestinal parasites. After asking for a pledge of strict confidence, Frank also told me he had been tested for the AIDS virus and was HIV-positive.

I can't say I was surprised. Because of the attention AIDS has received in the media, Americans probably know more about it than they know about the common cold. Where I would have a tough time discussing colds without some reference to chicken soup, I can speak knowledgeably about opportunistic infections, Kaposi's sarcoma, the side effects of AZT, and the immune system in general.

What Frank didn't realize when he asked for and got my pledge of secrecy was that the rumor mill had already conducted an amazingly accurate medical evaluation of his symptoms. There were a number of reasons for the widespread interest in his illness. First, he was highly visible in the organization. Second, everyone knew he was gay. Add the fact that he was the first suspected AIDS case in the office—at a time when the disease was getting extraordinary media coverage—and it's easy to see how idle speculation translated quickly into common knowledge.

Frank's case points up the difficulty any manager faces in maintaining employee confidentiality and in balancing human and organizational needs. I cannot begin to count the phone calls and visits I received from Frank's colleagues and subordinates seeking confirmation of their suspicions. Early on, I could respond to their often subtle questioning with a forthright, "I don't know." Once Frank told me he was HIV-positive, I resorted to dodging their questions.

As necessary as I thought they were, my evasions fooled no one. What they did do was weaken organizational credibility, increase everyone's discomfort and insecurity—except perhaps Frank's—and damage morale, more even than I realized at the time. Openness and honesty are vital; employee confidentiality is critical. In this typical AIDS-related trade-off, both suffered.

Telling Frank's staff was not the only problem. There was also the question of telling my supervisor. As Frank's absences from the office lengthened, productivity in his unit deteriorated. I took on much of the essential work myself, including Frank's budget planning, but I didn't have the time to supervise his unit's daily routine operations. As a new director, I was concerned about how top management viewed my own performance, so I very much wanted to discuss Frank's illness with my executive-level superior.

Without going into detail, I asked Frank for permission to tell my supervisor, and he gave it. Greatly relieved, I went to my boss and felt a tremendous burden lift from my shoulders. For the first time, I was able to talk openly about my own feelings and the work-related questions that Frank's illness raised. My supervisor was also concerned about declining unit performance, and he promised his support for whatever approach I thought best. I came away from the meeting reassured that he was aware of my difficulties and felt I was doing an effective job.

In late August, after another long hospitalization, Frank called on a Friday to tell me he would be back at work the following Monday. I'd seen him in the hospital only a few days before and was astonished to hear he felt well enough to come back to the office. Of course, I hoped his condition would take another turn for the better—many AIDS patients have periods of relative improvement in their long downhill struggle—but now I began to suspect that Frank didn't realize how sick he really was. He told me he would begin with a half-day schedule and that within a few weeks he hoped to return to work full-time. I told his staff to expect him on Monday.

Before Friday was over, his subordinates asked to see me, and I met with them late that afternoon. Several said how pleased they were to hear his condition had improved, but all confessed that they were worried about his return. One of them, apparently a designated spokesperson, said they all believed Frank had AIDS. They didn't ask me to confirm this, but they did want my assurance that they couldn't catch it in the office. One of them asked if it was safe to use the bathroom after Frank. Another even wondered about the water fountain. After all of the formal and informal AIDS education I knew they'd had, both in and out of the office, these two questions surprised me. I reminded them that AIDS could not be transmitted through casual contact, even assuming they were right about Frank's illness.

At the end of the meeting, I thanked them for their extra efforts during Frank's absence and said I hoped things would soon return to normal. I doubt I eased any of their fears, but I think just getting their anxieties into the open helped. To their credit, every one of them appeared for work on Monday.

As it turned out, Frank had to leave after only two hours on the job, and that was the last time he ever came to the office. He spent most of the next three months either alone in his apartment or in the hospital.

Frank still admitted only to being HIV-positive, but his two hours in the office convinced me he had an advanced case of AIDS and would never again be fully able to do his job. The visit also forced me into a decision I had been avoiding: whether to keep Frank on despite his illness or to take the steps necessary to replace him.

Since I'm lucky enough to work for an organization that puts a premium on employee health and well-being, this was not a question of termination. The Comptroller of the Currency has long had an official policy covering employees with life-threatening illnesses, and we fully support accommodations such as working at home, flexible hours, leave-sharing, and moving people to less stressful jobs. We also do our best to keep employees in paid positions for as long as they wish to work.

Although Frank's extended absences and loss of productivity gave us ample grounds for enforced retirement or some other removal action, I knew his sense of self-worth was almost completely tied up in his career. He had little contact with his family and, as far as I could tell, few close friends. His job was the most important thing in his life, and I had no desire to strip a dying man of what mattered to him most. I was convinced that any effort to take away his job would undermine his optimism and further shorten his life.

For the short term, I gave one of his subordinates a temporary promotion in order to have someone directing traffic. In addition, everyone rolled up their sleeves and pitched in to get the work done. But these were make-shift arrangements. In September, I finally decided to ask Frank to consider reassignment to a nonsupervisory position. Because of his seniority, he would have to make a formal request for a reduction in rank, and if he balked, I'd have to initiate a lengthy and potentially hostile removal process. I broached the subject on one of my hospital visits. I told him it wouldn't mean a cut in pay. I said I hoped it would relieve him of any concern he might have about his inability to manage his unit.

To my surprise, Frank immediately agreed to request the reassignment. It was sad to watch him relinquish his whole career without a murmur of protest, but I was enormously relieved.

From that day until his death in November, I visited Frank as often as I could. I helped him fill out his health-insurance claim forms, and I passed along the latest office gossip. He was failing rapidly, and he had the hospital put my name on the emergency contact list. At Frank's request, I called his younger brother, explained that Frank was near death, and asked him to come to New York to be with him.

Frank died two days after his brother's arrival. A group of us from the office made arrangements for a memorial service, and I wrote and delivered a eulogy. Except for Frank's brother, the only people who attended were from the agency.

I was saddened by Frank's death, but, at the same time, my superiors and colleagues praised my sensitive response to a difficult management crisis, and I have to admit that their approval pleased me. I felt I had set a standard for other managers to follow. No inner voice warned me that my approach to Frank's case might be of little value when I confronted AIDS a second time.

Immediately after Frank stepped aside in September, I began recruiting for his replacement. Jim, who had worked for me in Dallas, was one of my principal candidates. I had known him about four years, considered him a friend as well as a capable colleague, and was delighted when he agreed to transfer to New York. He arrived in January 1988.

Because he was familiar with our organizational priorities and my own management style—and because he was just plain good at his job—Jim quickly restored former production levels, improved morale, and generally made my life a lot easier. I was now able to focus on areas I had neglected over the previous six months and, being still relatively new as director for administration in a large and diverse operation, to go on discovering what I was director of. The next 18 months were comparatively easy ones for Jim and for me.

Then one morning in the spring of 1989, Jim walked into my office for a quarterly status reports meeting, sat down stiffly in his chair, and told me quite calmly that he had just learned he was HIV-positive.

I had a hard time taking it in, and when I did, I was more than surprised. I was devastated. Deep inside, I'm sorry to say, a selfish voice was saying, "Why me?" and "Not again!" Aloud I said, "I'm terribly sorry to hear that, Jim. Please let me know if there's anything I can do to help."

My response was superficial and inadequate, but it was the best I could do at that moment. Having been through this once before, my compassion was mingled with dread. I didn't want to watch Jim suffer, and I didn't want to grapple again with the problems that his suffering might cause for his staff and for me. Although he still looked the picture of health, I began mentally calculating the time remaining before he would have to leave his job.

Jim explained that he was beginning AZT treatments and that his doctor was optimistic about his ability to live a long life. Having seen Frank's health deteriorate rapidly over the course of five months, I had my doubts. I resolved to deal with the situation quickly and effectively.

I told Jim there were others in the organization who needed to know and that I would discuss his condition with my supervisor. He agreed to this limited release of information but was adamant that I tell no one else. He insisted he was not like Frank in any way and said he didn't want people in the office talking about him the way they had talked about Frank.

Despite my long professional association with Jim, I knew very little about his personal life. While we saw each other socially from time to time, it was usually at parties or office functions. Though I considered him a friend, to this day I have no idea how he became infected with the AIDS virus. His sense of privacy was exceptionally strong.

Several months passed without any noticeable decline in Jim's condition. I started hoping that he might enjoy many years of good health before his virus developed into AIDS. By late June, however, he was beginning to show the familiar signs of weight loss. When I asked him about it, he said he felt great. He said his doctor was adjusting his medication to improve his appetite.

I took him at his word. I now think Jim was in denial, but even I was cautiously optimistic. He seemed able to carry a full work load and was only occasionally absent from the office for doctor's appointments. Because I was focusing so intently on his physical health, I was slow to notice the decline in his performance and slow to remember Frank's initial denial of any performance problem.

By now, Jim's unit had begun to miss occasional deadlines, and I was hearing periodic complaints about unit response time. Given Jim's history of superior performance, I wrote these off to the increasing work load. Yet the complaints persisted, and new problems cropped up—simple errors uncorrected, critical organizational objectives ignored, major projects never completed and never assigned to subordinates. My supervisor started pressuring me about several projects that were stalled.

I mentioned these concerns to Jim without suggesting any link between his illness and unit performance. I believed at the time, and I still believe, that Jim had developed an active case of AIDS by June of 1989, but not because he told me so. In fact, Jim never acknowledged that his HIV had developed into full-blown AIDS. Absent that acknowledgment, I raised his performance problems the same way I would have raised them with any other manager. I had received complaints, I said, and I expected him to analyze and correct them.

Nevertheless, I was sufficiently worried about Jim's state of mind that I met with several members of his staff a few days later to get their views on whether or not Jim was losing his ability to function as a manager. One employee, whom I'll call Liz, was so candid that she forced me to recognize the truth: AIDS was affecting not only Jim's performance but also the performance of every one of his subordinates.

Liz was the senior staffperson in Jim's unit and had been extremely loyal to Jim personally. She and others had covered for him as best they could for several months, but now she'd had enough. Liz was also getting complaints—from the unit's internal customers as well as from our Washington headquarters for a number of late and inaccurate reports. But the final straw had come from Jim himself. According to Liz, Jim had recently told her that I was dissatisfied with unit performance and that he blamed her and the rest of the staff. He'd gone on to say that he would take corrective action unless there was immediate improvement.

Liz was in tears as she told this story. She and others had worked extra hours and run interference for Jim, and he'd laid the blame for the entire problem at their door. When I asked her why she hadn't told me earlier, Liz said she'd felt sorry for Jim, hadn't wanted to make more trouble for him, and, in any case, found it awkward to go over his head. She also told me that she and others had come to the conclusion that Jim had AIDS.

I tried to assure Liz that I didn't blame her or anyone else in the unit for declining performance, but I'm afraid the damage had already been done. Several days later, I found Liz ill in one of the office corridors—she was hyperventilating—and sent her home for the day. Several months later, she told me she had a job offer from another organization, and I encouraged her to accept it for the sake of her own health.

Because AIDS takes the lives of its primary victims, we naturally lose sight of the fact that it injures others as well. Unlike Frank and Jim, Liz didn't come close to dying, but she paid a price for their illness in stress and overwork. Others did too. During the four-year period from the onset of Frank's illness to the end of Jim's, we saw a 200% turnover in unit personnel. Today only one person remains who worked for both men.

One of the most difficult dilemmas a manager faces in this situation is how to weigh the obvious, painful needs of the dying person against the less dramatic but clearly compelling needs of the organization. I have no ready answers. I only know that managers will be plunged into moral and professional choices at the most mundane, specific level, that there will be little precedent for many of these choices, and that almost all will cause injury to someone. Fatal disease permits no win-win solutions, only lose-lose ones. A manager's task is to minimize the losses—to people and to organizations.

After talking to Liz, I was more troubled than ever about Jim's competence, his apparent paranoia, unit morale—and my own performance as his supervisor. Once again, confidentiality had lost its meaning as a protector of privacy and become a source of uncertainty and fear. Once again, subordinates were paying the price for Jim's denial. I had allowed the situation to go on too long. I decided it was time to replace him.

As in Frank's case, I never had to consider outright termination. I hoped Jim would accept reassignment to a less critical position the way Frank had. Alternatively, Jim had enough years of service to qualify for disability retirement. All things considered, I was naively confident that Jim would step aside graciously—if not for himself, then for the good of the organization. I was about to see a new face of denial.

I began my meeting with Jim by discussing his declining performance and suggesting a link with his health. But before I had a chance to offer him a different job, Jim vehemently rejected my appraisal of his work. If there were unit deficiencies, he said, they depended on the substandard performance of his staff and a work load too large for his unit to handle. As for the alleged complaints about his performance, people were simply blaming their own inadequacies on him. And since there was nothing wrong with his performance, AIDS was clearly not a contributing factor. He accused me of treating him unfairly because I was bitter about having to deal with two HIV-infected employees in a row.

I was stung. My spontaneous, angry reaction was to tell him he should consider himself lucky to be working for someone with experience in dealing with this situation. Then, cooling off quickly, I responded more professionally. I was determined to say what had to be said, even if it sounded cold and clinical.

In any case, Jim was not receptive to a change of title and position. I made the offer, and he turned it down. He reminded me that I would have to take formal action to remove him from his post. I said I was aware of the organizational requirements. I said I was prepared to take that course unless his performance immediately improved. It was now June; I gave him until September to demonstrate such improvement.

Several days after this stormy encounter, Jim put in a request for a month's vacation. I was surprised and angry all over again. If Jim was determined to resist my efforts to help him, I thought he should be spending more hours at work, not going on vacation. Fortunately, I was not so angry that I lost all perspective. I knew this might be the last vacation Jim would ever have, so despite my real convictions about organizational priorities, I approved his request.

As it happened, Jim became extremely ill on the plane and had to spend the first two weeks of his vacation in the hospital. He called to explain that he'd been diagnosed with meningitis, which he claimed was completely unrelated to his AIDS.

When he returned to the office, Jim looked awful. He had lost a great deal of weight, he was losing his hair, and he confessed to difficulty keeping down any food at all. Nevertheless, Jim seemed genuinely optimistic about the new medication he was taking for what he still insisted was meningitis and nothing more.

For that matter, his health actually seemed to improve for a time. But despite extraordinary efforts and long hours, Jim was unable to improve his performance. As we approached my September deadline, a flood of complaints rolled in from other managers about the unit and about Jim specifically. He simply wasn't getting the job done. Once again, I rolled up my sleeves, personally managed several program areas, and got our Washington headquarters to provide temporary staff assistance. But my efforts weren't enough. Jim's unit was central to the organization, and now its reputation was gone, its staff thoroughly demoralized, and its manager too ill to function. Worst of all, it was clearly my job to fix it. I had no alternative but to proceed with a formal performance action against him.

As a manager, it was the most agonizing task I ever faced. On the one hand, I knew that removing Jim was necessary to meet my responsibilities as a manager. On the other hand, I believed that taking action against him meant failing my responsibilities as a human being. Although I was well practiced in the art of terminating unproductive employees, I had never had to force the removal—or, in this case, the reassignment—of an employee who was facing death.

At the end of September, I handed Jim a formal notice of proposed performance action. It informed him that unless his performance improved significantly by year's end, he would be rated "unacceptable" and terminated, demoted, or reassigned. In early January, after the holidays, I presented Jim with an unacceptable rating. As expected, he disputed its accuracy.

Over the next several days, Jim and I carried on an intense and painful negotiation. My goal never was to fire him. The unacceptable rating was simply a way of getting him to ask for reassignment. I told Jim that if I had to force him out of his job, I would set out my reasons in plain English. But if he gave up his supervisory position of his own free will, he could name any reason he wished. I told him I would reconsider his unacceptable rating when I received his voluntary request for reassignment.

We talked several times a day, clarifying our respective positions, each of us trying to get the other to relent. In the end, "for reasons of health," Jim "volunteered" for reassignment to a nonmanagerial position. In return, I raised his performance rating to "acceptable." I felt manipulative, but I also felt I had done my job.

I would like to say that this solved the work-related problem. I was able to replace Jim with another proven manager, and the change improved staff morale and restored much of the unit's responsiveness and credibility. But Jim continued to dispute his performance rating even after I raised it to acceptable. He went so far as to file a grievance in order to get a rating high enough to carry a salary increase. The grievance procedure sustained my action, but it was a shallow victory. Jim avoided me; we rarely spoke unless I called for a formal meeting. Sadly, his performance continued to deteriorate even with reduced responsibility, so we had a series of stiff, formal meetings right through 1990. I was doing my job, but I had lost a friend and, I was afraid, a piece of my better self.

Things proceeded to get worse for both of us. Jim's absences grew longer and more frequent, and he was hospitalized several times. I'd minimized his diminishing effectiveness by limiting his responsibility, but Jim still couldn't do his job. At the end of the year, nevertheless, I gave him another acceptable rating so he could keep his new position. Although I considered it a gift—in fact, Jim's work was far from acceptable—he filed another grievance. At the very same time, however, he also submitted an application for disability retirement and went on sick leave pending its approval. When I asked him why he was contesting his rating when he meant to retire anyway, Jim explained angrily that he needed a better rating to find a new job. My supervisor was the grievance officer in his case, and, with my concurrence, he increased Jim's final rating to "fully successful."

Unlike Frank, Jim had solid support from his family and was able to return to his hometown and live with his mother for the last year of his life. He died in January 1992.

Every manager knows that people differ in their ability to accept constructive criticism and acknowledge performance deficiencies. Looking back, it amazes me that I expected the same reaction from Jim that I got from Frank. I suppose I was misled by their obvious similarities. Both were terribly sick, both lost their effectiveness, both fell into a clear physical category—AIDS victim—for which I felt trained and ready. But the dying are as different as the healthy. AIDS is not an "issue" but a disease, and the people who get it are human beings first and victims second. Some of what I learned in dealing with Frank applied equally to Jim. Much did not. The differences as well as the similarities have taught me some valuable lessons.

To begin with, there is a critical distinction to be made between employees who are HIV-positive and those who have developed active AIDS. Distressingly enough, my experience indicates that it is managers who must make this distinction, since the people affected may not volunteer or even admit to themselves how far their illness has progressed.

Employees who are HIV-positive are fully capable of providing normal, productive work. Supervisors should base every decision regarding their recruitment, evaluation, and promotion on merit alone and not on some imprecise notion of life expectancy or anticipated future decline in performance.

This much is basic. The real challenge for managers is dealing with employees in the advanced stages of AIDS, when performance is declining, attendance and dependability are haphazard, confidentiality has been jeopardized or swept aside by the rumor mill, and unit productivity and morale have begun to suffer serious damage. By extension, a manager's own performance will now be in question as well.

The broader issue is how to achieve a balance between organizational needs and the fair and compassionate treatment of a formerly successful employee. The narrower issues, unfortunately, tend to focus not so much on equity, counseling, and organizational success as on compromise, candor, and damage control.

Perhaps the most difficult aspect of AIDS for a manager is the inability or reluctance of AIDS victims to recognize how far their health has actually deteriorated. Both Frank and Jim tried hard to maintain their optimism. Both insisted that the variety of ailments they fell victim to were unrelated to AIDS. Both assured me repeatedly that new medications or new dosages would improve their condition. From time to time, I even shared their false hopes of recovery, and that was perhaps my greatest failing. The conflict between compassion and organizational efficiency is bleak enough without adding wishful thinking to the mix.

In Jim's case, clearly it would have been better for the organization if I had reassigned him earlier. Yet doing so would have required me to ignore or at least challenge his optimism about a partial or complete recovery, and I cannot believe I have the right to challenge that kind of hope. In the end, I had no choice but to proceed along the grueling and decidedly unsympathetic route of performance documentation.

Jim's case was further complicated by its duration. Only four months elapsed from the observed onset of Frank's disease until he agreed to step aside. Jim continued to work for some two years, his effectiveness diminishing more and more swiftly as time went on, before I forced him to accept reassignment. As medical breakthroughs improve the quality of life and prolong the careers of AIDS patients, the problem of decreasing job performance will probably grow more acute—and more distressing.

The next time I confront AIDS, especially in a supervisor, I will know that the disease affects everyone around it, not just the person who is ill. As performance flags, colleagues and subordinates will find themselves absorbing additional duties, redoing unsatisfactory work, and piecing together uncompleted projects. When the AIDS patient is a supervisor, a considerable amount of work may remain unassigned and simply fall through the cracks.

On top of the extra work load, productivity will suffer in other ways as well. People will discuss a coworker's deteriorating health, and if the nature of the illness is confidential, then they will spend additional time speculating about diagnosis, life-style, and the danger of infection. In the future, I will encourage employees with AIDS to consider seriously the advantages of confiding in their coworkers.

The next time I recognize performance impairment as a result of AIDS, I will also start focusing attention on the needs and concerns of the other workers in the unit. Had I paid closer attention to Jim's staff, I think I would have realized much sooner that they were covering for him.

The last lesson I learned was the importance of keeping my own supervisor informed of my difficulties. While I was quick to alert him to the existence of an AIDS case among my subordinates, I was slow to ask for help. There were two reasons for this lapse. The first was my training in the lean-and-mean school of management technique. The second was my miscalculation of the effect of AIDS on the unit as a whole. When I finally did seek support from my supervisor, my request for additional staff was approved without hesitation. I only wish I had asked sooner.

I am glad to say that once we stopped being subordinate and supervisor, Jim and I were able to recover some semblance of our past friendship. I am grateful to him for that. For me, one of the most numbing side effects of Jim's illness was my own anguish at having to put the interests of the organization ahead of Jim's need to take pride in his work and status.

I wished Jim well. I made mistakes, but short of neglecting my responsibility to the organization, I think I did all I could to ease his work life and eventual withdrawal. Yet in the end, I needed to know he forgave me for doing my job.

AIDS is a challenge to our humanity as well as to our reason because it robs us of a little bit of both.

PART

V

Emerging Issues in
Workplace Diversity

1
Dealing with the Aging Work Force

Jeffrey Sonnenfeld

The extension of mandatory retirement to age 70, signed into U.S. law last April, has caught most organizations off-guard and has surfaced latent fears about the general age drift in the work force. Management experts and journalists over the last year or so have become quite vocal in their prophecies about the changing complexion of the work force.

We used to hear predictions about the "greening of America." Now we hear references to impending problems resulting from the "graying of America," as the country belatedly awakens to the composite effects of demographic trends, improvements in life expectancy, and changes in social legislation. Executives are being warned to anticipate changes in employee performance and attitudes, performance appraisals, retirement incentives, training programs, blocked career paths, union insurance pensions, and affirmative action goals, among other worrisome issues.

Business managers have been the target of superficial and conflicting admonitions appearing in the press. As the chief executive of a leading paper company recently complained to me, "At first we were interested in the warnings. Now, they all say the same things. We hear all the fire alarms being sounded, but no one suggests where we should send the engines."

The needs of a very different work force overshadow many of the other issues of the 1980s for which managers must prepare their organizations. Just as other organizational activities must adapt to a changing environment, human resource planning dictates a major overhaul in recruitment, development, job structure, incentives, and performance appraisal. Thus management attention should now be focused on specific problems in mid- and late-career planning.

It is hard enough to comprehend the individual aging process without at the same time assessing the effects of an entire population growing older. If Congress and President Carter had not extended the work years, leaders of America's organizations would still have had to face troublesome human resource changes.

As a consequence of the 43 million babies born in the years immediately following World War II, a middle-aged bulge is forming and eventually the 35- to 45-year-old age group will increase by 80%. By the year 2030, this group will be crossing the infamous bridge to 65, increasing the relative size of that population from 12% of all Americans to 17%, a jump from 31 million to 52 million people.[1]

Some labor analysts point out that even those Department of Labor statistics are conservative, for likely changes downward in the mortality rate due to advanced medical treatment are not reflected in the predictions. Today, the average life expectancy is about age 73, which is 10 years longer than the years of life expected at birth in the 1950s.

On examining the rate of this change, one sees that the size of the preretirement population, between the ages of 62 and 64, will not be affected dramatically until the year 2000. Until that time, this group will expand at an annual rate of 7.6% above 1975 figures. Between 2000 and 2010, however, it will grow by 48%. For one to assume, however, that there are at least 22 years before major problems arise would be incorrect. This population bulge will be moving through several critical career phases before reaching the preretirement years.

One should pause and reflect on how, in just the next ten years, the population bulge will be lodged in the "mid-life crisis" age. This added strain will magnify the traditional work and nonwork problems associated with the sense of limited opportunity at that age. Even sooner, the decline in youth population, which is currently causing the consolidation of secondary schools, will shift the balance of power and the approach in company recruitment.

As a consequence, a dwindling young work force will make it more difficult to fill entry-level positions. Already there are predictions about shortages in blue-collar occupations by the mid-1980s.[2] It is not at all too soon for managers to start investigating their company demographics.

On top of the foregoing, the recent legislation on extending mandatory retirement further heightens the concern about job performance in the later years. Sooner than even the advocates of this legislation dreamed, business managers find themselves faced with contemplating the implications of long-tenured senior employees.

The immediate impact of this legislation depends, of course, on how older workers respond to the opportunity to remain on the job. Many companies are looking at the well-publicized trend toward earlier retirement, and concluding that this trend will counteract the effects of extended tenure possibilities. Labor force participation rates are dropping for workers age 55 and older and for those age 60 and over.

A retirement expert on the National Industrial Conference Board, a business research organization, said, "People want to retire while they are still young and healthy enough to enjoy the activities of their choice."[3] Another Conference Board researcher reported that these younger retirees are interested in education, in traveling, and in spending more and more money on themselves.[4]

Also, Victor M. Zin, director of Employee Benefits at General Motors, commented, "There used to be a stigma to going out. He was over the hill, but now it's a looked-for status. Those retirement parties, they used to be sad affairs. They are darn happy affairs now. The peer pressure is for early retirement."[5]

Research suggests, however, that such a trend reflects worker income, education, job conditions, and retirement security. Dissatisfied workers and those with better pension plans seem to be more likely to opt out earlier. The experience of Sears, Roebuck and Polaroid, and several insurance companies which have already introduced flexible retirement, shows that at least 50% of those workers reaching age 65 remain on the job. In contrast, only 7% of auto workers take advantage of the opportunity to continue past age 65.

Gerontologists also do not support an early retirement trend. They cite the greater political activity of older Americans, the increasing average age of nursing home occupants, and a 1974 Harris Poll survey of retirees over 65 who claimed they would still work if they had not been forced out.[6] Such a reversed trend might be strengthened as age 65 becomes early retirement and workers see extended career opportunities.

Mid-Career Considerations

With the projection of middle-aged workers shortly comprising a large part of the work force, and with greater numbers of older people a certainty later on, executives have good reason to be interested in relationships between age and performance.

Important age and performance considerations are manifest in younger workers well before they ever become established members of the "gray work force." In looking across the occupations of those in their mid-30s to mid-40s, one sees career drops in performance and morale, along with higher rates of turnover. There has also traditionally been higher mobility in these mid-life years as well.

Longitudinal career studies tracking people over ten-year intervals for the past three decades show that, despite growing barriers to employment in certain occupations, there has been an outstanding peak in job mobility for those in their mid-30s to mid-40s. This mobility may vary somewhat across occupations because of exceptionally high turnover rates in some jobs such as sales and service.

Candidates for second careers tend to be in their 40s and report a perceived discrepancy between personal aspirations and current opportunities for achievement and promotion. This gap widens as the opportunity for advancement decreases and results in major career frustration.

OCCUPATIONAL STAGNATION

A survey of over one thousand middle-aged men in managerial and professional positions found that five out of every six respondents endured a period of severe frustration and trauma which began in their early 30s. Work performance, emotional stability, and physical health were seriously affected. The study also found that one out of every six middle-aged workers never fully recovered from traumatic realizations that their sense of eternal youth had been replaced by physical deterioration and greater sensitivity to the inevitability of death. The loss of spirit led to lowered goals and diminished self-expectations.

Psychologist Erik Erikson first brought academic attention to this mid-career crisis, characterizing it as the locus of a conflict between feelings of "generativity versus stagnation."[7] The middle-aged worker senses that new starts in life are coming to an end.

Gerontologist Bernice Neugarten, reporting on her research that indicated a new perspective on "time" appears in the mid-to-late 30s, commented:

Life is restructured in terms of time-left-to-live rather than time-since-birth. Not only the reversal in directionality, but the awareness that time is finite is a particularly conspicuous feature of middle age.

Thus "you hear so much about deaths that seem premature—that's one of the changes that come over you over the years. Young fellows never give it a thought. . . ." The recognition that there is "only so much time left" was a frequent theme . . . those things don't quite penetrate when you're in your 20s and you think that life is all ahead of you.[8]

Harvard psychiatrist George E. Vaillant likens this period to the stresses of adolescence and rebellion against authority and structure. His original clinical research tracks people through 40 years of life, and provides a valuable in-depth analysis of adult development. Vaillant feels that, by 40, people "put aside the preconceptions and the narrow establishment aims of their 30s and begin once again to feel gangly and uncertain about themselves. But always, such transitional periods in life provide a means of seizing one more change and finding a new solution to instinctive or interpersonal needs."[9]

From his clinical studies of people progressing through their middle years, Yale psychologist Daniel Levinson argues, "This is not an extended adolescence, but a highly formative, evolving phase of adult life." He found that, while a smooth transition is indeed possible, more often dramatic chaos is likely to characterize mid-life transition. One's former life structure (e.g., occupation, marital life) suddenly seems inappropriate and new choices must be made.

According to Levinson, "If these choices are congruent with his dreams, values, talents, and possibilities, they provide the basis for a relatively satisfactory life structure. If the choices are poorly made and the new structure seriously flawed, however, he will pay a heavy price in the next period."[10]

Regardless of the causes of this stressful period, several events in society indicate that the symptoms will soon spread in epidemic proportions.

First, those persons reaching the mid-career period in the next ten years will have achieved far higher educational levels and associated higher aspirations than ever experienced by this group previously. By 1980, one out of four workers will have a college degree.

Second, the pattern of occupational growth suggests increasingly insufficient opportunities for advancement in a narrower occupational hierarchy. Unfavorable predictions of future needs through 1985 by the Bureau of Labor Statistics confirm the cause for distress. Professional positions will remain scarce, and the expanded demands of the 1960s for engineers, scientists, and teachers, which influenced so many young people to undertake higher education, will remain history. Clerical, sales, service, and operative workers are expected to be in demand.

Third, the size of the postwar baby boom means intense competition for whatever opportunities do exist. This competitiveness is due to the bulk of the population being at the same career point rather than being more evenly distributed.

Finally, the new legislation on mandatory retirement threatens to further limit opportunities for advancement.

Organizations should prepare now for the inevitable frustrations of career stagnation in the middle years. Already there are individual and organized complaints from those who say that somehow society has cheated them. After investing valuable years in expensive higher education, following glowing promises held out by society, graduates are entering a stagnant labor market. In many cases, academic degrees have become excess baggage to those recipients who are forced to enter the labor market at inappropriate levels.

Many research studies have warned about the growing expectations for self-fulfillment in work. Poor physical health, mental maladjustment, and social disenchantment are consequences of status conflict.

Some social analysts have suggested that anarchistic tendencies of the terrorists in Italy and other parts of Europe are expressions of rage against betrayal by the social order. The fury that burned college buildings in this country in the last decade may strike again in the coming decade, as that generation reacts in frustration to limited opportunities and a sense of defeat.

STEREOTYPED PERCEPTION

One of the fears of businessmen is that they will no longer be able to ease out older workers. Much of the initial reaction to the recognition of a graying work force has been to try to figure out new ways of "weeding out the deadwood." Pension inducements, less generous and "more realistic" performance appraisals, and other rationalizations for eliminating older, less desirable workers are being developed.

Who should be the target of those designs? Columnist William L. Safire has echoed the fears of many businessmen who link age to performance:

> . . . old people get older and usually less productive, and they ought
> to retire so that business can be better managed and more economi-

cally served. We should treat the elderly with respect, which does not require treating them as if they were not old. If politicians start inventing "rights" that cut down productivity, they infringe on the consumer's right to a product at the lowest cost . . .[11]

The Later Years

It is important to explore how much factual evidence there is to support the stereotyping and the prejudices that link age with senility, incompetence, and lack of worth in the labor market. Age 65 was an arbitrarily selected cutoff age used by New Deal planners who looked back historically to Bismark's social welfare system in nineteenth century Germany.

Certainly, one does not have to look hard to find the elderly among the greatest contributors to current society. The list is long of older citizens who have made major contributions in all fields including the arts, industry, science, and government, and who continue to be worthy and inspiring members of our society.

AGE-RELATED CHANGE

Physiological changes are most pronounced and most identified with old age, but vary markedly in degree between individuals of the same age. It is not clear what changes are actually a result of aging and what can be attributed to life-styles. Researchers indicate, however, that after age 50 life-style becomes a less influential factor in physiological change than aging itself.

Among age-related changes are declines in the sensory processes, particularly vision, failures in the immunity system that lead to cardiovascular and kidney problems, and degenerative diseases such as rheumatoid arthritis. While 85% of those workers over 65 suffer from chronic diseases, these are not sudden afflictions. Hence 75% of those 60 to 64 years old suffer from these diseases, many of which can be controlled by modern medical treatment. The major effects of these diseases are loss of strength in fighting off invaders and loss of mobility.

Reaction time seems to be affected by the increase in random brain activity, or "neural noise," which distracts the brain from responding to the proper neural signals. A fall in the signal-to-noise ratio would lead to a slower performance and increased likelihood of error. To correct for this possibility of error, performance is delayed to permit time to gain greater certainty. Research on cognitive abilities shows that older people are more scrupulous in the use of decision criteria before responding or forming associations required for decision making. Older people are less likely to use mnemonic or "bridging" mechanisms to link similar concepts. They require a 75% chance of certainty before committing themselves, while younger people will take far greater risks.[12]

When time pressure is not a relevant factor, the performance of older people tends to be as good, if not better, than that of younger people. In self-paced tests and in self-paced learning situations, older people do not have to make speed versus accuracy trade-offs and, consequently, their performance is higher.

Learning is also inhibited by the delayed signal-to-noise ratio since it interferes with memory. Most of the learning difficulties of older people stem from acquisition and recall rather than from retention. This relates to the two-step process of memory involving an initial introduction and a later retention period. That is, older people have a harder time holding information in short-term memory, awaiting long-term storage, due to neural noise. This is the same sort of problem older people have with recall.

However, once the information reaches long-term storage, it can be retained. The process of inputting the information, and retrieving it, can become blocked for intervals of time. Cognition is perhaps the most important difficulty of older workers and relates to problem solving, decision making, and general learning ability. Training in appropriate mental techniques can overcome many of these short-term memory blockages.

Similarly, intelligence tests often have age biases built in with the inherent speed versus accuracy trade-off. Recent researchers have tried to avoid such a bias and have found problem solving, number facility, and verbal comprehension to be unaffected by age. The ability to find and apply general rules to problem solving are more related to an individual's flexibility and education than to age.

WORK ATTITUDE

Research studies on all sectors of the American work force have found that age and job satisfaction seemed to bear positive relationships, but it has become apparent that it is hard to consider job satisfaction without considering what aspects of the work experience are important to the individual.[13] Organizations must carefully consider the type of satisfaction which they are measuring, and try to determine how both the more productive and less productive workers in different age groups vary. Perhaps the types of incentives built into a company's rewards package may encourage the less productive, rather than the more productive, older workers to remain with the company.

Along the same line, increasing monetary benefits but not expanding opportunities for job variety would be a serious mistake if the desired workers are more interested in personal growth and achievement than in financial incentives. Mastery and achievement are closely related to job satisfaction. As such, the need for mastery, or recognized accomplishment, becomes increasingly important.

Thus sudden change in job structure and social networks can be threatening to older workers. Their niche in society is defined largely by their contribution in the work place. The job presents friendship, routine, a sense of worth, and identity. Obsolescence and job change are major fears of older workers.

JOB PERFORMANCE

In reviewing studies of performance by occupation for different age groups, it is important to be aware of biases built into the performance appraisals themselves. On top of this, cross-sectional studies of different age groups are also viewing different individuals. It is quite possible that selection factors in older populations explain much of the difference between older and younger populations. In other words, the older workers staying on the job may be different somehow in their skills or interests in that they have managed to remain on the same job.

Looking first at *managers*, one once again sees the manifestation of the tendency toward caution with age. Victor H. Vroom and Bernd Pahl found a relationship between age and risk taking and also between age and the value placed on risk.[14] They studied 1,484 managers, age 22 to 58, from 200 corporations and used a choice-dilemma questionnaire. It seemed that the older managers were less willing to take risks and had a lower estimate of the value of risk in general.

These findings are supported by another study on determinants of managerial information processing and decision-making performance; 79 male first-line managers with ages ranging from 23 to 57 years (a median of 40 years) were measured by the Personnel Decision Simulation Questionnaire.[15] Older decision makers tended to take longer to reach decisions even when the influence of prior decision-making experience was removed.

However, the older managers were better able to accurately appraise the value of the new information. Hesitancy about risk taking was also supported in this study; older decision makers were less confident in their decisions.

Another study focusing on task-oriented groups also found that older group members once again sought to minimize risk by seeking more reliable direction.[16] Younger members were more willing to shift authority within the group and to make better use of the experience of others. In this way, younger members of the group were more flexible and more tolerant.

Studies of professionals generally concentrate on *scientists* and *engineers*. Perhaps this is because their output is so easy to measure (e.g., publications, patents). Such studies have found bimodal distributions of innovativeness as a function of age. That is to say, there were two peaks of productivity separated by ten-year intervals in research laboratories compared with development laboratories. The first peak in research laboratories occurred by age 40, and the second peak did not appear until age 50. In the development laboratories, the first peak occurred around age 45 to 50, and the second appeared around age 55 to 60.[17] These studies tracked contribution longitudinally over a person's career.

Wider studies of scholarship and artistic contribution revealed a similar first peak at about age 40 and a second peak in the late 50s. Looking more broadly at productivity, it is clear that creative activity was lowest for the 21- to 50-year old group and generally increased with age.[18] It is also a fact, however, that younger scholars and scientists have a more difficult time achieving recognition in the journal networks than do their senior colleagues.

Older people seem to have achieved superior standing among *sales workers* as well and to have remained higher performers. Reports from insurance companies, auto dealers, and large department stores suggest that age is an asset, if a factor at all, in performance.

In a large study of sales clerks in two major Canadian department stores, performance improved with age and experience, the actual peak performance of the sales clerks being about age 55.[19] In several organizations, particularly high technology companies, however, morale plummeted corresponding to length of service. These latter organizations may have used sales as a traditional entry position for managerial development. Those employees remaining on the job over ten years began to perceive frustration in their personal goals of managerial advancement.

Age has had surprisingly little effect on *manual workers*. In several studies, performance seemed to remain fully steady through age 50, peaking slightly in the 30s. The decline in productivity in the 50s never seemed to drop more than 10% from peak performance. Attendance was not significantly affected, and the separation rate (quits, layoffs, discharges) was high for those under age 25 and very low for those over 45.[20]

These findings may not only indicate greater reliability among older workers, but also suggest that those who have remained on the job are, in some way, the most competent. Such a sorting out of abilities may not take place equally well across all industries. While tenure among factory workers within industries is reduced with age, absenteeism rates in heavy industry and construction do increase with age. This may be a more evident consequence of mismatches between job demands and physical abilities.

Finally, the high variation of manual labor performance within age groups, compared with the variation between age groups, suggests that individual differences are much more important than age group differences. The need to evaluate potential on an individual basis, and not by age group, has been convincingly established in these studies.

Considerable variation within age groups is found in studies on *clerical workers* as well. A study of 6,000 government and private industry office workers found no significant difference in output by age. Older workers had a steadier rate of work and were equally accurate. Researchers in many studies found that older clerical workers, both male and female, generally had attendance records equal to that of other workers, as well as lower rates of turnover.[21]

CORPORATE EXPERIENCE

Many well-publicized reports identify particular companies in various parts of the country which have never adopted mandatory retirement policies yet have continued to be profitable and efficient with workers well into their 70s and 80s. For example, Thomas Green-wood, president of Globe Dyeworks in Philadelphia, who has retained workers hired by his grandfather, commented, "As long as a man can produce, he can keep his job."[22] The 87-year-old president of Ferle, Inc., a small company owned by General Foods, which employs workers whose average age is 71, commented, "Older people are steadier, accustomed to the working discipline."[23] Sales workers at Macy's department stores in New York have never had to conform to a mandatory retirement age, and have demonstrated no apparent decline in performance attributable directly to age.

Banker's Life and Casualty Company proudly points to its tradition of open-ended employment, retaining top executives, clerks, and secretaries through their late 60s, 70s, and 80s. Of the 3,500 workers in Banker's home office, 3.5% are over 65 years of age. Some have been regular members of the Banker's work force, while others have come after being forced into retirement from other companies. The company reports that older workers show more wisdom, are more helpful and thorough, and perform their duties with fewer personality clashes. Studies on absenteeism at Banker's Life and Casualty show that those over 65 have impressive attendance records.

Large companies that have changed to flexible retirement plans in recent years have had similar satisfactory performance reports. U.S. Steel has permitted more than 153,000 nonoffice employees to continue working as long as they can maintain satisfactory levels of performance and can pass medical examinations.

Polaroid has found that those employees who choose to remain on the job after age 65 tend to be better performers. Company retirement spokesman, Joe Perkins, explained, "If you like to work, you're usually a good worker." He added that attendance is also exemplary as older workers ". . . often apologize for having missed work one day, three years ago because of a cold. There is a fantastic social aspect as people look forward to coming to work." No one is shifted between jobs at Polaroid unless the worker requests a change. Even among older workers whose jobs entail heavy physical demands, high performance is maintained.

PERFORMANCE APPRAISAL

Generally the companies just mentioned have not had to deal with older workers who remain on the job despite poor performance. There is no guarantee that workers will always be able or willing to perform well, and to relinquish their jobs when they are no longer capable of fulfilling the job requirements. Even if both the company and the individual want to continue their relationship, it is not always possible to effectively match an employee's skills with the company's job opportunities.

This need to identify differences between more and less productive older workers is a difficult distinction to make with current performance measurement techniques. The process must be objective, consistent, and based on criteria that are uniformly applied and which will endure court challenges. Arthur C. Prine, Jr., vice president of R.R. Donnelley & Sons Company, recently explained, "As soon as you pick and choose, you'll scar a lot of people when they are most sensitive. I just dread the thought of calling someone and saying, 'You've worked for forty-five years and have done a wonderful job, but you've been slipping and you must retire.'"[24]

Instead of carrying less productive older workers near retirement on the payroll, employers may begin to weed them out earlier in an effort to deter age-discrimination charges. Richard R. Shinn, president of Metropolitan Life, forecasts that "employers are going to make decisions earlier in careers if it appears that someone is going to be a problem as time goes on."[25]

Thus predictions of future performance will be important criteria in performance appraisal. Even the use of formal standard evaluations does not eliminate age bias or avoid self-fulfilling prophecies which prejudice the evaluation process.

Such a bias was shown in a recent poll of managers. A 1977 questionnaire of *HBR* readers concluded that "age stereotypes clearly influence managerial decisions."[26] *HBR* readers perceived older workers as more rigid and resistant to change and thus recommended transferring them out rather than helping them overcome a problem. The respondents preferred to retain but not retrain obsolete older employees and showed a tendency to withhold promotions from older workers compared with identically qualified younger workers.

Part of this discrimination problem is that many companies consider an employee's potential to be an important element in his evaluation. As mentioned in the section on basic abilities, chronological age never has been a valid means of measuring a worker's potential and now is illegal under the Age Discrimination Employment Act. The strength of various faculties may slightly correlate with age in certain regards, but there is no categorical proof that age has an effect on capabilities.

Individuals vary greatly, and useful measures of potential must recognize such differences.

One of the best known functional measures was the GULHEMP system designed by Leon F. Koyl, physician from DeHaviland Aircraft.[27] This system had two dimensions, the first being a physical-mental profile and the second a job-demand profile. Workers were examined on seven factors of general physique, upper extremities, lower extremities, hearing, eye sight, mental features, and personality attributes. These individual factors were plotted on a graph and superimposed on similarly graphed job task profiles. Individuals were then viewed in relation to the job profiles available. While successful in its pilot experience, this federally supported project was not seen as a high priority government expenditure. Thus the project in functional age measurement was terminated.

Functional measures, however, are not the answer to the performance appraisal question. While they can provide the quantifiable "expert" criteria companies might need for age-discrimination suits, their strength lies in largely assessing the potentials of physical labor. The sensitive areas in performance appraisal are evaluations of the more nebulous factors.

Ratings of "mental abilities" and "personality attributes," which were the poorest factors on the GULHEMP scale, are the most sensitive areas in the appraisal process, and the only truly relevant dimensions in most white collar and managerial jobs. Some consulting firms have been assessing the important elements of successful job performance, appraising corporate personnel, and establishing appropriate organizational recruitment and development programs.

What Managers Can Do

How can companies resolve the kinds of frustration expressed at the beginning of this article by the chief executive of the paper company? Where can they send the fire engines? It is far easier to read about social trends than to perceive ways of preparing for them. It is clear that America's work force is graying. Older workers will tend toward caution, will experience far greater levels of frustration, and will show signs of age individually at very different rates.

However, companies are not fated for stodginess. In this section let us look at six priorities for managers to consider in preparing for the impending dramatic change in their own internal environments:

1. *Age profile.* It has been demonstrated that age per se does not necessarily indicate anything significant about worker performance. Instead, executives should look at the age distribution across jobs in the organization, as compared with performance measures, to see what career paths might conceivably open in the organizations in the future and what past performance measures have indicated about those holding these positions.

2. *Job performance requirements.* Companies should then more precisely define the types of abilities and skills needed for various posts. A clear understanding of job specifications for all levels of the organization is necessary to plan for proper employee selection, job design, and avoidance of age-discrimination suits. For example, jobs may be designed for self-pacing, may require periodic updating, or may necessitate staffing by people with certain relevant physical strengths.

Several companies have looked at the skills needed in various jobs from the chief executive down to reenlisted older and even retired workers who have the needed experience and judgment. For example, as Robert P. Ewing, president of Banker's Life and Casualty, stated, "Our company sets performance standards for each job and these standards are the criteria for employment. Age doesn't count. Getting the job done does."

Such an approach requires careful assessment of needed job competence where traits, motives, knowledge, and skills are all evaluated. When this information is considered in relation to the magnitude and direction of planned company growth, future manpower needs can be predicted. Obsolete job positions can be forecast and workers retrained in advance. Necessary experience cannot be gained overnight, and development programs should be coordinated with precise company manpower needs.

3. *Performance appraisal.* Corresponding with improved job analyses, companies must improve their analyses of individual performance as well. Age biases are reflected in both the evaluation format and the attitudes of managers. Management development programs should be aware of the need to correct these biases. Both Banker's Life and Polaroid have teams that audit the appraisals of older workers to check for unfair evaluations. These units have also been used to redress general age prejudice in the work place.

Companies need a realistic understanding of current work force capabilities for effective human resource planning. A company cannot adjust its development, selection, and job training strategies appropriately without knowing the current strengths and weaknesses of its workers. Additionally, potential courtroom challenges on staffing and reward procedures necessitate evidence of solid decision criteria.

4. *Work force interest surveys.* Once management acquires a clearer vision of the company's human resource needs, and what basic abilities its workers have, it must then determine what the current workers want. If management decides that it wants to selectively encourage certain types of workers to continue with the organization while encouraging turnover of other types, it must next determine what effects different incentives will have on each group.

In addition, management must be well aware of workers' desires and values so that it can anticipate and prepare for morale drops. Understanding work force aspirations is essential in reducing the harmful organizational and personal consequences of mid-career plateauing. For example, companies might offer counseling programs to those who frequently but unsuccessfully seek job changes, or might consider making alterations in the prevailing company culture and in the norms which link competence and mobility.

5. *Education and counseling.* Management may discover that its workers are also confronted with a variety of concerns regarding the direction of their lives after terminating current employment. Counseling on retirement and second-career development are becoming increasingly common to assist workers in adjusting to the major social disengagement following retirement.

IBM now offers tuition rebates for courses on any topic of interest to workers within three years of retirement, and continuing into retirement. Subject matter need not have any relation to one's job and many workers include courses in preparation for second careers (learning new skills, professions, and small business management).

Counseling is also important to address problems of the work force which remains on the job. Career planning to avoid mid-career plateauing, and training programs to reduce obsolescence, must be developed by each company. The educational programs must reflect the special learning needs of older workers. Self-paced learning, for example, is often highly effective. Older workers can learn new tricks, but they need to be taught differently.

6. *Job structure.* A better understanding of basic job requirements and employee abilities and interests may indicate a need to restructure

jobs. Such restructuring cannot be done, however, until management knows what the core job tasks are in the organization and what types of changes should be instituted. Alternatives to traditional work patterns should be explored jointly with the work force. Some union leaders have expressed reservations about part-time workers whom they fear may threaten the power of organized labor. Management, too, wonders about its ability to manage part-time workers. Some part-time workers have found that they "lack clout and responsibility" in their jobs in small companies.

Management may have more flexibility than anticipated in changing conditions like work pace, the length or timing of the work day, leaves of absence, and challenges on the job. With a tightened reward structure for older workers, satisfaction with the job may shift increasingly to intrinsic features of one's current job.

America's work force is aging, but America's organizations are not doomed to hardening of the arteries. Older workers still have much to offer but organizations must look at certain policies to ensure that their human resources continue to be most effectively used. Organizations must be alert to changing work force needs and flexible in responding to meet those needs.

Notes

1. U.S. Bureau of the Census, "Current Population Reports," Series P-25, No. 61, *"Projections of the Population of the United States, 1975 to 2050"* (Washington, D.C.: U.S. Government Printing Office, 1975).

2. Neal H. Rosenthal, "The United States Economy in 1985: Projected Changes in Occupations," *Monthly Labor Review,* December 1973, p. 18.

3. Jerry Flint, "Early Retirement Is Growing in U.S.," *New York Times,* July 10, 1977.

4. Jerry Flint, "Businessmen Fear Problems from Later Age for Retirement," *New York Times,* October 2, 1977.

5. Ibid.

6. "The Graying of America," *Newsweek,* February 28, 1977, p. 50.

7. Erik Erikson, *Childhood and Society* (New York: Norton, 1963).

8. Bernice Neugarten, *Middle Age and Aging* (Chicago: University of Chicago Press, 1968), p. 97.

9. George E. Vaillant, *Adaptation to Life* (Boston: Little, Brown, 1977), p. 193.

10. Daniel J. Levinson, "The Mid-Life Transition: A Period in Adult Psychosocial Development," *Psychiatry*, 40, 1977, p. 104.

11. William L. Safire, "The Codgerdoggle," *New York Times*, September 3, 1977, p. 29.

12. For an example of research on cognitive abilities, see A.T. Welford, "Thirty Years of Psychological Research on Age and Work," *Journal of Occupational Psychology*, 49, 1976, p. 129.

13. See, for example, John W. Hunt and Peter N. Saul, "The Relationship of Age, Tenure, and Job Satisfaction in Males and Females," *Academy of Management Journal*, 20, 1975, p. 690; also, Bonnie Carroll, "Job Satisfaction," *Industrial Gerontology*, 4, Winter 1970.

14. Victor H. Vroom and Bernd Pahl, "Age and Risk Taking Among Managers," *Journal of Applied Psychology*, 12, 1971, p. 22.

15. Ronald N. Taylor, "Age and Experience as Determinants of Managerial Information Processing and Decision Making Performance," *Academy of Management Journal*, 18, 1975, p. 602.

16. Ross A. Webber, "The Relation of Group Performance to Age of Members in Homogeneous Groups," *Academy of Management Journal*, 17, 1974, p. 570.

17. Ronald C. Pelz, "The Creative Years in Research Environments," Industrial and Electrical Engineering, Transaction of the Professional Technical Group on Engineering Management, 1964, EM-II, p. 23, as referenced in L.W. Porter, *"Summary of the Literature on Personnel Obsolescence,"* Conference on Personnel Obsolescence, Dallas, Stanford Research Institute and Texas Instruments, June 21–23, 1966.

18. Wayne Dennis, "Creative Productivity Between the Ages of 20 and 80 Years," *Journal of Gerontology*, 21, 1966, p. I.

19. *"Age and Performance in Retail Trades,"* Ottawa, Canadian Department of Labor, 1959, as referenced in Carol H. Kelleher and Daniel A. Quirk, "Age Functional Capacity and Work: An Annotated Bibliography," *Industrial Gerontology*, 19, 1973, p. 80.

20. U.S. Department of Labor, *The Older American Worker*, Report to the Secretary of Labor, title 5, sec. 715 of the Civil Right Act of 1964 (Washington, D.C.: U.S. Government Printing Office, June 1965).

21. See, for example, U.S. Department of Labor, Bureau of Labor Statistics, *Comparative Job Performance by Age: Office Workers*, Bulletin No. 1273 (Washington, D.C.: U.S. Government Printing Office, 1960); and U.S. Department of Labor, Bureau of Labor Statistics, *Comparative*

Performance by Age: Large Plants in the Men's Footwear and Household Furniture Industries, Bulletin No. 1223 (Washington, D.C.: U.S. Government Printing Office, 1957).

22. J.L. Moore, "Unretiring Workers, to These Employees, The Boss is a Kid," *Wall Street Journal*, December 7, 1977.

23. S. Terry Atlas and Michael Rees, "Old Folks at Work," *Newsweek*, September 26, 1977, p. 64.

24. Irwin Ross, "Retirement at Seventy a New Trauma for Management," *Fortune*, May 8, 1978, p. 108.

25. Ibid.

26. Benson Rosen and Thomas H. Jerdee, "Too Old or Not Too Old," *Harvard Business Review*, November–December 1977, p. 105.

27. Leon F. Koyl and Pamela M. Hanson, *Age, Physical Ability and Work Potential* (New York: National Council on the Aging, 1969).

2
Business and the Facts of Family Life

Fran Sussner Rodgers and Charles Rodgers

Business is a good thing.

Family is also a good thing.

These are simple, self-evident propositions.

Yet the awkward fact is that when we try to combine these two assertions in the new labor force, they stop being safe, compatible, and obvious and become difficult, even antagonistic. Sometimes the most complex and controversial challenges we face have commonsense truths at their roots.

Consider these variations on the same theme:

Our economy needs the most skilled and productive work force it can possibly find in order to remain competitive.

That same work force must reproduce itself and give adequate care to the children who are the work force of the future.

People with children—women especially—often find themselves at a serious disadvantage in the workplace.

Among Western democracies, the United States ranks number three in dependence on women in the work force, behind only Scandinavia and Canada.

In short, we value both business and family, and they are increasingly at loggerheads.

The Family as a Business Issue

At one time, women provided the support system that enabled male breadwinners to be productive outside the home for at least 40 hours every week. That home-based support system began to recede a generation ago and is now more the exception than the rule. The labor force now includes more than 70% of all women with children between the ages of 6 and 17 and more than half the women with children less than 1 year old. This new reality has had a marked effect on what the family requires of each family member—and on what employers can expect from employees. It is not only a question of who is responsible for very young children. There is no longer anyone home to care for adolescents and the elderly. There is no one around to take in the car for repair or to let the plumber in. Working families are faced with daily dilemmas: Who will take care of a sick child? Who will go to the big soccer game? Who will attend the teacher conference?

Yet employees from families where all adults work are still coping with rules and conditions of work designed, as one observer put it, to the specifications of Ozzie and Harriet. These conditions include rigid adherence to a 40-hour workweek, a concept of career path inconsistent with the life cycle of a person with serious family responsibilities, notions of equity formed in a different era, and performance-evaluation systems that confuse effort with results by equating hours of work with productivity.

Despite the growing mismatch between the rules of the game and the needs of the players, few companies have made much effort to accommodate changing lifestyles. For that matter, how serious can the problem really be? After all, employees still get to work and do their jobs. Somehow the plumber manages to find the key. We know that children and the elderly are somewhere. Why start worrying now? Women's entry into the labor force has been increasing for 20 years, and the system still appears to function.

Nevertheless, we are seeing a rapidly growing corporate interest in work-and-family issues. There are four principal *business* reasons:

First, work force demographics are changing. Most of the increase in the number of working women has coincided with the baby boom. Any associated business fallout—high turnover, lost productivity, absenteeism—occurred in the context of a large labor surplus. Most people were easily replaced, and there was plenty of talent willing to make the traditional sacrifices for success—like travel, overtime, relocation. With the baby boom over and a baby bust upon us, there are now higher costs associated with discouraging entry into the labor force and frustrating talented people who are trying to act responsibly at home as well as at work. In some parts of the country, labor is already so scarce that companies are using progressive family policies as a means of competing for workers.

Second, employee perceptions are changing. Unless we rethink our traditional career paths, the raised aspirations of many women are now clearly on a collision course with their desire to be parents. Before the emergence of the women's movement in the 1960s, many suburban housewives thought their frustrations were uniquely their own. Similarly, for 20 years corporate women who failed to meet their own high expectations considered it a personal failing. But now the invisible barriers to female advancement are being named, and the media take employers to task for their inflexibility.

This shift in women's perceptions greatly changes the climate for employers. Women and men in two-career and single-parent families are much better able to identify policies that will let them act responsibly toward their families and still satisfy their professional ambitions. Companies that don't act as partners in this process may lose talent to companies that do rise to the challenge. No one knows how many women have left large companies because of cultural rigidity. It is even harder to guess at the numbers of talented women who have never even applied for jobs because they assume big companies will require family sacrifices they are unwilling to make.

And it's not just women. In two studies at DuPont, we found that men's reports of certain family-related problems nearly doubled from 1985 to 1988. (Interestingly, on a few of these items, women's reported problems decreased proportionally, which suggests that one reason women experience such great difficulty with work-and-family issues is that men experience so little.)

In fact, men's desire for a more active role in parenting may be unacceptable to their peers. Numerous reports show that few men take advantage of the formal parental leave available to them in many companies. Yet a recent study shows that many men do indeed take time off from work after the birth of a child, but that they do so by piecing together other forms of leave—vacation, personal leave, sick leave—that they see as more acceptable.[1]

A third reason why more companies are addressing work-and-family issues is increasing evidence that inflexibility has an adverse effect on productivity. In a study at Merck in 1984, employees who perceived their supervisors as unsupportive on family issues reported higher levels of stress, greater absenteeism, and lower job satisfaction.[2] Other studies show that supportive companies attract new employees more easily, get them back on the job more quickly after maternity leave, and benefit generally from higher work-force morale.[3]

Fourth, concern about America's children is growing fast. Childhood poverty is up, single-parent families are on the increase, SAT scores are falling, and childhood literacy, obesity, and suicide rates are all moving in the wrong direction.

So far, the business community has expressed its concern primarily through direct efforts to improve schools. Yet in our studies, one-third to one-half of parents say they do not have the workplace flexibility to attend teacher conferences and important school events. It is certainly possible that adapting work rules to allow this parent-school connection—and trying to influence schools to schedule events with working parents in mind—might have as great a positive effect on education as some direct interventions.

For companies that want to use and fully develop the talents of working parents and others looking for flexibility, the agenda is well defined. There are three broad areas that require attention:

1. Dependent care, including infants, children, adolescents, and the elderly.
2. Greater flexibility in the organization, hours, and location of work, and creation of career paths that allow for family responsibility as well as professional ambition.
3. Validation of family issues as an organizational concern by means of company statements and manager training.

Few companies are active in all three areas. Many are active in none. The costs and difficulties are, after all, considerable, and the burden of change does not fall on only employers. There is plenty for government to do. Individual employees too will have to take on new responsibilities. Corporate dependent-care programs often mean purchasing benefits or programs from outside providers and may entail substantial community involvement. Workplace flexibility demands reexamination of work assumptions by employees as well as employers and often meets with line resistance. A corporate commitment to family takes time to work its way down to the front-line supervisory levels where most of the work force will feel its effects.

Dependent Care

Dependent care is a business issue for the obvious reason that employees cannot come to work unless their dependents are cared for.

Study after study shows that most working parents have trouble arranging child care, and that those with the most difficulty also experience the most frequent work disruptions and the greatest absenteeism. Moreover, the lack of child care is still a major barrier to the entry of women into the labor force.

Child-care needs vary greatly in any employee population, and most companies have a limited capacity to address them. But, depending on the company's location, financial resources, the age of its work force, and the competitiveness of its labor market, a corporate child-care program might include some or all of the following:

Help in finding existing child care and efforts to increase the supply of care in the community, including care for sick children.

Financial assistance for child care, especially for entry level and lower level employees.

Involvement with schools, Ys, and other community organizations to promote programs for school-age children whose parents work.

Support for child-care centers in locations convenient to company employees.

Efforts to move government policies—local and federal—toward greater investment in children.

Existing child care is often hard to find because so much of the country's care is provided by the woman down the street, who does not advertise and is not usually listed in the yellow pages or anywhere else. Even where lists do exist—as the result, say, of state licensing requirements—they are often out-of-date. (Turnover in family day care, as this form of child care is called, is estimated at 50% per year.) And lists don't give vacancy information, so parents can spend days making unsuccessful phone calls. Sometimes existing care is invisible because it operates in violation of zoning rules or outside of onerous or inefficient regulatory systems.

In other places—suburban neighborhoods where many women work outside the home or where family income is so high that few need the extra money—there is virtually no child care. Often, too, land prices make centers unaffordable. Infant care is especially scarce because it requires such a high ratio of adults to children. Care for children before and after school and during the many weeks when school is out is in short supply just about everywhere, as is care for "off hour" workers such as shift workers, police officers, and hospital employees.

In addition to the difficulty of finding child care, quality and affordability are always big questions. Cost depends greatly on local standards. In Massachusetts, for example, infant care in centers runs from $150 to more than $200 per week per child due to a combination of high labor costs and strict state licensing standards. Even the highest standards, however, still mean that an infant-care staff member has more to do all day—and more responsibility—than a new parent caring for triplets. In states with lower standards, one staff member may care for as many as eight infants at a time. Up to now, child care in many places has been made affordable by paying very low wages—the national average for child-care staff is $5.35 an hour—and by reducing the standards of quality and safety below what common sense would dictate.[4]

Given all these problems, is it any wonder the companies that want to help feel stymied? While few companies provide significant child-care support today, a very large number are exploring the possibility. We think that number will increase geometrically as the competition for labor grows and more members of the labor force need such support.

One increasingly popular way for companies to address these issues is through resource and referral services. Typically, such services do three things: they help employees find child care suited to their circumstances; they make an effort to promote more care of all types in the communities where employees live; and they try to remove regulatory and zoning barriers to care facilities. Resource and referral services (R&Rs) meet standards of equity by assisting parents regardless of their incomes and their children's ages. And R&Rs work as well for a few workers as for thousands. When the service is delivered through a network of community-based R&Rs, moreover, corporate involvement can also strengthen the community at large.

Although R&R programs can be very helpful, they have limitations. By themselves, they have little effect on affordability, for example, and only an indirect effect on quality, primarily through consumer education and provider training. Also, R&Rs cannot dig up a supply of care where market conditions are highly unfavorable.

A small but growing number of companies provide, subsidize, or contract with outside providers to operate on-site or near-site centers that are available to employees at fees covering at least most of the cost. A North Carolina software company, SAS Institute Inc., provides child care at an on-site center at no cost to employees. The company reports that its turnover rates are less than half the industry average and feels the center's extra expense is justified because it decreases the extremely high cost of training new workers.[5]

Companies that get involved with child-care centers, however, find themselves making difficult trade-offs as a result of the high cost of good care. Many companies won't associate themselves even indirectly with any child care that doesn't meet the highest standards, which means that without a subsidy, only higher income employees can afford the service. But if a company does subsidize child care, it must justify giving this considerable benefit to one group of parents while other parents, who buy child care in some other place or way, get none. One way of avoiding this dilemma is to give child-care subsidies to all lower income employees as an extension of the R&R service, the approach recently announced by NCNB, the banking corporation.

Companies sometimes capitalize centers by donating space or land along with renovation costs or by providing an initial subsidy until the centers are self-supporting. In this way, DuPont helped a number of community not-for-profit organizations establish and expand existing child-care centers in Delaware. Of course, costs can vary hugely. If a building is already available, renovation and startup costs could be as low as $100,000. In most cases, the bill will run from several hundred thousand to several million dollars.

Businesses are also working more closely with schools to encourage before-school, after-school, and vacation care programs. Such a partnership has been established between the American Bankers Insurance Group and the Dade County, Florida school system. The school system actually operates a kindergarten and a first- and second-grade school in a building built by the insurance company. In Charlotte, North Carolina, the 19 largest employers have joined forces with the public sector to expand and improve the quality of care.

In any case, employee interest in child care is great, and employees often fix on the issue of on-site care as a solution to the work-and-family conflicts they experience. But helping employees with child care, given the enormity of the problem in the society at large, is a complicated question. More and more companies are taking the kinds of steps described here, but as the pressure grows, business as a whole is likely to focus more attention on public policy.

Of course, dependent care is not just a question of care for children. Studies at Travelers Insurance Company and at IBM show that 20% to 30% of employees have some responsibility for the care of an adult dependent. Traditionally, the wife stayed home and cared for the elderly parents of both spouses, but as women entered the work force, this support system began to disappear. Since the most recent growth in the female work force involves comparatively younger women whose parents are not yet old enough to require daily assistance, the workplace has probably not yet felt the full effects of elder-care problems.

As in the case of child care, studies show that productivity suffers when people try to balance work and the care of parents. Some people quit their jobs entirely. The most immediate need is for information about the needs and problems of the aging and about available resources. Most young people know nothing at all about government programs like Medicare and Medicaid. More often than not, children know very little about their own parents' financial situations and need help simply to open communication.

Unlike child care, elder care is often complicated by distance. In our experience with some 12,000 employees with elderly dependents, more than half lived more than 100 miles from the person they were concerned about. Crises are common. The elderly suffer unexpected hospitalizations, for example, and then come out of the hospital too weak to care for themselves. A service that can help with referrals and arrangements in another city can spare employees time, expense, and anguish. Also, people often need to compare resources in several states where different siblings live in order to make decisions about such things as where parents should live when their health begins to deteriorate.

Conditions of Work

A study at two high-tech companies in New England showed that the average working mother logs in a total workweek of 84 hours between her home and her job, compared with 72 hours for male parents and about 50 hours for married men and women with no children. In other words, employed parents—women in particular—work the equivalent of two full-time jobs.[6] No wonder they've started looking for flexible schedules, part-time employment, and career-path alternatives that allow more than one model of success. For that matter, is it even reasonable to expect people who work two jobs to behave and progress along exactly the same lines as those with no primary outside responsibilities?

Until now, most companies have looked at job flexibility on a case-by-case basis and have offered it sparingly to valued employees as a favor. But increasing competition for the best employees will make such flexibility commonplace. A smaller labor supply means that workers will no longer have to take jobs in the forms that have always been offered. Companies will have to market their own employment practices and adapt their jobs to the demands of the work force.

We all know that the way we did things in the past no longer works for many employees. Our research shows that up to 35% of working men and women with young children have told their bosses they will not take jobs involving shift work, relocation, extensive travel, intense pressure, or lots of overtime. Some parents are turning down promotions that they believe might put a strain on family life. Women report more trade-offs than men, but even the male numbers are significant and appear to be increasing. In our study, nearly 25% of men with young children had told their bosses they would not relocate.

Interestingly enough, few employees seem angry about such trade-offs. They value the rewards of family life, and, by and large, they don't seem to expect parity with those willing to sacrifice their family lives for their careers. Nevertheless, they *are* bothered by what they see as unnecessary barriers to success. Most believe they could make greater contributions and go farther in their own careers—despite family obligations—if it weren't for rigid scheduling, open-ended expectations, and outmoded career definitions. They long for alternative scenarios that would allow them more freedom to determine the conditions of their work and the criteria for judging their contributions.

The question is whether a willingness to sacrifice family life is an appropriate screen for picking candidates for promotions. It would be wrong to suppose that these employees are any less talented or less ambitious than those who don't make the family trade-off. A study we conducted at NCNB showed no evidence of any long-term difference in ambition between people with and without child-care responsibilities. Since fewer and fewer people in our diverse labor force are willing to pay the price for traditional success, to insist on it is only to narrow the funnel of opportunity and, eventually, to lower the quality of the talent pool from which we draw our leaders.

Flexible Schedules. In addition to time away from work to care for newborn or newly adopted children, employees with dependent-care responsibilities have two different needs for flexibility. One is the need for working hours that accommodate their children's normal schedules and their predictable special requirements such as doctor's appointments, school conferences, and soccer championships. The other is the need to deal with the emergencies and unanticipated events that are part and parcel of family life—sudden illness, an early school closing due to snow, a breakdown in child-care arrangements.

The most common response to both needs has been flextime. Flextime can be narrowly designed to permit permanent alterations of a basically rigid work schedule by, say, half an hour or an hour, or it can be more broadly defined to allow freewheeling variations from one workday to the next.

Pioneered in this country by Hewlett-Packard, flextime is now used by about 12% of all U.S. workers, while half the country's large employers offer some kind of flextime arrangement. Its effects on lateness, absenteeism, and employee morale have been highly positive.[7] The effects on the family are not as easily measured, but most employees say they find it helpful, and the more scheduling latitude it offers, the more helpful they seem to find it.

A number of companies are considering ways of further expanding the notion of flextime. One alternative, called "weekly balancing," lets employees set their own hours day-to-day as long as the weekly total stays constant. In Europe, some companies offer monthly and yearly balancing. Clearly, this is most difficult to do in situations where production processes require a predictable level of staffing.

In November 1988, Eastman Kodak announced a new work-schedule program that permits four kinds of alternative work arrangements:

1. Permanent changes in regular, scheduled hours.
2. Supervisory flexibility in adjusting daily schedules to accommodate family needs.
3. Temporary and permanent part-time schedules at all levels.
4. Job sharing.

Aetna Life and Casualty too has recently launched an internal marketing effort and training program to help its supervisors adapt to, plan for, and implement unconventional work schedules.

Employees also must assume new roles. In the job-sharing program at Rolscreen Company, for example, employees are responsible for locating compatible partners for a shared job and for ensuring that the arrangement works and that business needs are met.[8] Also, employees are often expected to make themselves available when business emergencies arise. In the best flexible arrangements, employers and employees work as partners.

Part-Time Employment. Studies show that a third to half of women with young children want to work less than full-time for at least a while, despite the loss of pay and other benefits. Yet we have found in our work with dozens of companies that managers at all levels show firm resistance to part-time work. They seem to regard the 40-hour week as sacred and cannot imagine that anyone working fewer hours could be doing anything useful. Even in companies that accept the need for part-time work, we see managers who refuse to believe it will work in their own departments. Indeed, even the term "part-time" seems to have a negative connotation.

Research on part-time productivity is sometimes hard to interpret, but the studies we've seen indicate that the productivity of part-time workers is, in certain cases, better than their full-time counterparts and, in all cases, no worse. One study comparing part-time and full-time social workers found that, hour for hour, the part-time employees carried greater caseloads and serviced them with more attention.[9]

Part-time is not necessarily the same as half-time, as many managers assume. Many parents want 4-day or 30-hour workweeks. Many other assumptions about less than full-time employment are also unwarranted. For example, managers often insist that customers will not work with part-time employees, but few have asked their customers if this is true.

Another axiom is that supervisory and managerial personnel must always be full-time, since it is a manager's role "to be there" for subordinates. This article of faith ignores the fact that managers travel, attend meetings, close their doors, and are otherwise unavailable for a good part of every week.

Career-Path Alternatives. It takes a lot of ingenuity and cultural adaptability to devise meaningful part-time work opportunities and to give employees individual control of their working hours. But an even greater challenge is to find ways of fitting these flexible arrangements into long-term career paths. If the price of family responsibility is a label that reads "Not Serious About Career," frustrations will grow. But if adaptability and labor-market competitiveness are the goals, then the usual definition of fast-track career progression needs modification.

The first step, perhaps, is to find ways of acquiring broad business experience that are less disruptive to the family. For example, Mobil Oil has gradually concentrated a wide range of facilities at hub locations, partly in order to allow its employees a greater variety of work experience without relocation.

Another essential step is to reduce the tendency to judge productivity by time spent at work. Nothing is more frustrating to parents than working intensely all day in order to pick up a child on time, only to be judged inferior to a coworker who has to stay late to produce as much. For many hardworking people, hours certainly do translate into increased productivity. Not for all. And dismissing those who spend fewer hours at the workplace as lacking dedication ignores the fact that virtually all employees go through periods when their working hours and efficiency rise or fall, whether the cause is family, health, or fluctuating motivation.

Corporate Mission

Fertility in the United States is below replacement levels. Moreover, the higher a woman's education level, the more likely she is to be employed and the less likely to have children. The choice to have a family is complex, yet one study shows that two-thirds of women under 40 who have reached the upper echelons in our largest companies and institutions are childless, while virtually all men in leadership positions are fathers.[10] If we fail to alter the messages and opportunities we offer young men and women, and if they learn to see a demanding work life as incompatible with a satisfying family life, we could create an economy in which more and more leaders have traded family for career success.

There are four things a company needs to do in order to create an environment where people with dependents can do their best work without sacrificing their families' welfare. It needs to develop a corporate policy that it communicates to all its employees; it needs to train and encourage supervisors to be adaptable and responsible; it needs to give supervisors tools and programs to work with; and it needs to hold all managers accountable for the flexibility and responsiveness of their departments.

The key people in all this are first-line managers and supervisors. All the policies and programs in the world don't mean much to an employee who has to deal with an unsupportive boss, and the boss is often unsupportive because of mixed signals from above.

We have seen companies where the CEO went on record in support of family flexibility but where supervisors were never evaluated in any way for their sensitivity to family issues. In one company, managers were encouraged to provide part-time work opportunities, yet headcount restrictions reckoned all employees as full-time. In another, maternity leave was counted against individual managers when measuring absenteeism, a key element in their performance appraisals. As a general rule, strict absenteeism systems designed to discourage malingerers often inadvertently punish the parents of young children. Yet such systems coexist with corporate admonitions to be flexible. Where messages are mixed and performance measurement has not changed since the days of the "give an inch, they'll take a mile" personnel policy, it is hardly surprising that supervisors and managers greet lofty family-oriented policy statements with some cynicism.

Training is critical. IBM, Johnson & Johnson, Merck, and Warner-Lambert have all established training programs to teach managers to be more sensitive to work-and-family issues. The training lays out the business case for flexibility, reviews corporate programs and policies, and presents case studies that underline the fact that there are often no right answers or rule books to use as guides in the complicated circumstances of real life.

Perhaps the thorniest issue facing businesses and managers is that of equity. Most managers have been trained to treat employees identically and not to adjudicate the comparative merits of different requests for flexibility. But what equity often means in practice is treating everyone as though they had wives at home. On the other hand, it is difficult to set up guidelines for personalized responses, since equity is a touchstone of labor relations and human resource management. Judging requests individually, on the basis of business and personal need, is not likely to lead to identical outcomes.

Seniority systems also need rethinking. Working second or third shift is often the only entry to a well-paying job for nonprofessional employees, but for a parent with a school-age child, this can mean not seeing the child at all from weekend to weekend. Rotating shifts wreak havoc with child-care arrangements and children's schedules. Practices that worked fine when the labor force consisted mostly of men with wives at home now have unintended consequences.

Finally, the message top management sends to all employees is terribly important. In focus groups at various large companies, we hear over and over again a sense that companies pay lip service to the value of family and community but that day-to-day practice is another story altogether. We hear what we can only describe as a yearning for some tangible acknowledgment from top management that family issues are real, complex, and important.

Johnson & Johnson, which sees its 40-year-old corporate credo as central to its culture, recently added the statement, "We must be mindful of ways to help our employees fulfill their family obligations." DuPont has developed a mission statement that commits it, in part, to "making changes in the workplace and fostering changes in the community that are sensitive to the changing family unit and the increasingly diverse work force."

Throughout Europe, governments have required companies to treat the parenting of babies as a special circumstance of employment and have invested heavily in programs to support the children of working parents. In this country, recent surveys indicate almost universal popular support for parental leave. But our instincts oppose government intervention into internal business practices. We leave decisions about flexibility and the organization of work to individual companies, which means that the decisions of first-line managers in large part create our national family policy.

In this, the United States is unique. But then we are also unique in other ways, including the depth of our commitment to business, to fairness, to equal opportunity, to common sense. Many of our young women now strive to become CEOs. No one intended that the price for business success should be indifference to family or that the price of having a family should be to abandon professional ambition.

Notes

1. Joseph Pleck, "Family-Supportive Employer Policies and Men's Participation," unpublished paper, Wheaton College, 1989.

2. From research conducted by Ellen Galinsky at Merck and Company, Rahway, New Jersey, 1983, 1984, and 1986.

3. Terry Bond, *Employer Supports for Child Care*, report for the National Council of Jewish Women, Center for the Child, New York, August 1988.

4. Marcy Whitebook, Carollee Howes, and Deborah Phillips, "Who Cares: Child Care Teachers and the Quality of Care in America," National Child Care Staffing Study, Child Care Employee Project, Oakland, California, 1989.

5. "On-site Child Care Results in Low Turnover at Computer Firm," *National Report on Work and Family*, vol. 2, no. 13 (Washington, D.C.: Buraff Publications, June 9, 1989), p. 3.

6. Dianne Burden and Bradley Googins, *Boston University Balancing Job and Homelife Study* (Boston University School of Social Work, 1986).

7. Kathleen Christensen, *A Look at Flexible Staffing and Scheduling in U.S. Corporations* (New York: Conference Board, 1989); and Jon L. Pierce

et al., *Alternative Work Schedules* (Newton, Mass.: Allyn and Bacon, 1988).

8. *Work and Family: A Changing Dynamic* (Washington, D.C.: Bureau of National Affairs Special Report, 1986), pp. 78–80.

9. *Part-Time Social Workers in Public Welfare* (New York: Catalyst, 1971), cited in *Alternative Work Schedules*, p. 81.

10. *The Corporate Woman Officer* (Chicago, Ill.: Heidrick and Struggles, Inc., 1986); *Korn/Ferry International's Executive Profile: Corporate Leaders in the Eighties* (New York: Korn/Ferry International, 1986).

3
How Technology Brings Blind People into the Workplace

Julia Anderson

In these days of low unemployment, many corporate and other organizations find it necessary to track the whereabouts and profiles of underused sectors of the labor pool. One sector seldom tapped by business has an unemployment rate as high as 70%—even though the advent of new data-processing technology has opened a window of opportunity for the group. What's more, people in this sector who do find employment historically have had a lower than average turnover rate.

They are the thousands of sightless or visually impaired people who possess desirable skills but who have difficulty finding work, or at least work commensurate with their skills. Many of them have received training as computer programmers, but there are quite a few other functions where blind persons have worked effectively, including customer service and repair service representatives, staff writers, quality control inspectors, receptionists, and curriculum specialists.

The advent of the microchip has been a boon for people with vision loss. Information encoded as a magnetic signal in a computer can be variously decoded into speech (through a speech synthesizer), braille (through a hard-copy printer or a refreshable cassette tape), or enlarged print visible on the computer monitor. Other recently developed aids include a computerized tape recorder that enables the user to speed-read by ear and a talking calculator.

The result has been a virtual explosion of opportunity for independent reading and writing by people who cannot use print. No longer do they have to depend on someone else's eyes to translate printed information. This technology revolution has forced corporations to rethink notions of the physical limitations on job performance in information processing.

Let's look in on a job interview held by several skeptical telephone company division managers. The applicant, Russell, blind since the age of two, had had five years of experience as a customer service representative with a government agency before attending a computer programming school. Russell demonstrated a device attached to a computer that allows the information on the screen to be read in braille on a tactual display. While he talked about his research in adaptive devices, he wrote a program to perform a simple data sort and then inputted the names of his interviewers. As the screen displayed the sorted material, Russell read it aloud by means of the attached display.

Intrigued, the managers showered him with questions about debugging programs and the comparative versatility of braille and speech in accessing visually presented information. He answered them readily while he broke down the equipment and packed it up. As he left, Russell offered to show them "a piece of the most impressive technology ever developed," and in one motion he snapped his folded cane into extension.

Earlier, several of the managers had expressed reservations about bringing a blind person into the department. "What if there were a fire?" one asked. "How would he find his way to the restroom?" another wanted to know. But their interview with Russell convinced them that he would be an asset, so they offered him the job.

Gambling with the Unknown

One employment roadblock for the visually impaired job seeker is the view most sighted people hold about a blind person's dependence and passivity in the world. From this stereotype, it's a short step to the assumption that a fast-paced corporation is no place for a person without sight. It takes exposure to a person like Russell to explode these misconceptions; on the strength of his personality and his talent, he was able to put his listeners at ease.

To many managers, hiring a sight-impaired person is taking a big chance. An executive once said to me: "The main risk on my mind was that I might have to let her go. I figured this person had suffered enough in her lifetime, and now, what if she really can't perform? I don't think we would have fired her, but we would have found her a different job."

For three years in the mid-1980s, I coordinated the Perkins Project with Industry, a federally financed project to expand job opportunities in New England for people with visual disabilities. Together with our colleagues at the Massachusetts Commission for the Blind, we encouraged our corporate clients to expect the same quantity and quality of work from visually impaired employees as they would from sighted employees, and to supervise them accordingly.

The results of our placement efforts were various: some blind employees learned their jobs and stayed on; some moved up; others quit to return to school; some got laid off or never mastered their jobs and were terminated. The same happened to their sighted peers. But certainly, most of the people we helped are either still holding their initial jobs or have advanced to better positions in the same or different organizations.

It was crucial for the employers with whom we dealt to find out the reality of a blind person's independence, which belies the misperception of dependence. When someone who is sighted observes how a person with vision loss manages in the world, and manages differently from a sighted person when necessary, the demystification of the disability begins. At that point, the sighted person starts looking past the disability to see the person behind it.

The feeling that blind people are somehow different—as though in experiencing the world differently, they are living in a different world—is often responsible for the rejection of a candidate early in the job application process. The manager's question, "Will I be comfortable working with this person?" is a legitimate question, often answered negatively because of a lack of information and familiarity.

Few of us can view calmly the prospect of spending time with someone we perceive as being very different from ourselves, for we fear not knowing what to do. In not knowing what to do, we risk appearing foolish. The Project with Industry aimed to give employers the information they needed to become more comfortable, especially information about the disability and about the types of job adaptations in place around the country.

Time after time, we observed that once a manager had decided to make the move and incorporate a blind person into his or her work group, the climate there became a very positive one for the new employee. The failures were always due to factors other than vision limitations, factors that can disrupt any employer-worker relationship. Yet even in those cases, the work group often felt a strong desire to recruit another visually impaired or blind person. They had an investment in the cause.

Even so, the problem of social isolation in the work setting has to be dealt with. A month after hiring a blind individual, an executive described the social situation this way: "It's easy for a sighted person to go visit somebody in the next department. But Sharon can't do that. A sighted person can see that someone's busy and decide not to interrupt. So Sharon, as a result, just stays in her office. It's up to everyone else to come by and say, 'How are you doing?' And most of them won't because they feel embarrassed. Nobody asks her to go to lunch because that takes a little bit of effort: you've got to be able to guide her. It's very uncomfortable for somebody who isn't prepared for it, unless you're a strong personality."

This executive arranged for his group to participate in a workshop that featured role playing and discussion of the facts and misconceptions about blindness. Back in the workplace, the manager noticed that employees seemed to feel more at ease with Sharon, and she was less shy with them.

He also devoted some thought to how he could communicate with his subordinates in a way that would not exclude the worker with limited sight. He learned to use the office's electronic mail system instead of relying on handwritten or typed memos, and he encouraged everyone in the office to do the same. The result was clearer communication for the entire department. His supervision of the staff improved, he was convinced.

Corporate Initiative

In this age of 6% unemployment, organizations looking for talent may have to do some creative recruiting. Individuals with little or no eyesight can be prime candidates for those recruiting efforts.

The first step should be an analysis of the problem from a logistical standpoint. What are the visual requirements of the jobs available? Can any reading demanded in the job be done with a computer screen? Other factors include the layout of the building, the frequency of disruptive environmental changes, and the expectation of field travel or out-of-the-office meetings. None of these factors precludes consideration of a blind person, but it's important to discuss all these job components with the candidate.

Every job deserves to be considered with a particular person in mind, partly because it's essential to understand the applicant's visual capacities. Most legally blind individuals have enough functional vision to use large or regular print. The applicant will probably have a reading preference among the options of regular or large print, braille, or a personal reader. It is also important to determine whether the applicant gets eyestrain when reading from a computer screen.

The rehabilitation agency for the blind in any state, often called the Vocational Rehabilitation Commission, has specialists who help organizations in recruiting and in adapting jobs to the needs of candidates. Such agencies in many states lend adaptive devices to blind people to use on the job.

Rehabilitation specialists can help an employer investigate appropriate devices and can advise him or her on applications for tax advantages connected with purchases of this equipment. Another resource is the local Project with Industry, from which businesses can get help through networking activity.

In some states, rehabilitation agencies have built excellent communication networks with private-sector employers, and both benefit. In other states, rapport has not been established, and differences in vocabularies and technological expertise present obstacles. There are enough successful collaborations, however, to serve as models for any corporation interested in pursuing this idea.

When initiative from employers is backed with expertise from the public organizations specializing in help for visually impaired job seekers, this resource can be better exploited for the benefit of both employer and worker.

PART

VI

Managers Wrestle with the Issues

1

The Case of the Unequal Opportunity

Mary C. Gentile

Laura Wollen, group marketing director for ARPCO, Inc., a manufacturer of small electrical tools and appliances, telephoned London
from her Columbus, Ohio office. She was getting ready to recommend
her best product manager, Charles Lewis, for a position in the London
office, a job that would give Lewis the international exposure he
would need to progress toward senior management. She and David
Abbott, her counterpart in the United Kingdom, had had several conversations about Lewis's candidacy, and Abbott had seemed impressed.
Wollen simply wanted to touch base with him before making her
recommendation formal.

Only two candidates were serious contenders for the U.K. product
manager job: Frank Billings and Charles Lewis. Billings had joined
ARPCO the previous year as a product manager for the housewares
division. Before that, he had been a sales representative for one of
ARPCO's main competitors. Wollen knew Billings fairly well because
he had reported to her for several months on a special project. She
found him to be intelligent and hardworking.

Yet she believed that Lewis, who had reported to her for three years,
had the same innate talents but was better prepared for the job and
possessed a creative spark that Billings did not. With a bachelor's
degree in business administration and two years of experience selling
financial services, Lewis had joined ARPCO as a sales rep in the
Midwest. He immediately proved himself a winner. Marketing often
recruited high fliers from the sales force, so Lewis was soon offered a
job as product manager for power saws.

Within a year, Lewis had such command of his product management job that Wollen asked him to head the introduction of a charging system for ARPCO's new line of cordless power tools. The assignment required more than the usual amount of interdependence and collaboration, but Lewis worked carefully and cautiously to develop the relationships that he needed. The product introduction was a smashing success.

Now the company wanted to launch the charging system along with several cordless power tools in the United Kingdom. It was ARPCO's first entry into the British home workshop market. Its success was important because the company saw the do-it-yourself home maintenance market as a way to compensate for stagnant sales in the housewares division. The company also wanted to maintain visibility in the U.K. while waiting for the economy to recover and for the opportunities that 1992 would bring.

Jobs outside the United States were highly sought after at ARPCO, and only the high performers made the cut. When an opening occurred, marketing directors reviewed their product managers and selected the appropriate candidates. They then discussed the candidates informally with the director who was doing the hiring, and each could recommend one candidate to his or her divisional vice president. The vice presidents typically reviewed the recommendations and passed them on unchanged to the director in the host country. ARPCO encouraged managers to recommend their best people; it rewarded managers for the number of people they put on the fast track and for the performance of those fast trackers in their first six months on the job.

To Wollen's mind, Lewis was a natural for the job. Although she hated to lose him, she was glad he would have the opportunity to demonstrate his ability in such a visible position, and she was eager to play a role in his professional development. But her friendly conversation with Abbott suddenly took an unexpected turn as she learned that Abbott no longer shared her enthusiasm for Lewis.

"You're the group marketing director, Laura, so I can't tell you who to recommend for the position, but I'll go on record as preferring Billings to Lewis." Abbott's British enunciation had an insistent edge.

"That really surprises me," she responded. "I know Billings is bright and motivated and all of that, but his experience is in housewares, just as yours is. Lewis, on the other hand, has three years in the home workshop division. His experience can get the launch off to a good start, and I know how important that is to you."

"You're right, I do have a lot riding on this launch, and it will require a lot of coordination. That's why I'm trying to pull together a team of professionals who can work together in the British environment. I need people who are comfortable with our sales force, our research and support staff, and our buyers. When Billings was here on temporary assignment last fall, he demonstrated that ability. I'm sure he can learn the product line."

"But let's face it," Wollen said. "That assignment was a three-month fill-in in housewares and didn't include any client contact. Besides, Billings has been on line as a product manager for only eleven months. Compared with Lewis, he's less mature, less creative—"

"If you insist on recommending Lewis, fine, I won't refuse the hire," Abbott said crossly. "But I need someone who can work comfortably and constructively with the team I've put together, not some individual contributor whose main concern is the next rung on the career ladder."

Wollen hesitated, then trusting her instincts, said, "We're not really talking about the same thing here, are we David? This isn't about market knowledge or ego. It's about race. You're concerned because Lewis is black, aren't you?"

"You didn't even mention it in our earlier conversations! If one of my managers hadn't mentioned it, I wouldn't have known until he walked in the door for the interview two weeks from now."

"Does it matter? Is it relevant here?" Wollen asked.

"The only thing that matters is that my new product manager is able to work well with the other managers and that he—or she—is able to adjust to the culture. Other managers like Lewis have been uncomfortable here, and we can't afford to botch this introduction. It's the key to our presence in the whole market."

"Look, David," Wollen reasoned, "in the three years Lewis has worked for me, he's had to work with all kinds of coworkers and customers, and they all had their own concerns and assumptions about him. But he managed to build productive relationships despite all those things. If you think he's too sensitive or inflexible, I can point to—"

"Don't misunderstand me, Laura. Lewis looks very good on paper. I'm certain he's very talented and will go far with ARPCO. I just don't believe that he is the most appropriate candidate for this position at this time. And when a manager doesn't last, everyone suffers from the loss of continuity. It will set the product line back months. Our group can recover from that kind of setback, but what about you? A failed recommendation will become part of your record. And just think what it will do to Lewis's career."

Wollen winced. "What would have happened to my career if Ralph Jordan hadn't been willing to take a chance by putting a woman product manager in the home workshop division for the first time? That's all I'm asking of you, that you give Lewis the chance to show what he can do."

"Perhaps this one is a bit too close to home, Laura. Are you sure this isn't just a personal issue?"

Wollen regretted giving Abbott that opening and closed the conversation coolly: "I'll think about what you've said and submit my recommendation by the end of the day."

Wollen hung up the phone and dashed from her office up to the eighth floor conference room for a meeting with the rest of the home workshop marketing directors and Ralph Jordan, their divisional vice president. Much as she tried to shift gears and focus on their planning agenda, she kept thinking about Abbott's question, "Are you sure this isn't a personal issue?"

Wollen had been with ARPCO for nine years, and although she knew the company had its problems, she was proud of it. It was known for making high-quality tools and appliances and for being a responsible employer. The company was full of bright, dedicated people, many of whom had been with ARPCO for more than 20 years. But sitting across the table from Jordan, she found herself thinking about the time five years earlier when she nearly left in disillusionment and defeat. It was Jordan who convinced her to stay.

Having joined ARPCO fresh from her MBA program, Wollen came ready to make her mark on the organization. She was particularly interested in the relatively new home workshop division. Her father was a carpenter, and she had spent many evenings and weekends watching and helping him. She loved that time working quietly beside her father and was proud of the skills he had taught her. She saw the home workshop division as the perfect place for her to combine her talents and interests.

In interviews with the ARPCO recruiters, she had stated her interest in the home workshop division, but they urged her to take a position with housewares. They assured her that if she did well, she could circulate into another area. That began a four-year stint with food processors, vacuum cleaners, and electric knives. Wollen improved the performance of every product she managed, and every time she learned of an opening in the home workshop division, she notified her supervisor of her interest. She was consistently passed over. Finally, after being overlooked yet again, she was ready to leave. Before she did, she made a last-ditch effort by going over her director's head to Ralph Jordan, who was then the divisional vice president of housewares.

Jordan knew Wollen's record, and after listening to her story, he looked into the situation. Six days later, he told her she had an interview for product manager of ARPCO's power drills if she wanted it. She still remembered much of what he had said to her that afternoon: "Laura, you have an outstanding record in housewares, and you deserve to be circulated among other divisions and regions. You have great potential to do well here, both for yourself and for the company. And I'm committed to developing talent whenever I find it.

"But I want you to listen to what I say to you now. Home workshop has never had a woman product manager before, partly because of a lack of interest on the part of our women product managers and also because of a lack of imagination on the part of our marketing directors. At any rate, you'll be working with managers and customer reps who will find you an anomaly. You're taking a risk by leaving housewares. But if you succeed, you will be opening a whole new set of doors for yourself.

"I can't guarantee that you'll succeed. I can't even guarantee you a level playing field. But I can promise you that I will do everything in my power to provide you with the backing you deserve. I will give you the support and authority you merit, just as I would for any talented manager. I believe that the truest test of a manager is his or her ability to develop good people. That's where I prove my stuff. If you make it, I'll feel I've done my job well."

Wollen interviewed for the position, and when it was offered to her, she promptly accepted.

In a way, Wollen did have a personal stake in Lewis's situation. She had embraced Jordan's philosophy of developing talent. When Lewis first went to work for her, Wollen had reflected on the fact that he was the only black manager in her group and one of very few in the division. She was aware that he was not as well knit into the social fabric of the group as other managers hired around the same time. Although Lewis got along with his colleagues professionally, he didn't socialize with them and their families, except for formal ARPCO events.

When the opening arose for a product manager to introduce the charging system for ARPCO's new line of cordless power tools, Wollen had some concern that Lewis's outsider status would cause problems for the project if it meant that he couldn't work himself into the information loop with the other product managers. On the other hand, the social distance could give him a balanced perspective, free of personal loyalties that might complicate the task. Finally, she thought the charging system assignment might be just what Lewis needed to work his way into the product managers' informal network.

The posting provided the opportunity for Lewis and Wollen to begin to develop a close mentoring relationship. Wollen was frank with Lewis, and she made a point of checking in frequently with him during the first few months of his new assignment. This support was an important signal to Lewis and to the other product managers as well. They were made aware of how important the collaborative project was to the entire group. And in fact, this cordless segment of the power tools market had been growing at a rate five times that of the rest of the group over the past two years.

At about the same time Wollen had begun to look around for an international assignment for Lewis, she learned of ARPCO's plan to enter the British home workshop market with the cordless line. The timing and fit seemed perfect.

Back in her office after a difficult lunch discussing cuts in the research budget, Wollen tried to prepare for a 1:30 meeting with Charles Lewis. Lewis had requested the meeting hastily, which meant one thing: he wanted to get to Wollen before she submitted her recommendation. The two of them had discussed the position at great length when it first opened, and initially Lewis was excited but concerned— excited about the implications of such an assignment, concerned about the impact on his family. After many long conversations with his wife, who had just rejoined her law practice after a year-long maternity leave, Lewis had told Wollen that he was willing to make the one-and-a-half to two-year commitment. The concern had vanished, and then it was pure excitement.

As Lewis entered the office, Wollen could see that the concern was back.

"Thanks for seeing me on such short notice," Lewis started. "It's about the U.K. position, of course. I know you haven't promised me anything. . . ."

"But I told you you're high on the list. Go on."

"It's just that I've heard rumors from some of the guys over in housewares, and I don't know how much credence to give them."

"What exactly did you hear?" Wollen asked.

"Vague comments, really. When they found out I was being considered for the London slot, they shook their heads and said things like 'I hear it's real conservative over there' and 'Don't expect a lot of warmth.' I thought they were jealous. But then they got more explicit. They told me about a product manager who was assigned there—a black manager. He found the environment very difficult."

"You know we can't promise that all your client contact will be smooth sailing," Wollen said. "You deal with that all the time, and you've always been able to establish your credibility firmly and quietly."

"But that's just it," Lewis replied. "With this other manager, the customers weren't the problem, or not the only one. It was the other managers and even the supervisor, David Abbott. I know I can deal with difficult clients, but I've always counted on my boss's—on your—support. I've got to know there's some authority behind me. I'll need David Abbott's support."

Wollen hoped Lewis couldn't read her face. She knew Lewis was right about needing Abbott's support, and she was undecided about how to handle Abbott's message from the morning's call. She was also concerned about putting ARPCO in legal jeopardy. International assignments were still an evolving area in antidiscrimination law.

Wollen didn't know how much candor she could afford, so she proceeded cautiously. "You know, Charles, when U.S. companies send expatriate managers overseas, there are bound to be obstacles. Sometimes people are outright hostile, if only because they think you're taking opportunities away from them. When you—"

"That's not what I'm talking about," Lewis interrupted. He sat silent for a long, uncomfortable moment, then said, "I've given this opportunity a great deal of thought. My wife and I have considered the pros and cons for both of our careers, for our marriage, and for our daughter. We don't expect it to be easy, but we're ready to face the challenge."

"I'm not asking for any guarantees of success," Lewis continued. "But I am asking you to consider whether or not you think I truly have a shot in this slot. If you don't, then don't recommend me. I'll trust your judgment. Maybe I don't have the right to ask that of you, but you know more about the situation than I do, and I don't see that I have a choice."

Lewis and Wollen ended the meeting with a solemn handshake. Wollen's forced smile faded when Lewis closed the door behind him.

Earlier in the day, Wollen thought nothing could dissuade her from recommending Lewis. Now she sat at her desk poring through the personnel files looking for a reason to change her mind.

The company policies were clear: "promote the most qualified person, regardless of race, gender, or ethnic background" and "capitalize on the considerable investment ARPCO makes in its people by applying their skills in ways that will maximize benefit to the company and the individual." In Wollen's opinion, Lewis was the most qualified, and making him product manager in Britain would leverage his training and experience in the United States. She also wondered how long he would remain at ARPCO if he didn't get this opportunity. Lewis knew international circulation was critical to his career there.

The criteria used to evaluate her performance were also clear. Her vice president would consider the number of product managers she placed on the circulation track and how those managers performed in the first six months of their new assignments. Lewis was her best— virtually her only—shot.

But policies and her own career aside, there were other considerations, such as the realities of the London office and Lewis himself. Abbott was convinced that Lewis wouldn't work out, and Wollen knew that expectations beget reality. Abbott wouldn't have to thwart Lewis. If he believed that efforts to help Lewis would only postpone the inevitable, his passivity alone could do the trick.

Wollen wondered if she should go ahead and recommend Lewis and let him decide for himself whether to accept the position. Of course, if he refused such a competitive appointment, he would be knocked out of the running for some time.

Then she pondered how much support she could provide from a distance. Maybe she could talk to Jordan and enlist his help. But pronouncements from the top wouldn't necessarily improve the situation for Lewis. Real change usually came slowly.

If the lack of support got in the way of Lewis's performance, he was likely to leave the company. His departure would be a permanent loss of talent for ARPCO. And then there was the impact on Lewis himself. Wollen hated the thought of seeing a man with so much promise fail in a job he was basically well prepared to do. And while it would be painful for Wollen if Lewis didn't succeed, it would of course be all the more painful for Lewis and his family.

She had to assess Lewis's real chances for success and decide which candidate to recommend.

Should Wollen Send Lewis to England?

Four experts on international management discuss the dilemma.

JIM KAISER

On the skills side, this decision is a no-brainer. Lewis is the most qualified candidate; he deserves the assignment. His experience gives him the clear advantage, and company policy allows no alternative but "to promote the most qualified person, regardless of race, gender, or ethnic background." Wollen's challenge then is not assigning Lewis but making that assignment work by sorting out all biases and creating expectations for his success.

My international experience in countries such as Japan and France has reinforced my belief that race should not be a significant factor in decisions like this. Business skills should. Lewis should not have to worry about being black. I don't. In meetings, I think of myself and my business skills first and foremost; anyone who thinks of me primarily as being black is carrying that burden for me.

Along those lines, the most difficult cultural fit has to do with nationality rather than race. Though there are mitigating factors in this instance, Lewis's American identity is the toughest challenge he will encounter in any overseas assignment. When I was a senior executive in France, my biggest challenge was that I wasn't French. I was perceived as a temporary American manager from headquarters. I therefore spent as much time as possible learning about French culture and spent 18 months in intensive French language courses. I also made efforts to work through local channels, formally and informally, and made every effort to represent the French position, balancing it with global positions.

I learned that the best way for any foreigner to gain the credibility of local employees is to build relationships. That means adopting such simple and immediate practices as coaching those who need it, asking for help from those who can give it, and paying attention to informal matters like hanging out at the water fountain. For me, it meant having frank conversations with managers over what my appointment meant, especially when I became their superior.

The fact is, cultural biases must be identified clearly and then put in a proper perspective. Sometimes, managers can even use the misperceptions of others to their advantage. When I am in Japan, I am more able to play the part of the American and ask extremely direct questions because it is expected of an American.

Lewis, then, must seek a work environment where his skills are valued and where biases are put in their place. For his success, Wollen must directly challenge biases and create coaches, thereby allowing Lewis's business skills to become the criteria on which he is judged. There are several steps she can take to make this happen.

First of all, Wollen should solicit Jordan's support and mentorship for the position, telling him about the comments and implied threats Abbott has made to her. In her argument, she should stress company policy and the fact that Lewis is the most skilled candidate, and she should make the promotion conditional on Abbott's support. To back this up, she and Jordan could work the grapevine by phoning key colleagues to let them know what a great manager Lewis would make.

I would recommend that Lewis declare to all parties that he wants this position despite the rumors of a "cold welcome." He has already told Wollen he wants to go as long as he can get the support; he should behave as if he will receive it. He thus avoids turning down an attractive promotion because he is afraid of a tough assignment. This also forces Abbott to say where he stands on this issue and eliminates his ability to use Lewis's reluctance as an excuse for favoring Billings.

To make sure that all hidden agendas finally surface, Wollen should meet with Jordan and Abbott to discuss the recommended candidate, address any biases at play, and set expectations for Abbott concerning the project and the policy. It is important that Abbott be given a chance to declare his concerns and have the group address them. This allows everyone to share Abbott's risk, and by making explicit the source of his concern, sets the stage for actions to address it.

Once Wollen makes the decision to send Lewis, the management team can prepare him for success. First of all, Wollen and Jordan should create appropriate mentors. Lewis's most important contact will be Abbott: he should be able to look to Abbott for help on how to fit into the culture and team. Wollen and Jordan could also look for a "channel two"—somebody like Wollen who checks in periodically to see how Lewis is doing in his new position. He should also try to use the local human resource manager as an ombudsman.

As a final though vital step in this process, Wollen, Abbott, and Lewis need to develop a success plan for Lewis that establishes clearly defined criteria for success—both what and how. This plan should pay strict attention both to what is expected and how it should be done. Some candidates who are not groomed to succeed may pass the "what" side of a performance appraisal but then they get nailed on the "how." By defining clear objectives in this situation, the entire team gives Lewis a real chance to succeed.

JEFFALYN JOHNSON

Few African-Americans who climb the corporate ladder escape a dilemma like Charles Lewis's. David Abbott's resistance to Lewis is common, as is Laura Wollen's vacillation between recommending Lewis and protecting him from potential failure in the face of prejudice.

I base this conclusion on a study of African-American executives I recently conducted for the Executive Leadership Council. The participants in the study are successful: they have titles like president, vice president, general manager, and director, and more than 70% of them are employed by major industrial companies. But throughout their careers, they have faced barriers of several kinds—paternalistic attitudes, misconceptions about their acceptance overseas, and the use of "soft" evaluation criteria—that are rooted in false assumptions about the resistance they would meet, their abilities to build relationships, and their willingness to rise to stiff challenges.

Most of these executives said they had been denied an opportunity for promotion, even when they were the most qualified. The excuse managers often used for not recommending them was that they wanted to protect the candidate from the risk of failure. The reaction to such protectiveness was one of frustration and resentment. As one senior vice president in the study said: "Twice I have been blocked by paternalistic managers who made the decision not to recommend me for promotion because the hiring manager felt that I—or any person of another race or culture—would not fit in and would fail. I still resent a former boss denying me an opportunity because he felt he knew what was best for me. His responsibility was to make the decision based on my qualifications, not on the prejudices of my prospective boss. . . . I believe that any attempt to play father, mother, or God in an effort to protect an employee against risk and possible failure by denying opportunity when he or she is clearly the best qualified is not good management."

Qualified minorities are often denied opportunities overseas because managers assume that the other culture will resist them. Yet that assumption is often wrong. Many of the African-American executives have taken jobs in other countries despite vigorous warnings from their managers, and a number of them noted that the environment turned out to be less hostile than predicted. The fact that 48% of the executives have responsibility for international operations demonstrates that African-Americans can be and are successful in offices and markets throughout the world. The misperception about minorities' chances of succeeding overseas is particularly troubling because international experience has become an increasingly common prerequisite for advancement.

Another barrier for minorities arises when managers use subjective criteria to evaluate job candidates. Many managers favor candidates who appear to be like themselves. It makes them feel that they understand the person and can trust him or her. They often use words like *comfort, fit,* and *team* to express that desire. In discussing Lewis's suitability for the job in the London office, for instance, Abbott talks about comfort, fit, and teamwork. Those are code words for the "in group," the "club," or the "old boys' network."

Concern about teamwork is, of course, legitimate, but personal prejudice can often cause managers to underestimate the interpersonal skills of those who are "different." Abbott didn't consider Lewis's record of developing relationships with many kinds of people, including difficult clients. Ironically, Lewis probably developed his interpersonal skills in part *because* he is different. As many African-American managers stated, minorities often need those skills to survive in the corporate world. A number of them said that they had learned to rely on their interpersonal and collaborative skills to manage in nonsupportive or even racist environments. They said it was especially important for them to use collaboration to exert influence in order to avoid having the majority group label them as "pushy," "too aggressive," or "difficult to work with."

The tendency to use subjective criteria becomes more problematic at higher levels of an organization because all the contenders for the top jobs are high performers on objective measures. This may in part explain why African-Americans have been able to progress to certain levels in corporations—but no farther.

Getting back to the case, Wollen must make her decision based on facts rather than suppositions. Lewis has earned the right to an opportunity for advancement. He and only he must make the decision about whether to accept the risks.

BRIAN HARVEY

Laura Wollen faces an ethical dilemma on several levels. Personally, she faces a conflict between her desire to do the right thing for Charles Lewis and her own sense of immediate self-interest. Managerially, she must balance the risks of promoting Lewis with the potential good he could do both in the job and for ARPCO as a whole.

Wollen's choices in this extremely political situation run the spectrum from cowardice to heroism. The best we can expect from her is bravery, which would result in her leveling with Charles Lewis about her conversation with Abbott. Laying it on the line with Lewis—thus confirming the rumors he has heard—respects his right to be treated as an end in himself rather than a means to Wollen's and Abbott's success. She should then nominate Lewis only if he is willing.

There are real risks in selecting Lewis. If Wollen persists in recommending Lewis, her selection could backfire. Abbott's concerns about Lewis's fit could turn out to be valid: a hostile work environment could leave Lewis frustrated and deter him from a successful stint in the U.K. He has expressed a reluctance to go into a difficult environment, and his concern should be respected.

Additionally, by stepping outside of her role and pushing too hard for Lewis, Wollen could harm her career and others involved in this decision. She could generate resentment from Abbott and the entire U.K. team by seeming to ignore his opinion. If Abbott feels pushed around, he may take it out on Lewis. Also, the distance between Lewis and the United States prevents Wollen from being able to act as a mentor in the manner Jordan did with Wollen.

On a managerial level, sending Lewis could be a mistake for ARPCO's success in England if he does not work out. Wollen's decision would then have sacrificed both the success of an important new project and the career of a promising executive in order to salve her conscience. Lewis, whose career is important to ARPCO, could leave the company.

Corporate exigencies would thus dictate that she conform to what she recognizes as "the way things are done around here" and play the rational, battle-hardened manager. Faced with the decision of minimizing risk or following her moral sense of what is right, Wollen should opt for the bravest choice—of leveling with Lewis but going no farther. Ethical principles (that Lewis has a right to be treated as an end in himself and not as a means to her own success) call for her to:

1. Level with Lewis, and confirm the rumors he has heard (in the same way Jordan once did for her).
2. Write a case in support of Lewis, setting out all the factors she has considered. This leaves open the possibility of a response by her superiors.
3. Recommend Lewis only if he still voices an interest in the job.

Should she go even further and try to "manage" the relationship with Abbott herself—perhaps via Jordan? I think not. The most important thing she can do is reach some sort of consistency between her personal ethical standards and the demands of the management role. She cannot realistically go further still and put the strategic and ethical issues on ARPCO's policy agenda. That is the responsibility of the CEO, whose job it is to ensure that values are on the corporate agenda and that the company is not "running blind" on matters of corporate responsibility and managerial ethics.

NANCY J. ADLER

Myths—such as Abbott's belief that Lewis "won't be able to adjust to the culture" of the British position—still affect many managerial decisions today and keep companies from developing their human resources in the most productive manner. While women do not confront the identical issues of bias in the workplace that blacks do, my research on women reveals that many senior human resource managers who assign managers internationally fail to take advantage of their diverse work force because they allow false assumptions to take precedence over business reality. Wollen should take note.

Lewis is the most qualified candidate and deserves the job. He is intelligent, hardworking, creative, experienced, and has a track record of success. These skills lead one to believe that he would do an excellent job in the new position. In her recommendation, Wollen's job is to prevent the myth—that Lewis's ethnic background will hinder him as a manager—from interfering with his selection.

As one woman said, summarizing her experience as well as that of many other female expatriate managers, "The most difficult aspect of an international assignment is getting sent, not succeeding once sent." Three important findings from my research explain this situation. First, many managers mistakenly assume that there are so few female managers abroad because women don't want to go. Second, many managers rightly assume that companies refuse to send women abroad. The third prevailing assumption is that the "real" problem is foreign managers and clients who are so prejudiced that they will sabotage the women's assignments.

To test the first assumption, over 1,100 men and women were asked about their interest in global careers and international assignments. The results revealed "no significant difference": men and women are equally interested in working internationally, with the only difference being that both married men and married women are less interested in foreign assignments than are their unmarried colleagues.

Unfortunately, it is true that companies are hesitant to send women abroad; my survey of senior human resource managers in 60 large global companies revealed that 54% were hesitant. Although such an attitude is clearly illegal, three-quarters of the human resource managers supported it by citing the obstacles that they believe dual-career marriages pose and their belief that foreigners are too prejudiced to let women managers succeed.

While dual-career marriages clearly pose new dilemmas for companies that transfer employees both domestically and internationally, they do not pose greater challenges for women than for men.

To test the belief that foreigners would not let women succeed, I interviewed 100 female expatriate managers. The result was an overwhelming success story—in fact, only two reported less than full success. (In comparison, one-quarter of men's expatriate assignments are judged unsuccessful by their companies.) Why did they succeed? Because the assignments were high-risk, the company sent superbly qualified candidates: women with skills for success such as top graduate degrees, fast-track backgrounds, good interpersonal skills, and experience with other cultures. They also demonstrated the most important quality for success: a desire to go. Perhaps equally important, foreigners are not as prejudiced against expatriate business women as many executives had feared.

Lewis demonstrates these traits already. Beyond being the most qualified candidate and being highly enthusiastic about his position, he has proven his ability to succeed in an environment that has very few black professionals and is not free of racism—the United States. Additionally, given that the most common reason for a person's failure on an international assignment is dissatisfaction on the part of the spouse, Lewis's wife's enthusiasm bodes well for his success.

In planning for Lewis's success, ARPCO could learn from the experience of women expatriate managers, whose work abroad turned up several surprises: first, a "halo effect"—based on their being different— actually helps them. That is, the foreign executives and clients assumed that these women—who did not fit the typical image of white male expatriates—had to be especially qualified to have been sent and so expected them to do well. Moreover, locals reacted to female managers as foreigners first and foremost and then as women. Thus assumptions based on how people treat their own minorities and women are not a particularly good predictor of expatriate success.

Finally, Lewis and Wollen should not confuse naïveté with malice. In dealing with racism or sexism—both at home and abroad—it is important to remember that racists do not necessarily make bad business decisions. Some people may feel uncomfortable with Lewis socially, but that does not mean they will not buy ARPCO's products or work with him.

Note

At the time of this article's publication Jim Kaiser was senior vice president and general manager, Technical Productions Division and Latin America and Asia Pacific Exports at Corning Inc. Jeffalyn Johnson was assistant to the president for institutional planning and evaluation at the University of Northern Florida in Jacksonville. Brian Harvey was a reader in management studies at Nottingham University, Nottingham, England, and honorary secretary of the European Business Ethics Network. Nancy Adler was a professor of management at McGill University, Montreal.

2
A Case of AIDS

Richard S. Tedlow and Michele S. Marram

The Hiring Decision, 11-1-89

Greg van de Water leafed through the applications one more time. After weeks of interviewing, he had narrowed the field to two young men, both of them internal candidates seeking promotion to Greg's sales and customer service team.

Hiring, he believed, was the most important decision he made as team leader. Since taking over three years ago, he had hired four of the six team members, and he had chosen well. Now again he was faced with a choice that would affect team performance for better or worse. Subjective judgments about how people would work together, how they would feel about each other, how deeply they would buy into company values like openness, honesty, mutual respect, and support were just as important as the sales ability, communication skills, knowledge of the industry, energy, and enthusiasm that the job called for on paper. Greg also knew that teamwork and attitude produced results and that members of a sales team could easily become destructively competitive unless their commitment to each other was genuine.

The folder on top belonged to Peter Kroll. Peter had worked his way up through the company and understood its products and its product strategy. He was bright, eager, and came highly recommended. Greg was confident that he could handle the job and handle it well.

The second folder was Joe Collins. On paper, Joe and Peter looked much the same, but after meeting them both, Greg preferred Joe. On the minus side, Joe hadn't been with the company as long—only two years. On the plus side, Joe had worked well under the kind of group-compensation system Greg's sales team utilized. Moreover, Joe seemed to have more self-confidence than Peter. Joe also struck him as a better listener and a more sensitive person—important qualities in teamwork and communication. Finally, although neither had much sales experience, Joe somehow seemed a natural salesman.

So that was that—except for one thing. In the strictest confidence, Joe had revealed that he was HIV infected. Greg was not panicked by the news. He knew there was no danger of contagion from casual office contact, and he knew an HIV-positive person could live and work productively for years without developing an active case of AIDS. Moreover, the company guidelines stated clearly that "physical disabilities and chronic health conditions" were not to be considered in hiring and promotion decisions unless they interfered directly with performance.

But was it really that simple? Joe had shown no symptoms yet, but Greg was worried about hiring him and then having his health deteriorate. How could Joe work up to speed if he was recovering from a bout of pneumonia? Wasn't there at least a chance that the pace and the pressure of this job would be detrimental to his health? Moreover, how could Joe keep his secret from the other people on the team?

Except for HIV, the choice was easy: hire Joe. But was there any such thing as "except for HIV"?

JONATHAN MANN

Greg van de Water should hire Joe Collins—with or without his HIV infection. Like all other people, some HIV infected are excellent workers and some are not. It is wrong to assume that when people become HIV infected, they immediately and irrevocably fall into a category of people who can't work well. Joe proves that HIV infection need not handicap one's performance.

Obviously, the "hidden" issue here is transmission. Will other workers be safe in the workplace? In this case, the answer is absolutely unanimous and unequivocal: there should be no concern for transmission in the workplace. (The exceptions are professions that involve exposure to blood and, in two instances that transcend the workplace but that I mention for the sake of completeness, people having sexual intercourse and sharing needles.) So it's important to put that concern to rest.

It's also important to put the hiring decision into the context of the expected lifespan of a person who is infected with HIV. The facts are that ten years after being infected, half of HIV-positive people will develop AIDS, while half will not—and this is without treatment. With treatment, depending on a number of factors related to individuals that we don't fully understand, that picture is improved in several ways.

There is an issue of a potentially reduced work life. While that's a real concern, consider how important any condition—HIV infection, hypertension, smoking, a family history of cancer—should weigh upon a hiring decision where there is a clear, or felt, superiority of a candidate. HIV infection doesn't tell you whether someone can or can't do a job well.

The employee's ability counts most. Greg should hire Joe because Joe is the most qualified candidate. At the same time, he should discuss the future with Joe. Finally, having the information that he does, Greg should find out if the company has an AIDS policy in place. If it doesn't, he should push for one. Because in the United States, with over one million people who are HIV infected, the idea that it won't happen in your company is fantasy. It's just a matter of time.

JAMES W. NICHOLS

Greg van de Water should not take Joe Collins's HIV infection into account when hiring him. He should hire on abilities, not disabilities. Besides, who is to say that Peter Kroll, the other candidate, isn't HIV positive as well?

I know that many of the roughly 1.2 million people infected with the AIDS virus in this country are productive workers. For five and a half years after receiving my HIV diagnosis, I continued to contribute to my company as an employee and a manager. My company knew my health status throughout. In allowing me to continue working, the company not only benefited from my work but also fueled my will to live.

My experience taught me that the only way for companies to handle the issue of HIV infection is for the company and the employee to work together. Like work, AIDS takes place in the context of personal relationships. It needs to be *comanaged*, not merely managed. When Greg hires Joe, then, he should establish that he will work with Joe as his illness develops or when other considerations arise. Greg could say, "Joe, I can't tell you how important your honesty has been to me, and I believe that knowledge of your HIV status should be held in the strictest confidence."

"But when you are ready to tell people you have HIV, or if your productivity slips to the point that people approach me, I would hope, Joe, that you and I can work together to solve the problem."

It is absolutely critical for HIV-positive employees to know that they're going to have the support of their company. When I tested positive, I had a very good relationship with the head of my division. After I told him of my infection shortly after I was diagnosed in the spring of 1985, he said to me, "Jim, I have to tell you this makes me very sad."

He went on to say that the bank was ready to deal with AIDS. It had already rewritten its life-threatening illness policy to include AIDS. It was willing to support me in my work. My boss said: "We want the decisions made about you to be decisions that we make about you, not decisions that the bank is going to make for you, not decisions that you're going to make on your own."

As I began living and working with HIV, my company continued doing its work behind the scenes. The bank produced an AIDS-in-the-workplace training program for all employees. It provided brochures on AIDS for the home and workplace, directed toward both singles and families, and produced them in several languages.

All this made me feel like a million dollars. I don't believe the bank kept me because it liked me—but because keeping me was fair.

LEE SMITH

Joe Collins should get the job. In terms of professional skills and "fit," he is the most qualified. And perhaps as important, there is no reason *not* to pick Joe. His HIV status should not count against him for the same reason we don't consider the projected health status of an older employee or the possibility of pregnancy for a female employee. Also, the Americans for Disability Act of 1990 now includes HIV infection as a disability, which means it is illegal for Greg to use HIV as a basis for not hiring Joe.

Once Greg hires Joe, he must respect Joe's confidentiality. Unfortunately, HIV-positive individuals today are subject to terrible discrimination in the workplace and in the rest of their lives. They face fear and stigmatization from colleagues, friends, even family, and as a direct or indirect result, they lose their jobs, their insurance, and other work-related benefits.

On the other hand, disclosure represents the first step for a company and an individual to manage HIV together. I encourage people like Joe to be open about their illness. A partnership of concerned individuals can manage this illness far more effectively than can individuals on their own.

Disclosure is not an easy step: I am not sure that I could follow my own good advice if faced with this situation. Disclosure, moreover, doesn't work without a supportive and well-informed workplace. Levi Strauss & Co. took its first steps toward establishing its AIDS corporate policy in 1982, when the epidemic was in its early stages. It was evident that an appropriate AIDS strategy had to be included in Levi's philosophy about the treatment of employees with any life-threatening illness: all employees are to be treated with dignity and respect. This clearly included an employee with HIV. Employee groups began volunteer activities and fundraising to support people with AIDS. This effort created opportunities for communication and education about the disease, about fear, and about people living and working with the virus.

Since then, we have rolled out a companywide policy of education, support, and involvement in AIDS causes. These education efforts go beyond the company to the employees and their families, to other businesses and community organizations. Initially, we designed a program for managers and employees that we customized to regional and cultural differences.

Today AIDS education is ongoing: most Levi employees in the United States have attended, on company time, a minimum of a one-hour education program about AIDS in the workplace. New employees attend AIDS awareness trainings. Managers and work groups receive specialized training and consultation as needed.

The Confidentiality Crisis 11-1-90

Greg van de Water looked up in surprise. Harry Lopez, who'd been a member of the sales team for four years, had come into Greg's office and was closing the always-open door.

"Greg," he began as he turned to face him, "I've got to talk to you about Joe."

"Sit down, Harry," Greg said casually, trying to remain expression-less and hide his concern. "What seems to be the trouble?"

"Well, I don't know exactly, but something's wrong. I hate to say it, but Joe's been letting us down. Now, don't get me wrong. We all like him. We liked him the moment he came on board last year. He was fun and easy to work with, he contributed more than his share of new leads, he knows the merchandise. He pulled his weight and then some. He made us look better than we'd ever looked before. And with sales up, we were making more money than ever before."

Lopez paused, took a deep breath, and went on. "But that's all changed. I want to be fair, but lately he's been, well, taking advantage of the team. You know what I'm talking about. He comes in late or he leaves early—not every day but two or three times a week. A couple of times last month, and again yesterday, he didn't come in at all. No phone call, no explanation, just never showed up.

"Worse yet, he's preoccupied and unpredictable. I heard him yell at a customer last week, and Friday we had a real argument about who would take care of one last caller. I ended up handling it myself.

"It's reached the point where we're all having to work harder be-cause of Joe's behavior. We're still a team, so we still cover for him, but nobody likes doing it. And nobody can talk to him anymore. Greg, he's just not himself. You know what I'm talking about. You've got eyes."

Harry paused for a moment and cleared his throat. "In fact," he went on, "I wonder if you know something about Joe that you're not telling the rest of us."

"Like what?" Greg said lamely. He'd been trying hard not to see Joe's increasing delinquencies. He dreaded the prospect of talking to Joe and addressing the issue of his apparently emerging illness—if that's what it was. And then there was the issue of Joe's privacy to consider. Of course he'd known when he hired him that this day would probably come sooner or later, but who would have thought Joe would get sick so soon?

"You tell me," Harry said. "Maybe there's a family crisis. Maybe he's got a drinking problem. For all I know, he could have AIDS—and I've been sharing a cubicle with him for a year. Whatever it is, you owe us an answer. This team lives and dies on honesty and openness and mutual respect. We've never kept secrets from each other. Whatever it is that's going on violates everything we stand for."

Greg needed time. "You're right, Harry," he said. "I'm glad you brought it up. I have noticed some of the things you're talking about, but I didn't know it was this serious. I'll talk to Joe. Thanks, Harry. We'll work it out."

JONATHAN MANN

Forget HIV infection for a second. Greg's got an employee who's dysfunctional. The question is: What's really going on? Jumping to the conclusion that Joe has AIDS is premature. Though his behavior could be related to the symptoms of HIV infection, I can think of many reasons why someone would be unreliable or irritable—and they have nothing to do with HIV.

The point is that Greg does not have to diagnose the condition. He just has to help Joe do his job. As a first step, he needs to open up the channel of communication. Greg could approach Joe in a supportive way and point out that his work has been suffering. It's unlike him to miss work, Greg could say. Is there anything he could do to help? Greg thus begins a process of easing Joe toward the evaluation and care he might need.

At the same time, Greg needs to become what I call "literate about AIDS." People at his level in a corporation should know what the disease is, how it spreads, how it acts in the body. Most important, Greg should know how and where to learn about AIDS. He needs access to accurate and updated AIDS information independent of Joe—a doctor, for instance, whom he can call to ask any and all questions without embarrassment. Because AIDS is a constantly evolving health and social issue, it mandates access to sound and up-to-date technical information in order to make informed decisions.

Facts are important; leadership is equally vital. Harry's aside shows that Greg should also start pushing the company to develop an ongoing educational program on AIDS in the workplace. He needs to take a leadership role so that company discussion is a coming together and not a witch hunt. Greg might make a symbolic gesture such as walking into the educational meeting with his arm around Joe.

Greg should not tell Harry about Joe's situation without Joe's consent. First of all, Joe deserves to have his immediate problem evaluated and brought under control. Then he and Greg can discuss disclosure. Given that transmission is not an issue here, neither Greg nor Joe has a legal or public health obligation to disclose that Joe is HIV infected. But for the sake of group dynamics, Greg and Joe might want to consider informing the team about Joe's health status, which can be done in a way that builds on the supportive environment of the team.

JAMES W. NICHOLS

Greg van de Water needs some fundamental training on how to manage people. No one can make a positive contribution to AIDS in the workplace unless teamwork already exists. And teams are built by professional managers who respect and build the self-esteem of their employees. Clearly, Greg has not learned this.

As a general rule, managers should attack problems, not employees. Greg did the opposite by agreeing with Harry that Joe's work has suffered. He should have merely thanked Harry for offering his opinion. And rather than playing the paternalistic manager who fixes employee's problems, Greg could have asked Harry for his solution.

When Greg does talk to Joe he should focus on his failing productivity and show him the same respect he shows Harry—that is, give him the chance to solve the problem. Asking Joe what he thinks should be done may force him to concede that HIV has slowed him down, but it also respects his abilities.

Let me add that Joe's declining productivity may be AIDS related but does not necessarily reflect his own health. My own productivity dropped so low at one point that the bank could have fired me in 30 seconds. I was performing so poorly primarily because I was suffering from bereavement overload.

Bereavement overload and grief are two of the biggest problems for employees who have AIDS. My brother was the thirty-fifth person I knew who died of AIDS. After him I quit counting. It got to the point where one day I exploded at work over an incident that had nothing to do with work and everything to do with my anger; it took a sympathetic worker to say to me, "Jim, it's not the teller you can't take. You can't take having lost so many friends." Her reaction, which was to gather the troops and tell them I was having personal troubles—without mentioning my health—helped me immensely.

You don't have to be infected to be affected by AIDS. The HIV factor is a hidden productivity crippler to the brothers, sisters, parents, friends, and lovers of those who have the disease. Unfortunately, the stigma associated with AIDS forces those people to cope with AIDS privately, secretively, and from a distance.

LEE SMITH

Greg van de Water's missed opportunities are coming back to haunt him. Because Greg didn't develop a plan, educate his work team, or work with Joe more openly, he now faces a volatile situation.

He has abrogated the stated company standards of honesty, openness, and forthrightness and chosen the path of avoidance. There's absolutely no question that the best approach with this disease is proactive rather than reactive. It is easier for people to grapple with the issues surrounding an HIV-infected coworker before he or she begins showing symptoms and performing poorly.

Of course Greg is dealing with a thorny issue: balancing Joe's right to confidentiality with the expectations, needs, and rights of the other team members. First of all, Greg should talk with Joe about his situation; after all, Greg can't be sure that the recent performance delinquencies are due to the illness. Then Greg should use all his skills to convince Joe of the benefits of confiding in the work group. Much can be gained by sharing this information. A team can manage this situation far better than one individual fighting it quietly, secretly, alone. Work teams really mount an effort to help individuals in trouble: there are times in all of our lives when colleagues cover for us, whether the problem is AIDS or something else. Sharing information that affects the work group can bring out the best in everyone.

At Levi Strauss, I work with an HIV-positive man by the name of Alan Philip. Right now he is asymptomatic. In fact, he's a marathon runner. With his input and participation, we disclosed Alan's HIV status to selected managers and are running small, informal meetings with Alan and his close coworkers to discuss any issues involving HIV and their own work group. We want to provide a safe place for everyone on the staff to be informed and to be able to explore their own feelings.

Greg and Joe shouldn't miss this opportunity to teach the work team about HIV infection in all its complexities. Talking about AIDS is very different from watching it happen to someone you know. Few people turn their backs on the person who sits next to them day after day.

I remember how Keith Coppin, a Levi Strauss employee who recently died of complications related to HIV infection, was apprehensive about telling his work group about his illness. When he did, people were initially scared and uncertain; some were angry with his manager for not revealing his condition earlier. But Keith and his manager, Paula Dueball, worked to create an environment where people could talk about their feelings and clarify assumptions they had made about what Keith could and should do. Eventually, Keith felt there was a normalcy to his daily working life.

The Long-Term Question 11-1-91

Joe Collins was sitting in Greg van de Water's office, grinning broadly. "Tell me the truth, Greg," he said. "Have you ever had a better sales team? Or a better salesperson? Admit it, I'm 110% of my old self, and those numbers prove it!"

Greg laughed at Joe's good humor as he scanned Joe's most recent sales figures. "No question about it, Joe," he said. "You've really bounced back from last year. I don't know if it's the medication or if it's just you and your attitude, but I have to admit, the work you've done in the last six months has been super."

"I was hoping you'd say that," Joe said. "As a matter of fact, that's what I came to talk to you about." He paused briefly to signal the beginning of a more serious discussion. "I've been here two years now, and frankly, Greg, I think that I'm ready for a change."

Greg nodded attentively, so Joe went on. "I feel as though I've pretty much done everything I can do here. I was looking through the job listing sheets, and I think I came across one that's right up my alley. It's right here," Joe said, handing him the internal job listings. "I've got it circled."

Greg read the job description: "Senior Sales Representative, Western States Region. Top-level sales and customer service job covering our fastest growing markets. Requires full knowledge of our product line. Candidate must be prepared for extensive travel and fast-paced customer demands. As the company grows, we will look to this individual—and the team that comes together under his/her leadership—to form long-term relationships with Western customers and to steer us into the markets of the future. Compensation commensurate with contribution to the company's future! Who wants it???"

Greg looked up. "I don't know, Joe," he said slowly, trying to hide his surprise. "When you said you wanted a change . . . I was expecting . . . well, I kind of thought that after the rough time you had last year, you might want to slow down a bit."

Greg knew he had to be gentle. Joe had confirmed he had AIDS and was likely to get sick again, and he seemed to be in denial. But Greg also knew he couldn't recommend Joe for a job he couldn't handle.

That would hurt the company, and it wouldn't do much for Greg's reputation, either.

"It seems to me," Greg said carefully, "that this job calls for the kind of long-term commitment you might not want or be able to make right now. Tell me the truth, Joe, do you really want to add all this stress to your life? And all that travel?

"You're such a good salesman," he went on, "I was thinking we could design a special job just for you—maybe a training and teaching job so you could help some of our younger people. You know, a chance for you to pass along some of your ideas and techniques. The hours would be flexible, you could work whenever you felt like it, and you could design the course to meet your own health needs. But this job," Greg looked back down at the job description in his hands. "I don't know about this job. This isn't slowing down, Joe. This is going into overdrive."

Joe fixed Greg with a long, searching look. "Greg," he said, "I know what you're thinking, but I'm not kidding myself. I'm just a long, long way from giving up—or from having to. I've still got a life to live. God knows I've still got drive. And I still do terrific work, which matters a lot to me and ought to matter to the company. I want my career."

He sat back in his chair and grinned. "I'll tell you what, Greg. Stop and think about it again. I'm going to give you another chance."

JONATHAN MANN

HIV workers who are not ill should be handled like all other workers who are not ill; HIV infected workers who are ill should be handled like all other workers who are ill. Greg's problem is that he is operating on what he expects rather than what the facts of the disease and the infection indicate. He sees a worker working well. Why should Greg assume Joe wants to slow down?

Even for people who have developed clinical AIDS, survival can be quite long. I have a friend who had clinical AIDS diagnosed almost ten years ago. And though he is the exception rather than the rule, it is important to know that exceptions exist. We're talking about biology, not mathematics.

If Joe can do the job and is the most qualified, Greg should recommend him. For Joe's sake, if he believes he'll be happy with the extra work and travel, if he'll be satisfied and fulfilled, then this job might actually be more important than eight hours of sleep. Stress is *not* necessarily unhealthy for Joe: some people work better and are in fact happier with a certain amount of external stress.

Greg's alternative comes across as a way of "parking" Joe. The real question is: What does Joe's future look like? Will he live longer and be healthier if he feels his career's over or if he's working extra hours as the head of a team? I think the answer lies somewhere between the two extremes: maybe what works for him now is the high-stress travel, and later he'll take another position with less stress and fewer hours.

Above all, Greg and Joe must use the facts of Joe's condition to make the decision. Now if Joe is clinically ill and can work only two days a week, the situation is easier to resolve: How could he possibly take this job? But until then, I recommend Greg follow this principle: if Joe's clinically sick, treat him like any other sick worker. If he's well, treat him that way.

Can Joe handle a long-term commitment? The question for me is, How long is long term? In today's work force, where mobility has become the norm, even a five-year commitment is considered long term. When you start to think about a job with a ten-year or fifteen-year commitment, then I would ask another question: How do you make decisions about the long term? Would it matter if Joe smoked or had hypertension? We don't figure those questions into the equation now, why should we with AIDS?

That is especially true today, as one can legitimately offer hope to a person who develops AIDS. It used to be that a person diagnosed with AIDS had an average life expectancy of about one year. Now it's a couple of years. And with the ability to prevent some life-threatening illnesses, it is becoming quite common to see people who have suffered their first AIDS-related illness return to relative health for a long period of time.

JAMES W. NICHOLS

Greg has offered Joe the ultimate in reasonable accommodation. Again, I speak from the perspective of an employee with HIV and AIDS. Greg has offered Joe a training position with flexible hours, with no cut in pay or benefits, without the stress of sales goals, and without competition from his peers.

As manager, Greg's role is to assess Joe's work performance and then provide choices. It certainly is his right to offer, or push for, reasonable accommodation. I was appalled when Joe offered Greg "a second chance." Joe has got it backwards. Employees don't give managers second chances. Besides, Greg has already given Joe a second chance. When his productivity declined, Greg gave him the opportunity to stay with the company and keep his job.

Joe appears to be very poorly educated about how HIV operates. I say this because I agree with Greg's original assumption: Joe is in serious denial. Joe seems to be denying the spiraling health-care costs associated with AIDS. He appears not to know that stress is a major cofactor in the replication of the virus and that fatigue is a major symptom. Beyond that, if he takes the new job and fails, he could be fired on the spot—losing his salary and benefits. Joe's hope for the future is overshadowing his assessment of the present.

Greg has given Joe options—and only with options can Joe still maintain control. In fact, Greg's offer sounds exactly like the deal my bank offered me two and a half years ago. At that time, my boss said I had a decision to make. My productivity had gone to hell, and I was not acting as a good manager. I had the choice of quitting—or turning my attitude around and keeping a job at the bank. I was not given the choice of keeping my old job, however. The bank offered me a new job, at the same salary and benefits, yet without the stress of managing people or meeting sales goals.

The way the bank handled my illness was vital to my continued productivity. If employees want to work and can, companies should let them. If you take away a person's job unnecessarily, you not only rob the company of potentially valuable work, you also take away much of what sustains that person's will to live.

LEE SMITH

Greg should take the "second chance" Joe's offering him by putting Joe up for the promotion. If Joe can perform, has shown the ability to do so, and is qualified for the promotion, I can think of no other relevant consideration. AIDS or not, he is entitled to his career.

Joe may not be able to work indefinitely, but I'm betting that he can perform well in this job for a reasonable amount of time, providing a return on the investment. If he becomes too ill to work, then reasonable accommodation can be worked out by all parties.

But it's not only Joe that worries me. I'm also concerned about

Greg. He talks about the company's openness and honesty, and yet he still seems to be acting solely to protect himself. Although I applaud him for being more explicit with Joe, he is still making assumptions about Joe's *future* health.

Ultimately, this situation is an opportunity for the company to find out whether it really cares about individuals in the organization or whether it cares strictly about output. Joe's situation presents the company with a tremendous chance to educate fellow employees, to bring compassion to the workplace, and to treat people with dignity in the face of a life-threatening illness.

There are also solid business reasons to keep and promote people in Joe's condition. First of all, employees in companies such as ours stay for an average of five or more years. We have a huge investment in those people, and losing them suddenly to disease means an absolute loss. We also incur the expense of training replacements. So it is cost-effective to leave HIV-positive workers in place as long as they continue to be productive. And we benefit in terms of insurance and medical outlays by intervening earlier to help individuals stave off the higher costs of the later stages of the disease.

Additionally, we have an opportunity to educate people about the disease and in so doing help prevent the spread of AIDS. For many adults, the workplace is the only place they receive this lifesaving information. We gain financially if we save even one employee from becoming infected. And by creating a more supportive work environment, we allow people who might otherwise be fearful to get on with their jobs and work side-by-side with someone who is HIV positive.

Note

At the time of this article's publication Jonathan Mann was professor of epidemiology and international health at the Harvard School of Public Health and director of the International AIDS Center of the Harvard AIDS Institute. Lee Smith was president of Levi Strauss International. James W. Nichols, an assistant vice president of the American Security Bank in Washington, D.C., died of AIDS-related complications in October 1991, while the article was in production.

3
Is This the Right Time to Come Out?

Alistair D. Williamson

George Campbell, assistant vice president in mergers and acquisitions at Kirkham McDowell Securities, a St. Louis underwriting and financial advisory firm, looked up as Adam Lawson, one of his most promising associates, entered his office. Adam, 29 years old, had been with the firm for only two years but had already distinguished himself as having great potential. Recently, he had helped to bring in an extremely lucrative deal, and in six weeks, he and several other associates would be honored for their efforts at the firm's silver anniversary dinner.

As Adam closed the door and sat down, he said, "George, I'd like to talk to you about the banquet. I've thought about this very carefully, and I want you to know that I plan to bring my partner, Robert Collins, as my escort."

George was taken aback. "Well, Adam," he said, "I don't quite know what to say. I have to be honest with you; I'm a little surprised. I had no idea that you were gay. I would never have guessed." He looked at Adam for clues on how to proceed: his subordinate did seem nervous but not defiant or hostile.

Though only a 50-person operation, Kirkham McDowell had long since secured its status as one of the region's leading corporate financial advisers. The firm's client roster included established and successful regional companies as well as one of the country's largest defense contractors, a very conservative company for which the firm managed part of an impressive pension portfolio. Representatives of Kirkham McDowell's major clients and many of the area's most influential political and business leaders were expected to attend the banquet. All this raced through George's mind as he asked Adam, "Why do you want to do this? Why do you want to mix your personal and professional lives?"

"For the same reason that you bring your wife to company social events," Adam replied.

A look of confusion flickered across George's face while Adam continued. "Think about it for a moment, George. Success in this business depends in great part on the relationships you develop with your clients and the people you work with. An important part of those relationships is letting people know about your life away from the office, and that includes the people who are important to you. Some of the other associates already know Robert. Whenever his schedule permits, he accompanies me when I'm invited by one of my colleagues to have dinner with his or her spouse. Granted, that isn't very often— Robert is a corporate attorney, and his work is very demanding—but he joins me whenever he can."

"But, Adam, a wife isn't the same thing as a—"

"It *is* the same thing, George. Robert and I have made a commitment to each other. We have been together for almost five years now, and I would feel very uncomfortable telling him that I was going to a major social event alone—on a weekend, no less."

"Well, I'm sure you'd agree that it wouldn't be appropriate for an associate to bring a date—someone he barely knows—to such an event."

"Come on, George. I think you know me well enough to realize that I have better judgment than that. If Robert and I had known each other for only six months, I wouldn't be having this conversation with you right now. But, as I said, we've been together for over five years!"

George thought for a moment. "Adam," he said slowly, "I'm just not sure you should try to make an issue of this at such an important time for the company. Why bring it up now? Think of our clients. We work with some very conservative companies. They could very well decide to give their business to a firm whose views seem to agree more with their own. You're not just making a personal statement here. You're saying something about the culture at Kirkham McDowell, something that some of our clients might fundamentally oppose. How are they going to react?"

Adam leaned forward. "This is only an issue if people make it an issue," he said. "I have resolved never to lie about myself or about anything that is important to me—and that includes my sexuality.

Since I joined the firm, as I've become comfortable sharing details of my personal life with certain colleagues, I've come out to them and often introduced them to Robert. If people ask me if I'm gay, I'm honest with them. Likewise, if people ask me if I have a girlfriend, I tell them about my relationship with Robert. With the silver anniversary celebration coming up, I thought the time was right to speak with you. This is the first large social event the company has held since I started working here. And after a lot of discussion with Robert and some of the associates here, I've decided that I need to be as open at the banquet as I have tried to be in other areas within the organization.

"It's not a decision that I've taken lightly. I've seen what has happened to some of my gay friends who have come out at work. Even at much less conservative companies, some are never invited to important social events with colleagues and customers, no matter how much business they bring in. They'll never know whether or not their bonuses have been affected by prejudice related to their sexuality. I know my career could be adversely influenced by this decision, but I believe that my work should stand on its own merits. George, I've been a top contributor at this firm since I walked in the door. I hope I can rely on you to back me up in this."

Adam stood up but waited for George to reply. "You've given me a lot to think about," George said. "And I don't want to say anything until I've had a chance to consider all the implications. I appreciate the confidence you've shown in me by being so open. I wish I had something conclusive to say at this point, but the fact of the matter is that I have never had to face this issue before. I am one of your biggest supporters here at the firm. Your work has been exemplary. And, until today, I would have said that you could look forward to a very successful career here. But I'm concerned about how this will play with our clients and, as a result, about how senior management will react. I personally don't have any problems with your being gay, but I'd hate to see you torpedo your career over this. It's possible that this could jeopardize some of our relationships with significant clients. Let me think about it for a few days. We can have lunch next week and map out a strategy."

After Adam left his office, George sat in silence for a few minutes, trying to make sense of the conversation. He was unsure of his next move. Adam clearly had *not* come into his office looking for permission to bring his lover to the banquet. George realized that he could do nothing and let events simply unfold. After all, Adam had not asked that Robert be included in his benefits coverage nor had he requested a specific managerial decision. There was no company policy on paper to guide him through his dilemma. But Adam wouldn't have come to him if he hadn't wanted a response of some kind. And shouldn't he at least tell his superior in order to head off any awkward moments at the banquet?

Just how negative an effect could Robert have on Adam's career with the firm and on the firm's relationship with its clients? Wasn't it possible, even likely, that the party would come off without incident? That the issue would blow over? That even the firm's most conservative clients wouldn't realize the significance of Adam's guest or would simply decide that it was a personal issue, not a business one? Or would George's worst fears be realized? Adam had to recognize that the potential risks were great. It was one thing for him to come out of the closet at the office. But wasn't he pushing things too far?

How Should George Respond to Adam's Disclosure?

Seven experts examine issues of discrimination in the workplace.

JAMES D. WOODS

As lesbian and gay workers become an increasingly visible part of the work force, sooner or later every manager will stand in George Campbell's shoes. Some of them, like George, will be asked for their advice or blessing as a subordinate plans his or her exit from the closet. Others will encounter the issue more obliquely. They will participate in a promotion, compensation, or hiring decision involving a lesbian or gay worker. They will have to revisit a nondiscrimination policy that ignores sexual orientation or reevaluate a benefits program that excludes same-sex couples. They will be sought as mentors, tennis partners, and lunch companions by coworkers who they know or suspect to be gay. Like George, they may find themselves on unfamiliar turf.

Above all, managers should guide their responses by a commitment to fairness. To his credit, George has already focused on the central facts of Adam's situation. Kirkham McDowell has invited employees to bring their spouses to its silver anniversary dinner. Adam wants to bring his partner, Robert, a man with whom he shares a serious and committed relationship. Ethically speaking, the solution is obvious: Kirkham McDowell must encourage Adam to bring Robert, extending to him the same invitation given to other guests. Anything less amounts to discrimination, plain and simple.

Some will say, of course, that it is inappropriate for Adam to be so public about his sexuality, that he should strive to keep personal and professional matters apart. Yet this objection, however familiar, is based on a blatant double standard. If the firm is to be fair, it owes Adam the same opportunities given to his heterosexual peers, including the right to be frank about his sexuality. In most work settings, heterosexuality is continuously on display, ubiquitous to the point that we often fail to notice it. It is alluded to in benefits policies, in dress and self-presentation, in jokes and gossip, in symbols like wedding rings and baby pictures. Coworkers discuss their families, friends, and loved ones, and the sharing of sexual information often grounds such intangibles as rapport, loyalty, and trust.

Indeed, much "work" is in fact the management of relationships, which means that men and women's personal qualifications are inevitably part of the job. When judging the professional competence of our peers, for example, we routinely take so-called personal traits into consideration. We ponder how well a particular coworker fits in with the group, what kind of chemistry he or she has with customers, or how well he or she sees eye-to-eye with a particular client, all without realizing that there is a sexual dimension to these questions. As Adam points out, business is based on relationships, and relationships wither when one is evasive about personal, family, or romantic matters. Given the countless ways in which personal and professional lives overlap, it is disingenuous to argue that it is Adam who is confusing the two by bringing his partner to a company dinner.

However, there is a second consideration that involves not ethics but the bottom line. One can hardly fault George for worrying about how Adam's gesture will be received by clients. When he frets about the potential cost to the firm, he is simply being a responsible manager. What George should reconsider, however, is his definition of these costs. Rather than ask if Kirkham McDowell can afford to be fair, George should consider what the alternative would cost his firm.

First, George should realize that his decision will send a message to a potentially large number of men and women. As a percentage of the labor pool, lesbian and gay workers probably outnumber Hispanics, Asian-Pacific Islanders, the disabled, and others whom we have traditionally classified as minorities. (If we accept the standard estimate that 10% of the population is lesbian or gay, they also outnumber African-Americans, who represent 12.5% of the population but only 5.6% of the professional work force.)

That message, therefore, could have serious consequences for the performance of a large number of employees. Over the past three years, my own study of gay professionals identified several negative consequences of discrimination on the basis of sexual orientation. Most obviously, lesbian and gay workers are less productive when they are consumed by the fear of exposure. To protect themselves, some invent elaborate schemes to disguise their sexuality, deceptions that waste precious time. Others try to avoid the subject of sexuality altogether by withdrawing from the social life of the office but find that this too has its costs. They pay for their privacy with limited interpersonal effectiveness, reduced job satisfaction, and feelings of isolation. Even those who come out, as Adam did, sacrifice time and energy to the task. How many hours did Adam spend worrying about whom to tell, how they would respond, and what it would mean for his career? As Adam points out, "It's not a decision I've taken lightly." Kirkham McDowell has gained nothing by making the decision difficult.

Over time, some of these men and women will simply abandon their employers, taking with them whatever investment has been made in their development. Some will migrate toward more hospitable employers, ensuring a talent drain at those companies that make them feel unwelcome. Others will abandon large organizations altogether, some to accept "safe" jobs beneath their abilities, some to start their own businesses. My own survey found, for example, that half of all lesbian and gay professionals took sexual orientation issues into consideration when selecting their current place of employment. Many had left or turned down jobs with companies that they considered to be homophobic. In Adam's case, there can be little doubt that these issues are a key consideration. If his request to bring Robert is rebuffed, the firm should expect, sooner or later, to lose him.

Finally, George should not be too quick to assume the worst of his clients. Some may be offended by the sight of a male couple, just as some are offended by other ethnic, religious, or political groups in our increasingly diverse labor pool. Yet lesbians and gay men who come out in the workplace very often find the opposite to be the case. For many, their disclosure precipitates a flood of support. New opportunities emerge. Alliances materialize in unexpected places. Key relationships deepen. Clients and coworkers applaud them for their courage.

It is possible, of course, that Kirkham McDowell will lose a client or two. But, on balance, discrimination is never good for business. Some of George's clients are undoubtedly gay. Many of them have friends, children, or parents who are lesbian or gay, as do many of his potential clients. A growing number of companies—including AT&T, Levi Strauss & Co., 3M, and Digital—currently have nondiscrimination policies that include sexual orientation and select their business partners accordingly. By choosing the ethical solution, Kirkham McDowell stands to gain at least as much as it risks to lose.

George is absolutely right when he says that Adam would be "saying something about the culture at Kirkham McDowell" by bringing his partner to a company function. By welcoming Robert into its extended family, the firm would be saying that it respects the dignity of its employees, that it values the diversity of its work force. It would send a clear message, to clients as well as employees, that bigotry has no place within its walls. What will Kirkham McDowell be saying, both to Adam and to its clients, if it doesn't?

JOHN M. CONLEY AND WILLIAM M. O'BARR

We are struck initially by the fact that Adam and George agree on one fundamental point: the importance of non-financial factors to their firm's success in the financial world. Adam argues that the firm's business depends on personal relationships with clients and that disclosure of one's personal life helps foster such relationships. George counters that Adam's proposed disclosure would make a statement about Kirkham McDowell's culture that might be false, displeasing to clients, or both. Will pension fund managers and other clients actually base their evaluation of Kirkham McDowell on anything but the firm's investment performance?

The answer is an emphatic yes. An anthropological study of large pension funds that we recently completed shows compellingly that as long as money management firms perform within a broad band of respectability, pension executives judge them on the basis of ad hoc personal and cultural assessments. Adam's hopes and George's fears are *both* well-grounded.

Predicting the cultural values of a hypothetical group of clients is necessarily complex, but a few observations about pension funds are in order. Public pension funds are suffused with the values of the political bureaucracies of which they are a part. To know the larger political culture is to understand a great deal about the culture of the fund. In the political climate of, say, New York City, we would be astonished to see a public pension official revealing the slightest hint of intolerance, let alone acting on it. In our own state of North Carolina, our expectations would be quite different. Among private funds, it is the culture of the sponsoring company that sets the tone of the fund. Here, George's worst fears may be realized. Relationships with financial advisers are indeed important, but these relationships are most often based on traditional male-bonding activities such as golf, hockey games, and expensive steak dinners leavened with dirty jokes.

As anthropologists, however, we don't think that it is either economically necessary or morally justifiable for financial organizations to conform to the meaner aspects of their clients' cultures. The *pandering-to-the-customer* defense is nothing new. Elite law firms long justified their exclusion of women and minorities by saying, "We'd like to, but the clients wouldn't stand for it." But firms did begin to diversify, and the clients stood for it. The clients continue to complain about the price and quality of the work but not about the race and gender of the people doing it. On the contrary, the firms that once dragged their feet now pay a heavy price in recruiting talent with attendant consequences for their work product.

Perhaps the law firms simply underestimated their clients, which suggests that George may be doing the same. But perhaps these firms *really* underestimated their own capacity to lead and influence. When law firms or financial advisers or advertisers or television producers raise the pandering-to-the-customer defense, they implicitly argue that they are only responding to cultural values that they are powerless to change. Institutions do influence one another, however, and those that are willing to exercise leadership can shape cultural values rather than merely reflect them.

Kirkham McDowell, in the person of George, has been presented with an opportunity for leadership. We believe that the firm is morally bound to seize that opportunity. The history of elite law firms suggests that, in the long run, the moral choice will be the lucrative one as well. When major changes in cultural values take place, it pays to be leading the trend rather than running behind making excuses.

MICHAEL R. LOSEY

Adam has already made a thoughtful and important decision. Unfortunately, George and the management of Kirkham McDowell do not seem prepared to deal with the issue of sexual orientation in the workplace, though one could assume that sooner or later it would demand attention. The question is, can George and Kirkham McDowell, in the void created by their own lack of direction, live with Adam's actions?

If Kirkham McDowell intends to compete in a world where the level of success or failure depends on the skills and abilities of an increasingly diverse global work force, the answer must be a resounding yes. In fact, the firm's managers should not only support Adam's decision but also use this opportunity to reexamine their own assumptions and competitive practices. They will find that many employers have adopted policies on this issue. A recent poll of human resource professionals, conducted by the Society for Human Resource Management, showed that more than 65% of the 145 people surveyed work for companies that have well-understood policies against employment discrimination based on sexual orientation.

Struggling to manage without an explicit policy, George is wrestling with the same kind of issues raised a few decades ago when the public began debating the proper treatment of women and minorities in the work force. Anyone who worked in a personnel office in those days (before we had human resource departments) can remember when women were expected to resign when their pregnancies became visible or when African-American candidates were often at a disadvantage despite their qualifications and abilities. And it wasn't so long ago that airlines employed only female flight attendants because passengers supposedly preferred to be served by women.

By breaking down barriers for women and minorities in the workplace, we have learned that a policy of inclusion results in more creativity, greater productivity, and a larger applicant pool from which to draw qualified candidates. That's why it is so important to eliminate barriers that keep people out of the work force for reasons unrelated to their basic abilities. In fact, the longer an organization takes to recognize these barriers and eliminate them, the more that organization is at risk.

It simply makes good managerial sense to identify and utilize the best qualified people to support and improve an organization's competitive status. If George steps back and views his decision from that standpoint, the solution becomes clear. Adam has a proven track record of success. There can be little doubt of his value to the organization, especially when we recall that Adam is not to attend the dinner simply as a guest, but as a guest of honor for his efforts on behalf of the firm.

If George tells Adam that he may *not* bring his partner to the dinner, Adam may decide to leave Kirkham McDowell and join a competitor. If Adam does stay under those circumstances, chances are that the emotions surrounding the issue will build and affect his attitude toward his job, his performance, as well as the opinions and morale of fellow workers. Either option is a heavy price to pay. When all is said and done, does George really believe that companies doing business with his firm care more about Adam's sexual orientation than how he has helped them succeed? And doesn't George realize that in his desire to protect the firm's business with certain clients, he may jeopardize future business with other clients?

Even if the worst case scenario occurs and certain clients object to Adam's continued involvement simply because of his sexual orientation, Kirkham McDowell's decision to study the issue and determine a policy will ultimately prove useful. And if the organization is steadfast in its support of Adam, the majority of clients will accept its decision sooner or later. They may even learn something in the process.

CHARLES COLBERT AND JOHN WOFFORD

It's important to understand the developing legal context of this case. In April 1993, Minnesota became the eighth state to outlaw discrimination based on sexual orientation, joining California, Connecticut, Hawaii, Massachusetts, New Jersey, Vermont, Wisconsin, and the District of Columbia. A number of governors have addressed the subject by issuing executive orders covering public employment. And more than 100 cities have similar ordinances, including St. Louis, where Kirkham McDowell is located. In fact, the board of aldermen in St. Louis added sexual orientation to its list of protected minority categories—race, religion, age, gender, national origin, and disability—in October, 1992. Adam is thus legally protected from discrimination in all the terms, conditions, and privileges of his employment. Admittedly, however, no one would start a lawsuit solely over the dinner issue.

More than 70 million Americans are now covered by these laws, orders, and ordinances that seek to protect homosexuals from discriminatory action. Under these laws, sexual orientation is irrelevant to the entire range of employment activities from hiring to firing.

As such, sexuality is a private matter, and Adam is not flaunting his orientation by discussing it with George. He is merely presenting himself in his entirety. His sexual orientation is just as much a part of him as color or religion or national origin is a part of any other person. We would not accuse the light-skinned African-American who had "passed" as white and the Jewish person with a "gentile" name of flaunting, if they later chose to reveal their true selves. We would call it courage and honesty. And gay people who come out of the closet are at last gaining the courage to be honest in precisely the same way.

Right now, George and Adam need to think through the social dynamics of the banquet and its aftermath. Will spouses of other employees be recognized from the platform? If so, Adam will want his partner to be treated similarly. And now that the firm officially knows that Adam has a domestic partner, Robert's name should appear in the firm directory if spouses of heterosexual employees appear. Corporate America, albeit slowly, is getting used to "Mr. and Mr." and "Ms. and Ms."

As an openly gay couple, we have experienced this crumbling of discriminatory walls firsthand. Yes, we initially faced a barrier of discomfort, as well as our own ambivalence about raising the issue. For a time, when attending workplace and client functions together, we felt somewhat on display. But by taking the initiative ourselves in a non-threatening way, we all—ourselves, employers, and clients—were able to adjust to this new social dimension in business.

Undoubtedly, some Kirkham McDowell employees and clients will demonstrate strongly held objections to homosexuality. George needs to prepare carefully for this issue. Everyone is entitled to his or her moral views on issues of sexuality, but they should be checked at the office door. The workplace should be an essentially secular environment. Just as people work side by side with others who may hold different beliefs about and engage in different practices concerning divorce, abortion, premarital sex, contraception, interracial marriage, or the use of alcohol, so people who differ fundamentally on the issue of homosexuality can get along and work together productively. Acceptable behavior, not acceptable beliefs, is the appropriate workplace standard.

ELIZABETH MCNAMARA

Though George Campbell may not realize it, Adam Lawson has very politely presented him with an ultimatum: either immediately accept his decision to be open about his sexuality or eventually accept his resignation. What George must decide is whether or not his fears about the consequences of Adam's declaration are more important than the contribution Adam makes to Kirkham McDowell Securities.

To do that, George will have to examine his own assumptions, prejudices, and insularity. Why, for example, would he think that Adam—obviously an ambitious, successful professional whose judgment has already carried him far—would turn up at an important event with someone he just met at the gym? Because even if he knows better intellectually, George's gut response to a situation that makes him uncomfortable is to think of homosexual stereotypes: desperate, lonely people unable to sustain important relationships. Why is a lover of five years not like a wife of five years? The difference is only in the eye of the heterosexual beholder.

George must also understand that if he decides to support Adam's decision, there is no way to foresee, much less to control, people's reactions. He may experience, in a small way, what gay people who are open about their sexuality face every day. What impact does this information, aired publicly, have on my life? What decisions are made? What promotion or raise didn't I get? What gossip goes on?

George must have the courage of his convictions. He might want to tell his superior, but he must consider what he will do if ordered to rein Adam in. As for clients, if they are going to bolt over a gay companion, it seems unlikely that they were a solid bet to begin with.

Note

James D. Woods, assistant professor of communications at the College of Staten Island/CUNY, is the coauthor of *The Corporate Closet: The*

Professional Lives of Gay Men in America. John M. Conley holds the Ivey Research Chair at the University of North Carolina Law School and is adjunct professor of cultural anthropology at Duke University. William M. O'Barr is professor and chair of cultural anthropology at Duke University and adjunct professor of law and anthropology at the University of North Carolina at Chapel Hill. Michael R. Losey is president and CEO of the Society for Human Resource Management in Alexandria, Virginia. Charles Colbert is a management consultant in strategic human resources and workforce diversity in Cambridge, Massachusetts. John Wofford is a lawyer and mediator at ENDIS-PUTE, Inc., in Boston. Elizabeth McNamara is a member of the law firm of Lankenau Kovner & Kurtz in New York City.

Suggested Further Reading

Adler, Nancy J. *International Dimensions of Organizational Behavior*. Boston, Mass.: PWS-Kent, 1986 (rev. 1991).

Baron, S. Alma. "What Men Are Saying About Women in Business: A Decade Later." *Business Horizons*, July–August 1989, pp. 51–53.

Copeland, Lennie. "Valuing Diversity. Part I: Making the Most of Cultural Differences at the Workplace." *Personnel*, June 1988, pp. 52–60.

———. "Valuing Diversity. Part II: Pioneers and Champions of Change." *Personnel*, July 1988, pp. 44–49.

Cox, Taylor, Jr. *Cultural Diversity in Organizations: Theory, Research, and Practice*. San Francisco: Berrett-Koehler, 1993.

Ellis, Catherine, and Jeffrey A. Sonnenfeld. "Diverse Approaches to Managing Diversity." Center for Leadership and Career Studies, Emory University, 1993.

Emery, Alan. "The Workplace Profiles Project: Common Features and Profiles of HIV/AIDS in the Workplace Programs." Washington, D.C.: The National Leadership Coalition on AIDS, 1993.

Fagenson, Ellen A., ed. *Women in Management: Trends, Issues, and Challenges in Managerial Diversity*, vol. IV. Newbury Park, Calif.: Sage, 1993.

Fernandez, John P. *Managing a Diverse Workforce: Regaining the Competitive Edge*. Lexington, Mass.: Lexington Books, 1991.

———. *The Diversity Advantage: How American Business Can Outperform Japanese and European Companies in the Global Marketplace*. Lexington, Mass.: Lexington Books, 1993.

"Gay in Corporate America: What It's Like and How Business Attitudes are Changing." *Fortune*, December 16, 1991.

Gudykunst, William B. *Bridging Differences: Effective Intergroup Communication.* Newbury Park, Calif.: Sage, 1991.

"Harassment: Views in the Workplace." *The Wall Street Journal,* October 10, 1991, p. B1.

Harris, Philip R., and Robert T. Moran. *Managing Cultural Differences: High-Performance Strategies for Today's Global Manager.* Houston, Tex.: Gulf, 1979 (rev. 1987).

Hofstede, Geert. "Motivation, Leadership, and Organization: Do American Theories Apply Abroad?" *Organizational Dynamics,* vol. 9, no. 1, Summer 1980, pp. 42–63.

Jackson, Susan E. and Associates. *Diversity in the Workplace: Human Resource Initiatives.* (Society for Industrial Organizational Psychology.) New York: Guilford, 1992.

Jamieson, David, and Julie O'Mara. *Managing Workforce 2000: Gaining the Diversity Advantage.* San Francisco: Jossey-Bass, 1991.

Johnson, Alicia. "Black Managers Still Have a Dream." *Management Review,* vol. 76, no. 12, December 1987, pp. 20–27.

———. "Old Stereotypes Die Hard." *Management Review,* vol. 76, no. 12, December 1987, pp. 31–43.

Johnston, W. B., and A. H. Pacher. *Opportunity 2000: Creative Affirmative Action Strategies for a Changing Workforce.* Prepared by Hudson Institute for Employment Standards Administration, U.S. Department of Labor, September 1988.

Kanter, Rosabeth Moss. *Men and Women of the Corporation.* New York: Basic Books, 1977 (rev. 1993).

Leonard, Jonathan S. "The Changing Face of Employees and Employment Regulation." *California Management Review,* vol. 31, no. 2, Winter 1989, pp. 29–38.

Loden, Marilyn. "Recognizing Women's Potential: No Longer Business As Usual." *Management Review,* vol. 76, no. 12, December 1987, pp. 44–46.

Loden, Marilyn, and Judy B. Rosener. *Workforce America!: Managing Employee Diversity as a Vital Resource.* Homewood, Ill.: Business One Irwin, 1991.

"Managing AIDS: How One Boss Struggled to Cope," and "Why AIDS Policy Must Be a Special Policy." *Business Week,* February 1, 1993, pp. 48–54.

Minow, Martha. "On Neutrality, Equality, and Tolerance: New Norms for a Decade of Distinction." *Change,* January/February 1990, pp. 17–25.

Morrison, Ann M. *The New Leaders: Guidelines on Leadership Diversity in America.* San Francisco: Jossey-Bass, 1992.

Morrison, Ann M., and Mary Ann Von Glinow. "Women and Minorities in Management." *American Psychologist*, vol. 45, no. 2, 1990, pp. 200–208.

Morrison, Ann M., Randall P. White, Ellen Van Velsor, and The Center for Creative Leadership. *Breaking the Glass Ceiling: Can Women Reach the Top of America's Largest Corporations?*. Reading, Mass.: Addison-Wesley, 1987.

Riger, Stephanie. "Gender Dilemmas in Sexual Harassment Policies and Procedures." *American Psychologist*, May 1991, pp. 497–505.

Rothenberg, Paula J. *Racism and Sexism: An Integrated Study*. New York: St. Martin's Press, 1988.

Sims, Ronald R., and Robert F. Dennehy, eds. *Diversity and Differences in Organizations: An Agenda for Answers and Questions*. Westport, Conn.: Quorum Books, 1993.

Swiss, Deborah J., and Judith P. Walker. *Women and the Work/Family Dilemma: How Today's Professional Women Are Finding Solutions*. New York: John Wiley, 1993.

Tannen, Deborah. *You Just Don't Understand: Women and Men in Conversation*. New York: Ballantine Books, 1990.

Thiederman, Sondra. *Bridging Cultural Barriers for Corporate Success: How to Manage the Multicultural Work Force*. Lexington, Mass.: Lexington Books, 1992.

Thomas, David. "Impact of Race on Managers' Experiences of Gaining Mentoring and Sponsorship." *Journal of Organizational Behavior*, vol. II, no. 6, 1990, pp. 479–492.

———. "Racial Dynamics in Cross-Race Developmental Relationships." *Administrative Science Quarterly*, vol. 38, no. 2, June 1993, pp. 169–194.

Thomas, Roosevelt R., Jr. *Beyond Race and Gender: Unleashing the Power of Your Total Work Force by Managing Diversity*. New York: AMACOM, 1991.

Thompson, Donna E., and Nancy DiTomaso. *Ensuring Minority Corporate Management*. New York: Plenum, 1988.

Woods, James D., with Jay H. Lucas. *The Corporate Closet: The Professional Lives of Gay Men in America*. New York: Free Press, 1993.

"Work and Family: Companies Are Starting to Respond to Workers' Needs—and Gain From It." *Business Week*, June 28, 1993, pp. 80–88.

"Work and Family." *The Wall Street Journal Reports*, Eastern Edition, June 21, 1993, pp. R1–R13.

About the Contributors

When her article first appeared in the *Harvard Business Review*, **Julia Anderson** was a doctoral student in clinical psychology at Boston University. She was affiliated with the Perkins School for the Blind in Watertown, Massachusetts for more than a decade.

Gary E. Banas is director for administration for the northeastern district of the Comptroller of the Currency.

Mary C. Gentile has been studying, teaching, writing, and consulting on diversity issues for almost a decade. She designed and taught the first elective course on the subject at the Harvard Business School. Dr. Gentile is the author of the custom coursebook *Managing Diversity: Making Differences Work* (Harvard Business School Publishing 1995) and the casebook *Managerial Excellence Through Diversity* (1995), as well as the content expert for *Managing across Diversity*, an interactive multimedia CD-ROM for management development from Harvard Business School Publishing (1996).

When his article first appeared in the *Harvard Business Review*, **William B. Johnston** was a senior research fellow at the Hudson Institute. He is also the author of *Workforce 2000*.

Edward W. Jones, Jr. is the founder of Corporate Organizational Dynamics, Inc., a consulting firm specializing in organizational effectiveness. He is also the author of *Managing the Dynamics of Difference*.

David L. Kirp is a professor of public policy at the University of California, Berkeley. His latest books are *Learning by Heart: AIDS and*

271

Schoolchildren in America's Communities and *AIDS Among the Industrialized Democracies*.

Terry L. Leap is a professor of management in the College of Commerce and Industry, Clemson University, where he teaches personnel management.

Michele S. Marram is the former director of research and information systems, Baker Library, at the Harvard Business School.

Charles Rodgers is a principal of Work/Family Directions, Inc., and president of Rodgers and Associates, Inc.

Fran Sussner Rodgers is CEO of Work/Family Directions, Inc., which manages dependent-care programs and consults on issues related to the changing labor force.

A lawyer and former counsel to the U.S. Senate Subcommittee on Labor, **George P. Sape** has written extensively about the effects of equal opportunity legislation on employment practices.

At the time his article was published in the *Harvard Business Review*, **Robert Schrank** was a product specialist for the Ford Foundation, where his major responsibility was to monitor and evaluate employment training and related educational programs.

Felice N. Schwartz is founder and former president of Catalyst, a national not-for-profit research and advisory organization that works with business to affect change for women. In addition to her consulting work, she is the author of *Breaking with Tradition—Women and Work, The New Facts of Life*.

Larry R. Smeltzer is a professor and chairman of the business administration department at Arizona State University, where he specializes in managers' communication styles and strategies.

Jeffrey Sonnenfeld is a professor of organization and management and Director of the Center for Leadership and Career Studies at the Emory Business School. He is the author of several books, including *The Hero's Farewell: What Happens When CEOs Retire*.

Richard S. Tedlow is professor of business administration at the Harvard Business School and former editor of the *Business History Review*. His publications include *Keeping the Corporate Image: Public Relations and Business, 1900–1950, The Coming of Managerial Capitalism: A Casebook on the History of American Economic Institutions*, with Alfred D.

Chandler, Jr., and *New and Improved: The Story of Mass Marketing in America*.

R. Roosevelt Thomas, Jr. is founder and president of The American Institute for Managing Diversity, a research and education enterprise with the objective of fostering effective management of employee diversity.

Alistair D. Williamson is an editor at the Harvard Business School Press, where he acquires books in the areas of workplace diversity, family business, and business history, among others. He is also the editor of *Field Guide to Business Terms* and its companion volumes in the Harvard Business/The Economist Reference Series.

INDEX

Absenteeism, and family policy, 210–211
Adler, Nancy J., 236–238
Aetna Life and Casualty, 208
Affirmative action
    colorism and, 81
    among human resource priorities, 66
    at low vs. high levels of management,
        68
    premises underlying, 27
    recruitment-oriented cycle in, 29–33,
        42–43
    role of, in diversity management,
        40–41, 44, 45–46
    societal changes and, 27–28
    as transitional intervention, 28–29
    wage discrimination and, 119
AFSCME v. State of Washington, 107–108,
    114, 116, 117
Age Discriminiation Employment Act,
    191–192
Aging work force
    age-related physiological changes and,
        185–186
    corporate experience and, 189–190
    globalization of work force and, 10–13
    job performance and, 180, 184–185,
        186, 187–189, 193
    management priorities and, 192–195
    mid-career considerations and,
        181–185
    performance appraisal and, 193–194
    work attitudes and, 186–187
AIDS education
    general access to, 159
    HIV-positive employees and (case
        study), 242–243, 245, 247

at Pacific Bell, 142–143, 147–149, 155,
    157–160
AIDS Education Task Force (Pacific Bell),
    142–143
AIDS in workplace. *See also* AIDS
        education; HIV-positive employees
    AIDS education videos and, 149,
        153–155, 157, 158
    company policy on, 145–155,
        158–161, 241, 243
    coworker costs and, 169–170, 174
    coworker fears and, 144, 146–147,
        166, 243–248
    denial of issue and, 143–144
    grief and, 144, 246
    impact of, 143–144, 145
    management of, 163–176
    San Francisco conference on (1986),
        149–150, 154, 155, 160
Alexander, Ralph, 145, 153–154, 155,
    159
American Bankers Insurance Group, 205
American Institute for Managing
    Diversity, 42
Americans for Disability Act of 1990, 242
American Society for Personnel
    Administration, 143, 160
Anxiety, and black managers, 59
Assimilation, 33
Assumptions, false. *See also* Corporate
        culture; Stereotypes
    AIDS in workplace and, 252
    blind employees and, 217
    diversity management and, 36–38,
        236–238
    gay employees and, 264

275

Assumptions *(continued)*
    race barriers to promotion and,
        233–235, 236–238
Attitudes. *See also* Assumptions, false
    colorism and, 72–76
    diversity management and, 46
    organizational climate for black
        managers and, 69–70
    paternalism and, 233–234
    sexual orientation discrimination and,
        263
    women in work force and, 136–138
Avon, 41–42
Awareness training. *See also* AIDS
        education
    AIDS and, 163–164
    diversity management and, 41–43, 45

Banker's Life and Casualty Company,
        190, 193
Barnard, Chester, 60
Black managers
    balancing act required of, 80–81
    barriers to promotion and, 67–76,
        81–83
    colorism and, 72–76
    conformity pressures on, 76–81
    experience of discrimination by, 49–64
    international management and (case
        study), 223–238
    organizational process and, 61–63
    proportion of, 65
    race as issue and, 76–77
    support for other minority players
        from, 76–78
    women managers and, 78–80
Black women, and promotion, 79–80
Blind employees, 215–219
Boyd, Bill, 94
Briggs v. City of Madison, 116
Business mainstream
    blacks and, 75–76
    composition of, 27, 28
    women and, 129

Career development. *See also* Promotion
    black managers and, 49–64
    diversity management and, 38, 232
    family life and, 207, 209–210
    frustrations of stagnation and, 183–184
    HIV-positive employees and (case
        study), 239–252
    international promotion of black
        manager (case study), 223–238
    mid-career considerations and, 181–185
    older workers and, 194

Charley Brothers Company (case). *See*
    Taylor v. *Charley Brothers Company*
Child care, 131, 202–206
China, 9
City of Madison (case). *See Briggs* v. *City of*
    Madison
Clerical workers, and age, 188–189
Clients
    part-time employees and, 209
    sexual orientation discrimination and,
        258–261
Cobbs, Price, 76–77, 79, 80–81
Cognition, and aging, 186
Colbert, Charles, 262–264
College graduates, 15, 19, 20, 183
Colorism, 72–76, 81. *See also* Prejudice
Comanagement, and HIV-positive
        employees, 241–242, 243
Communication channels, 62, 68, 76–77,
        82, 217
Comparable worth, 107–121. *See also*
        Wage discrimination
Compensation system. *See also* Wage
        discrimination
    aging work force and, 186–187
    pay disparity safeguards in, 120
Confidentiality, and HIV-positive
        employees, 164–165, 168, 170,
        242–248
Conformity, and black managers, 76–81
Conley, John M., 259–261
Corning, 41–42, 126
"Corporate apartheid," 79, 81–82
Corporate culture. *See also* Assumptions,
        false
    diversity management and, 36–37
    equal opportunity and, 82
    HIV-positive employees and, 145–146,
        150
    HIV-positive employees and (case
        study), 239–252
    sexual orientation discrimination and,
        259
Corporate mission, and family, 210–212
Corporate policy
    on AIDS, 142–143, 145–155, 158–161,
        241, 243
    "color-blind," 67–76
    on harassment, 89–90
    on sexual orientation discrimination,
        261–262
    on women's issues, 125–126,
        133–138, 210–212, 261
Costs
    aging work force and, 10–11, 13
    of gender segregation in jobs, 127–133
    HIV-positive employees and, 146, 149,
        160–161, 252

of infant care, 204
Coulter, Steve, 151–152, 153, 154, 155, 156
The County of Washington v. *Gunther*, 110–111, 117
Courts
  harassment and, 85
  pay disparity and, 107–109, 110–113, 116–117
Cream-to-the-top assumption, 31, 32, 38
Cultural barriers
  black managers and, 59, 60
  global work force flows and, 23
  international management and, 231–233, 234, 236–238

Dade County, Florida, 205
Dannemeyer, William, 157
DeButts, John, 76
Decision making, and age, 187–188
Dependent care, 202–206
Deukmejian, George, 157
Developed vs. developing countries
  aging of work force in, 10–13
  education of work force in, 13–19
  women in work force in, 6–7
  work force growth rates in, 5–6
Developing countries
  age of work force in, 10
  economic growth in, 19
  economic pressures toward emigration in, 19–21
  education of work force in, 13, 14, 15, 16, 18
  mass migration of workers from, 23–24
  work force growth in, 5
Digital, 43–44
Disabilities. *See* Blind employees; HIV-positive employees; Maternity leave
Diversity management
  compared with affirmative action, 30
  cultural heterogeneity and, 36, 45
  empowerment and, 38–39
  false assumptions and, 36–38, 236–238
  guidelines for, 33–41
  management training and, 46
  motivations for, 34
  Pacific Bell and, 151–152
  at specific companies, 41–46
  system modification and, 38
  vision for, 34–36
Doer Model, 38–39
Donnelley & Sons Company, R. R., 191
Dragotta, Janice, 158
DuPont, 201, 205, 211

Eastern Europe, 19, 23
Eastman Kodak, 208
Economic growth, and globalization of work force, 9, 19, 23
Education. *See also* AIDS education; Awareness training; Training
  aging work force and, 194
  AIDS in workplace and, 142–143, 147–149, 242–243, 245, 247
  business support for, 202, 205
  global work force and, 13–19
EEOC. *See* Equal Employment Opportunity Commission (EEOC)
Elder care, 205–206
Emery, Alan, 157
Emigration, economic pressures toward, 19–21
Empowerment, 33–34, 38–39
Entrepreneurship, and women, 130, 137
Equal Employment Opportunity Commission (EEOC), 85, 108–109, 110, 125
Equal opportunity
  achievment of, 81–83
  black perceptions of lack of, 67–70, 74, 81
  candor about race and, 68, 76–77, 82
  case study in, 223–238
  diversity management and, 35
  ethical issues and, 235–236
  organizational structure for, 61–63
  performance standards and, 37
  racial harassment and, 85–90
Equal Pay Act, 109, 118
Equity, 211
Eriksen, Michael, 142, 144–148, 152, 153, 154, 155
Erikson, Erik, 182
Ethical issues
  race discrimination and, 235–236
  sexual orientation discrimination and, 257–259
Europe
  cross-national flows of workers and, 4, 23
  work-and-family issues in, 208, 212
European Community, 4, 25
Ewing, Robert P., 193
Executive Leadership Council, African-American executives study, 233–235

Fair Labor Standards Act, 109
Fairness, 66, 83, 107, 256–257
Family
  as business issue, 130–131, 199–202
  career path and, 209, 210

Family *(continued)*
  conditions of work and, 206–210
  dependent care and, 202–206
Family assumption, 37
Feagin, Joseph, 73
Federal National Mortgage Association, 126
Ferle, Inc., 190
Flexible schedules, 131, 132, 134, 135–136, 206, 207–208, 211
Flextime, 208

Gannett, 126
Gay employees. *See* Sexual orientation discrimination
General Motors, 181
Germany, 9, 23
Global work force
  aging of, 10–13
  educational levels of, 13–19
  labor market redefinition and, 5–19
  pressures toward emigration and, 19–21
  women in, 6–10
  work forces in developed vs. developing countries, 5–6
Globe Dyeworks, 190
Goodenough, Dave, 141–142
Governments, and globalization of work force, 25–26
Green, Gordon W., 114
Greenwood, Thomas, 190
Guest workers, 23
GULHEMP system, 192
Gunther. See The County of Washington v. *Gunther*

Haas, Bob, 149, 153
HACER, 152, 157
Hahn, Kurt, 94–95
"Halo effect," 238
Harassment
  racial, 85–90
  sexual, 130, 137
Harvey, Brian, 235–236
Hazing, 89–90
Health policy. *See also* HIV-positive employees; Maternity leave
  case management approach and, 146
  medical vs. wellness approach and, 148, 161
Henderson, Jim, 146, 152
Hewlett-Packard, 208
Hidden agendas, 232–233
Hiring. *See also* Recruitment
  AIDS and, 239–252

blind applicants and, 216
HIV-positive employees. *See also* AIDS education; AIDS in workplace
  career development and (case study), 239–252
  company AIDS policy and, 144–155, 241, 243
  coworker costs and, 169–170, 174
  coworker fears and, 144, 146–147, 166, 243–248
  denial and, 165–166, 169, 170–171, 174
  differences among, 173–175
  performance crises and, 243–248
  problems faced by, 246
  promotion of, 248–252
  support and, 142, 158–159, 242, 245
  vs. those with active AIDS, 174
Houghton, James R., 42
Humor, vs. racial harassment, 86, 89

IBM, 126, 205, 211
Immigration, economic benefits of, 21–23
Immigration policies, 4, 23, 24
Industrialized countries
  aging of work force in, 10–11, 13
  benefits of worker immigration and, 21–23
  education of work force in, 12, 13, 15, 19
  labor shortages in, 5, 20, 127, 136, 200–201
  women in work force in, 9
Informal organization, and black managers, 60–63
International management
  dual-career marriages and, 237–238
  gender discrimination and, 236–237
  nationality vs. race as issue in, 231–232
  race discrimination case, 223–238
Italy, 9
IUE v. *Westinghouse Electric Corporation*, 110–111, 112

Japan, 9, 11, 23, 129
Jimenez, Lynn, 157
Job performance. *See also* Performance appraisal; Productivity
  aging work force and, 180, 184–185, 186, 187–189, 193
  AIDS and, 169–173, 174–175
  enabling of, 33–34
Job satisfaction, 186–187

Job segregation, 110, 113, 115, 118, 120, 121
  costs of, 127–133
Johnson, Jeffalyn, 233–235
Johnson & Johnson, 211

Kaiser, Jim, 231–233
Kearns, David T., 45–46
Korn Ferry International, 66
Koyl, Leon F., 192
Krone, Charles, 151
Kuwait, 24

LaRouche, Lyndon, 155–156, 157
Latno, Art, 156
Leadership
  AIDS in workplace and, 150, 155–158, 245–246
  sexual orientation discrimination and, 260–261
Legal compliance
  diversity management and, 34, 42
  pay disparity and, 107–109, 110–113, 116–117, 120–121
  racial harassment and, 85–90
  sexual orientation discrimination and, 262–263
Levinson, Daniel, 183
Levi Strauss & Co., 149, 153, 243, 247
Losey, Michael R., 261–262
Luttgens, Leslie, 153, 154, 155

McBee, Gary, 156
Machismo, 104
McNamara, Elizabeth, 264
Macy's department stores, 190
Mann, Jonathan, 240–241, 245–246, 249–250
Manual workers, and age, 188–189
Massachusetts Commission for the Blind, 217
Maternity-leave policy, 134–135, 210
Melting pot metaphor, 33, 38
Memory, and aging, 186
Mentoring
  minority employees and, 232
  women and, 137
Merck, 201, 211
Meritocracy, 28–29
Metropolitan Life, 191
Mexico, 25
Minorities. *See* Affirmative action; Black managers
Moberg, Jim, 152, 153, 154–155

Mobil Oil, 209
Mulready, Terry, 158
Myths. *See* Assumptions, false

NAACP, 152, 154
National Academy of Sciences, 110
National differences
  international assignments and, 231–232, 238
  women in work force and, 7–9
National Industrial Conference Board, 181
NCNB (banking corporation), 205, 207
Networks, and minority managers, 42, 74–75
Neugarten, Bernice, 182–183
"Neural noise," 185–186
Neutrality, and racism, 73
Nichols, James W., 241–242, 246, 250–251

O'Barr, William M., 259–261
O'Hara, Tim, 142, 147, 158
Olberg, Diane, 148
Organizational structure
  change at Pacific Bell and, 150–155
  equal opportunity for advancement and, 61–63
Outward Bound rafting expedition, 93–105

Pacific Bell, 141–161
  evolution of AIDS policy at, 144–155
  HIV-positive employee at, 141–143
  public leadership on AIDS at, 155–158
Pacific Telesis Foundation, 149, 153–155, 157, 159
Pahl, Bernd, 187
Pandering-to-the-customer defense, 260
Parental-leave policy, 134, 135–136, 201
Part-time workers, 195, 208–209
Paternalistic attitudes
  AIDS in workplace and, 246
  as race barrier, 233–234
Pay disparity. *See* Comparable worth
Payne, Ted, 46
Pension funds, 259–261
Performance appraisal. *See also* Job performance; Productivity
  aging work force and, 190–192, 193–194
  black manager's experience of, 52, 54–55, 56, 57, 58
  diversity management and, 37, 38, 234
  HIV-positive employees and, 172–173

Performance appraisal. *(continued)*
  manager's contribution to equal
    opportunity objectives and, 62
  manager's sensitivity to family issues
    and, 210–211
  networks and, 74–76
  subjective criteria in, 52, 234
  white vs. black managers' confidence
    in, 70
Perkins, Joe, 190
Perkins Project with Industry, 217
Pioneering perspective, 39–40
Pivotal jobs, 46
Polaroid, 190, 193
Power, and male perceptions of women
  managers, 103–105
Prejudice, 63, 67–68, 69, 70–72. *See also*
  Colorism
Premature plateauing, 31, 32, 35
Prine, Arthur C., Jr., 191
Procter & Gamble, 44–45
Productivity. *See also* Job performance
  AIDS in workplace and, 175, 246, 251
  creative activity and age and, 188
  diversity management and, 35–36
  work-and-family issues and, 201–202,
    206, 209–210
Promotion. *See also* Career development;
    Performance appraisal
  affirmative action cycle and, 30–33
  cultural bias and, 231–233
  HIV-positive employee and (case
    study), 248–252
  international assignment of black
    manager and (case study), 223–238
  performance standards and, 37
  race barriers to, 67–68, 233–235
  risktaking and, 235–236
  special consideration and, 40
  sponsorship and, 38
  subjective criteria and, 66, 73
Proposition 64 (California anti-AIDS
  initiative), 155–157
Proposition 102 (California anti-AIDS
  initiative), 157
Puckett, Sam, 157

Quality
  recruitment and, 31, 32, 38, 217
  women in management and, 128–129

Racial slurs, 85–90
Reaction time, and aging, 185–186

Recruitment
  affirmative action and, 27, 28, 30–31
  aging work force and, 180
  blind persons and, 218–219
  costs of, and job segregation, 131–132
  diversity management and, 44–45, 46
  quality and, 31, 32, 38, 217
  race discrimination and, 50–51
Relationships. *See also* Networks
  international management and,
    231–232, 234
  between men and women managers,
    103–105
  openness about, 257, 259
Resource and referral services (R&Rs),
  204–205
Retirement
  flexible plans, 181, 189–190
  mandatory age of, 179, 180, 184
  trend toward early retirement, 181
Risks
  AIDS in workplace and, 240
  hiring of sight-impaired persons,
    216–218
  promotion of minority managers and,
    235–236
  willingness to take, and age, 186,
    187–188
Rolscreen Company, 208
R&Rs. *See* Resource and referral services
  (R&Rs)

Safire, William L., 184–185
Sales workers, and age, 188–189
San Francisco AIDS Foundation, 143,
  147–148, 153, 154
San Francisco Business Leadership Task
  Force, 153, 154
SAS Institute Inc., 204
Science, global educational trends in, 15,
  17, 18
Seniority systems, 211
Sexist behavior, 130
Sexual orientation discrimination. *See
  also* AIDS in workplace; HIV-positive
    employees
  case study on, 252–265
  at Pacific Bell, 152
Shinn, Richard R., 191
Shuttlesworth, Todd, 149
Skilled workers, global labor market for,
  20–21
Skin color, impact of, 60
Smale, John, 45
Smith, Lee, 242–243, 247–248, 251–252

Spain, women in work force in, 9
Spaulding v. *University of Washington,*
112–113, 116
Special consideration test, 40
State of Washington (case). *See AFSCME* v.
State of Washington
States, and wage discrimination
legislation, 14
Stereotypes, 73, 79, 184–185, 191, 216.
See also Assumptions, false
Stockholders, 132–133
Subjective criteria
in performance appraisal, 52, 234
in promotion, 66, 73
Support
black managers and, 52–53, 55–56, 73
family policy and, 201–202, 204,
210–211
HIV-positive employees and, 142,
158–159, 242, 245
women managers and, 103–105

Taylor, Jean, 146, 158
Taylor v. *Charley Brothers Company,* 108,
112, 113
Top management
AIDS policy and, 160–161
involvement in equal opportunity
process, 61–63, 82, 137–138
minority participation in, 65–66
women in, 128, 132, 210
work-and-family issues and, 210, 211
Training
of black manager, 51–52
costs of, and job segregation, 131–132
in diversity management, 42, 45
for women, 136, 137
work-and-family issues and, 211
Travel, international, 4, 13
Travelers Insurance Company, 205

Unassimilated diversity, 33
Underemployment, 23, 28, 215
United States
benefits of worker immigration and,
21, 23
education of work force in, 15, 17
labor shortages in, 127, 136, 200–201
women in work force in, 129, 212
U.S.-Mexico free trade agreement, 25
U.S. Steel, 190
Unskilled workers, global labor market
for, 20–21
Update (Pacific Bell newspaper), 148–149

Vaillant, George E., 183
Values
black managers and, 76–78
client, 133, 259–261
male vs. female, 120
of workers, 194
Vroom, Victor H., 187

Wage discrimination
burden of proof in, 111–113
court rulings on, 107–109, 110–113,
116–117
criteria for pay disparities and, 115–116
evolution of comparable worth and,
109–113
job segregation and, 110, 113, 115,
118, 120, 121
management approach to, 117–121
settlements involving, 107–109
standards for, 110–111
Warner-Lambert, 211
Washington Business Group on Health,
146
Waxman, Henry, 154
"Weekly balancing," 208
Wofford, John, 262–264
Women. *See also* Affirmative action;
Wage discrimination; Women
managers
corporate changes and, 133–138
corporate policy and, 125–126, 261
entrepreneurship and, 130, 137
global participation in work force, 6–10
underemployment of, 23
working conditions and, 9–10, 25,
206–210
Women managers
childless, 210
corporate costs of job segregation and,
127–133
international assignment of, 236–237
male undermining of, 103–105
proportion of, 65
race barriers to promotion and, 78–80
rafting expedition experience and,
103–105
in top management positions, 66
Woodman, Chuck, 142–143, 159
Woods, James D., 256–259
Work force. *See also* Global work force
factors in globalization of, 4
growth rates of, in developed vs.
developing countries, 5–6
interest surveys and, 194
Work force *(continued)*

labor shortage and, 5, 20, 127, 136, 200–201
Working conditions
racial harassment and, 85–90
women in work force and, 9–10, 25, 206–210
Work teams, 247. *See also* Outward Bound rafting expedition
Worthing, Marcia, 41

Xerox, 45–46, 126

Zaleznik, Abraham, 59, 81
Zimmerle, Alan, 44
Zin, Victor M., 181

DATE DUE